TAKE THE LAW INTO YOUR OWN HANDS™

C0-APX-862

How to Modify Your Florida Divorce Judgment

With Forms

Third Edition

Includes
Alimony
Child Support
Child Custody and Visitation

Edward A. Haman
Attorney at Law

SPHINX PUBLISHING
Sphinx International, Inc.
Post Office Box 25
Clearwater, FL 34617
Tel: 813-587-0999
Fax: 813-586-5088

SPHINX®
is a registered trademark of Sphinx International, Inc.

Note: The law changes constantly and is subject to different interpretations. It is up to you
to check it thoroughly before relying on it.
Neither the author nor the publisher guaran-
tees the outcome of the uses to which this
material is put.

Copyright © 1992, 1995, 1996 by Edward A. Haman

All rights reserved. No part of this book, except for brief passages in articles that refer to author
and publisher, may be reproduced without written permission of the author. Purchasers of the
book are granted a license to use the forms contained herein. No claim of copyright is made in
the forms which were promulgated by The Florida Bar or in any other official government forms
which are reproduced herein.

Third Edition 1996

ISBN 1-57248-056-4
Library of Congress Catalog Number: 96-69197

Manufactured in the United States of America.

This publication is designed to provide accurate and authoritative information in regard to the
subject matter covered. It is sold with the understanding that the publisher is not engaged in
rendering legal, accounting or other professional services. If legal advice or other expert
assistance is required, the service of a competent professional person should be sought.

-From a Declaration of Principles jointly
adopted by a Committee of the American Bar
Association and a Committee of Publishers.

Published by Sphinx Publishing, a division of Sphinx International, Inc., Post Office Box 25,
Clearwater, Florida 34617-0025. This publication is available by mail for $22.95 plus $3.00
shipping, plus Florida sales tax if applicable, postpaid. For credit card orders call 1-800-226-5291
or fax 1-800-408-3291.

Table of Contents

Introduction 5

Using Self-Help Law Books 6

Chapter 1   **The Legal System** 7
    Theory vs. Reality
    Legal Research and Additional Forms

Chapter 2   **Modifying a Divorce Judgment**.................................9
    Alimony
    Child Support
    Child Custody
    Child Visitation
    Asking Your Ex-Spouse

Chapter 3   **Basic Procedures** 13
    Legal Forms
    Filing with the Court Clerk
    Notifying Your Ex-Spouse
    Default
    Setting a Court Date
    Hearing Notices
    Preparing Your Case
    The Hearing
    When You Can't Afford Court Costs
    Good Things to Know

Chapter 4   **Lawyers**..27
    Do You Want a Lawyer?
    Selecting a Lawyer
    Working With a Lawyer

Chapter 5   **Alimony**..31
    How Alimony is Determined
    Evaluating Your Situation
    Petition to Modify Alimony
    Affidavit Regarding Alimony
    Family Law Financial Affidavit
    Interrogatories and Financial Disclosure
    Filing with the Court Clerk, Etc.
    Preparing and Presenting Your Proof
    Order Modifying Alimony
    Order Requiring Payment Through Central Depository

Child Support Income Deduction Order
Final Disposition Form

Chapter 6   Child Support..39
How Child Support is Determined
Evaluating Your Situation
Petition for Modification of Child Support
Family Law Financial Affidavit
Child Support Guidelines Worksheet
Interrogatories and Financial Disclosure
Filing with the Court Clerk, Etc.
Preparing and Presenting Your Proof
Final Judgment Modifying Child Support
Order Requiring Payment Through Central Depository
Child Support Income Deduction Order
Motion for Health Insurance Coverage
Order for Health Insurance
Instructions to Employer or Other Person Provided Health Insurance

Chapter 7   Custody..47
How a Change in Custody is Determined
Petition to Modify Custody
Financial Disclosure Documents
Uniform Child Custody Jurisdiction Act (UCCJA) Affidavit
Guardian Ad Litem
Filing with the Court Clerk, Etc.
Preparing and Presenting Your Proof
Final Judgment of Modification of Parental Responsibilty and Visitation

Chapter 8   Visitation...55
Supplemental Petition to Modify Visitation
Other Forms
Filing with the Court Clerk, Etc.
Preparing and Presenting Your Proof
Final Judgment of Modification of Parental Responsibility and Visitation

Appendix A: Florida Statutes and Court Rules 57

Appendix B: Forms 65

Index 171

Introduction

The child support, custody and visitation, and alimony provisions of a divorce judgment can affect your life for many years. As children grow older, their needs change. As time passes, financial conditions change. These aspects of a divorce judgment can also be changed to reflect these new circumstances.

This book makes it possible for you to request a change in your alimony, child support, child custody, and visitation without hiring a lawyer. Even if you do hire an attorney, this book will help you to work with him or her more effectively. This is not a law school course, but a practical guide to get you through "The System" as comfortably as possible. Legal jargon has been nearly eliminated. The emphasis is on practical information in plain English. For ease of understanding, the term "ex-spouse" is used to refer to your ex-husband or ex-wife (whichever applies), and the terms "child" and "children" are used interchangeably.

Please keep in mind that different judges, and courts in different counties, may have their own particular (if not peculiar) procedures and ways of doing things. The court clerk's office can often tell you if they have any special forms or requirements. Court clerks cannot give legal advice, but they will tell you what their court or judges require. This book cannot turn you into a lawyer and cannot cover every possible situation. But it will provide you with valuable information and forms that can get you through most situations.

The Supreme Court of Florida has stated that it should not be necessary to hire a lawyer every time you need to go to court. A few years ago, the Supreme Court ordered The Florida Bar (which is the Florida lawyers' organization) to create forms relating to divorce and other family law matters. It is obvious that they created these forms reluctantly, because they were sometimes poorly drafted and were not accompanied by any truly useful instructions or an explanation of the law. Now, these forms have been revised (apparently to make them more complicated), and incorporated in the offical court rules, along with some instructions but still lacking an explanation of the law. The lack of instructinons in the first set of forms, and the unnecessary complexity of the new forms, makes one wonder how serious the Supreme court really is about helping people handle their own legal matters. However, where possible, these official forms have been used in this book, as the author and the publisher believe that these forms are more likely to be accepted by the judges and court clerks in Florida.

Chapters 1 through 4 will give you an overview of the legal system, discuss what is involved in modifying a divorce judgment, give you basic information and instructions for procedures common to all modifications, and discuss lawyers. Chapter 5 discusses the details of modifying alimony. Chapter 6 concerns child support, Chapter 7 relates to child custody, and Chapter 8 to visitation. If you are trying to modify more than one of these items, you will need to read each related part. Appendix A contains selected portions of the Florida law. Although these provisions are discussed in the book, it is sometimes helpful to read the law exactly as the legislature wrote it. Appendix B contains the forms you will complete. You will not use all of the forms. This book will tell you which forms you need and give you detailed instructions on how to complete them.

**BE SURE TO READ THE SECTION ON "LEGAL FORMS" IN CHAPTER 3
BEFORE YOU USE ANY OF THE FORMS IN THIS BOOK**

Using Self-Help Law Books

Whenever you shop for a product or service you are faced with a variety of different levels of quality and price. In deciding what to buy, you make a cost/value analysis based upon your willingness to pay and the quality you desire.

When buying a car, you decide whether you want transportation, comfort, status, or sex appeal, and you decide among such choices as a Geo, a Lincoln, a Rolls Royce, or a Porsche. Before making a decision, you usually weigh the merits of each against the cost.

When you get a headache, you can take a pain reliever such as aspirin or you can go to a medical specialist for a neurological examination. Given this choice, most people, of course, take a pain reliever, since it costs only pennies, whereas a medical examination costs hundreds of dollars and takes a lot of time. This is usually a logical choice because rarely is anything more than a pain reliever needed for a headache. But in some cases a headache may indicate a brain tumor, and failing to go to a specialist right away can result in complications. Should everyone with a headache go to a specialist? Of course not, but people treating their own illnesses must realize that they are taking a chance, based upon their cost/value analysis of the situation, that they are choosing the most logical option.

The same cost/value analysis must be made in deciding to do one's own legal work. Many legal situations are very simple, requiring a simple form and no complicated analysis. Anyone with a little intelligence and a book of instructions can handle the matter simply.

But there is always the chance that there is a complication involved that only a lawyer would notice. To simplify the law into a book like this, several legal cases often must be condensed into a single sentence or paragraph. Otherwise, the book would be several hundred pages long and too complicated for most people. However, this simplification necessarily leaves out many details and nuances that would apply to special or unusual situations. Also, there are many ways to interpret most legal questions. Your case may come before a judge who disagrees with the analysis of our author.

Therefore, in deciding to use a self-help law book and to do your own legal work, you must realize that you are making a cost/value analysis and deciding that the chance that your case will not turn out to your satisfaction is outweighed by the money you will save by doing it yourself. Most people handling their own simple legal matters never have a problem, but occasionally people find that it ended up costing them more to have an attorney straighten out the situation than it would have if they had hired an attorney to begin with. Keep this in mind while handling your case, and be sure to consult an attorney if you feel you might need further guidance.

Chapter 1
The Legal System

This chapter gives you a general introduction to the legal system. Learn to accept these realities and avoid frustration.

Theory vs. Reality

Our legal system is a system of rules. There are basically three types of rules:
1) Rules of Law: such as a law telling a judge how to calculate child support.
2) Rules of Procedure: such as those requiring court papers to be in a certain form, or filed within a certain time.
3) Rules of Evidence: these rules require facts to be proven in a certain way.

The theory is that these rules allow each side to present evidence most favorable to that side, and an independent person or persons (the judge or jury) will be able to figure out the truth. Then legal principles will be applied to that "truth" which will give a fair resolution of the dispute. These legal principles are supposed to be relatively unchanging so we can all know what will happen in any given situation and can plan our lives accordingly. This will provide order and predictability to our society. Any changes in the legal principles are supposed to occur slowly, so that the expected behavior in our society is not confused from day to day. Unfortunately, the system doesn't really work this way. What follows are a few of the problems in the *real* system:

The law changes constantly. Each year new laws are passed, and the appeals courts issue new rulings.

The system is not perfect. Contrary to how it may seem, legal rules are attempts to make the system as fair and just as possible. Unfortunately, these attempts have resulted in a complex set of rules. Sometimes the rules don't give a fair result in a certain situation. Also, judge's can make bad decisions and people can lie.

The system is slow. Even lawyers get frustrated at how long it can take to get a case completed (especially if they don't get paid until it's done). Whatever your situation, things will take longer than you expect. Patience is required to get through the system with a minimum of stress. Be calm and courteous.

Judges don't always follow the rules. This is a shocking discovery for many young lawyers. After spending three years in law school learning legal theory, countless hours preparing for a hearing, and having the law on your side, you find that the judge isn't going to pay any attention to legal theories and the law. Many judges are going to make a decision simply on what they think seems fair under the circumstances. Unfortunately, what "seems fair" to a particular judge may depend upon his personal ideals and philosophy.

No two cases are alike. Just because your friend's case went a certain way doesn't mean yours will have the same result. The judge can make a difference, and more often the circumstances will make a difference. Just because your co-worker makes the same income as you and has the same number of children, you can't assume you will be ordered to pay the same amount of child support. There are usually other circumstances your co-worker doesn't tell you about and possibly doesn't understand.

Half of the people lose. Remember, there are two sides to every legal issue, and there is usually only one winner. Don't expect to have every detail go your way.

Legal Research and Additional Forms

The law relating to divorce, as well as to any other area of law, comes from two sources: 1) the *Florida Statutes*, which are the laws passed by the Florida Legislature, and 2) past decisions of the Florida courts. A complete set of *Florida Statutes* is published every two years (1995, 1997, 1999, etc.), with supplements published during the years in between (1996, 1998, etc.). This book is designed so that you won't need to look up the law in most cases, but if you do decide to look something up be sure you have the most current edition. A set of *Florida Statutes* can usually be found at your local library. The laws for divorce are in Chapter 61 of the *Florida Statutes*. Portions of this law relating to alimony, child custody, and child support can be found in Appendix A of this book. You may also find *Florida Statutes Annotated*, which includes summaries of court opinions and other information about each section of the Florida Statutes. The Florida court decisions are much more difficult to locate and follow. For most situations the law is clearly spelled out in the statutes, and the past court decisions are not all that important. If you need to look up these decisions, you will need to go to your county's law library, which are usually located in the county courthouse or nearby. If you happen to live near a law school, you can also find a law library there.

In the law library you will also find the court rules, and books on divorce and modifying divorce judgments. These will include additional information about specific problems you may have, as well as additional forms. Ask the librarian where to find materials on divorce. The following is a list of primary sources of information:

Florida Rules of Court. These are the rules which are applied in the various courts in Florida, and they also contain approved forms and instructions. These rules mainly deal with forms and procedures. You would be primarily concerned with the "Family Law Rules of Procedure" and "Rules of Civil Procedure."

Florida Digest. This is a set of books containing short summaries of court opinions, and giving the place where you can find the court's full written opinion. The information in the digest is arranged alphabetically by subject. Find the chapter on "Divorce," then look for the subject you want (such as "alimony," "child support," etc.).

Southern Reporter. This is a set of books which contain the full written opinions of the appeals courts. There are two sets, or "series" of the reporter, the older cases being found in the *Southern Reporter* (abbreviated "So."), and the newer cases being found in the *Southern Reporter, 2d Series* (abbreviated "So.2d"). For example, if the digest tells you that the case of *Smith v. Smith* is located at "149 So.2d 721," you can find the case by going to volume 149 of the *Southern Reporter, 2nd Series*, and turning to page 721.

Florida Jurisprudence. This is a legal encyclopedia. You simply look up the subject you want ("Dissolution of Marriage") in alphabetical order, and it gives you a summary of the law on that subject. It will also refer to specific court cases which can then be found in the Southern Reporter.

Other sources. Four books you may want to ask for at the law library are: *Florida Family Law Practice Manual*, by D& S Publishers, Inc.; *Florida Family Law*, by Abrams (published by Matthew-Bender); *Florida Dissolution of Marriage*, by the Florida Bar Continuing Legal Education; and *Florida Civil Trial Practice*, by the Florida Bar Continuing Legal Education. These will explain the law and provide additional forms.

Chapter 2
Modifying a Divorce Judgment

Although the official term in Florida is "dissolution of marriage," this book will also use the term "divorce" to mean the same thing. For example, what is actually titled the "Judgment Dissolving Marriage" will also be referred to as the "divorce judgment."

Only certain parts of a divorce judgment may be modified. These parts are those relating to alimony, child support, child custody, and child visitation. (Property settlement provisions may not be modified except in a few uncommon situations. If you are thinking about modifying your property division, you should consult a lawyer). The main requirement for modifying a divorce judgment is that there has been some change in circumstances since the judgment was entered. The only exception is where you and your ex-spouse agree to the change. Where there is no agreement, the procedure to seek modification is as follows:

Filing the petition. This is nothing more than a written request for the judge to issue an order modifying your divorce judgment. Petition forms are provided in Appendix B of this book, and full instructions are also provided in the following chapters. Once the Petition is filled out and signed, it is taken to the court clerk to be filed. There may also be other papers which must be filed with the Petition depending upon the circumstances.

Obtaining a hearing date. Once all of your paperwork is in order and has been filed, you need to set a date for a hearing. A hearing is simply a meeting with the judge so that he or she can review the circumstances of your case and decide whether to change the divorce judgment. This is done by contacting the judge's secretary or the court clerk and asking for a hearing date. This can often be done over the telephone.

Notifying your ex-spouse. After you've filed the Petition you need to officially notify your ex-spouse. Even though your ex-spouse may already know that you are filing for a modification of your divorce judgment, you still need to have him or her officially notified. This is done by having a copy of your Petition delivered to your ex-spouse. There are certain requirements for how this must be done, which will be explained in detail later.

The hearing. Finally, you go to the hearing. The judge will review the papers you have submitted, hear anything you want to say, consider any additional information you have, and make a decision about whether to change your divorce judgment.

Alimony

A change in alimony requires a significant change in the circumstances of one or both parties since the current alimony award was made. Alimony is determined by the needs of the party receiving alimony and the ability of the other party to pay. In order to increase alimony, the party receiving alimony must prove that he or she needs an increase and that the other party has the ability to pay more. Merely showing that the paying party has increased income is not enough to justify an increase.

In order to decrease alimony, the party paying it will have to prove either that he or she is no longer able to pay the originally ordered amount, or that the receiving party no longer needs as much. For a decrease, it may be enough for the paying party to show that he or she has suffered a decrease in income.

Child Support

Child support is generally determined by taking the combined income of both parents and reading a chart to determine the needs of the children. Then, each parent's contribution to those needs is determined by each parent's share of their total combined income. Occasionally, additional special needs of the children are added. As with alimony, a change in child support also requires a change in needs and ability to pay. However, since it is the income of the parents that determines the needs of the children, a change in income alone will be enough to justify an increase or decrease in the amount of child support. An increase can be justified by either an increase in the income of the paying parent or a decrease in the income of the custodial parent. A decrease can be justified by either a decrease in the income of the paying parent, or an increase in the income of the custodial parent. A change in the special needs of a child may also justify a change in child support.

Child Custody

Unlike the other areas of divorce judgments, custody cannot be changed merely because of a change in circumstances. Generally, the party with custody must be proven to be unfit, or a danger to the child, before custody will be changed against that party's will. The main thing the judge will decide is whether a change in custody is in the best interest of your child. However, there is a strong presumption that the child is best off in a stable environment, which favors the child remaining where he or she is.

Child Visitation

The question of visitation is probably the least clearly defined area of divorce law. It is clear that the law strongly favors a child maintaining a relationship with both parents. While it is difficult to terminate visitation, it is not difficult to obtain a clearly defined visitation schedule. Most people begin with a divorce judgment simply stating that the non-custodial parent "shall have reasonable and liberal" visitation. This leaves it up to the parents to work out a flexible visitation schedule to suit their needs. However, this also leaves much room for argument and problems. If "reasonable and liberal" is not working, it may be necessary to modify the judgment to establish a more clearly spelled-out and rigid schedule.

Also, if you already have a detailed schedule ordered, it may be necessary to change this schedule if there is a change in circumstances which makes the current schedule no longer workable. Examples of changes in circumstances which would justify a change in visitation are the increasing age of the children, a change in a parent's working schedule, or a parent moving a significant distance away from the other parent.

In cases of abuse or neglect, it may also be necessary to ask the court to order supervised visitation or to terminate visitation altogether. This is much more difficult and requires proof similar to that for changing custody due to abuse or neglect.

Asking Your Ex-Spouse

The easiest way to make any of these changes is to agree on the change with your ex-spouse. Reaching an agreement you both can live with is much better than placing the matter in the hands of a third party (the judge), which can lead to a result neither of you will be happy with.

It is beyond the scope and ability of this book to fully present a course in negotiation techniques. However, a few basic rules may be of some help:

Ask for more than you want. This always gives you some room to compromise and still get what you really want. For example, if the issue is child support, your first step is to figure out what support would be under the child support guidelines discussed in Chapter 6. This will tell you what you should be expecting and what the judge will probably order if you go to court. Your second step is to ask your ex-spouse for more (if you want an increase) or less (if you want a decrease) than is called for by the support guidelines. Third, if your spouse rejects your first proposal, you can negotiate up or down to reach what the guidelines call for. If your ex-spouse won't settle for something very close to the guidelines, give up trying to work it out and let the judge decide. The same method should be followed for alimony, although you won't have a table to help you arrive at a figure.

Generally, child custody tends to be something which cannot be negotiated. It is often used as a threat by one of the parties in order to get something else, such as lower child support or alimony. If the real issue is one of these other matters, don't be concerned by the threat of a custody fight. In these cases the other party probably doesn't really want custody and won't fight for it (attorneys charge a lot of money for custody fights). If the real issue is custody, you probably won't be able to agree and will have to let the judge decide anyway.

Let your ex-spouse start the bidding. As a general rule, the first person to mention a dollar figure loses. Try to get your ex-spouse to name the amount he or she thinks it should be first. If your ex-spouse starts with a figure almost what you had in mind, it will be much easier to get to your figure. If your ex-spouse begins with a figure far from yours, you know how far in the other direction to begin your bid. If you absolutely must start the bidding, remember to ask for more than what you really want.

Give your ex-spouse time to think and worry. Your ex-spouse is probably just as afraid as you about the possibility of losing to the judge's decision. Don't be afraid to state your "final offer," then walk away. Give your ex-spouse a day or two to think it over. Maybe he or she will call back and make a better offer. And if not, you can always "reconsider" and make a different offer in a few days. However, don't be too willing to do this or your ex-spouse may think you will give in even more.

Know your bottom line. Before you begin negotiating you should try to set a point which you will not go beyond. If your ex-spouse won't meet your bottom line, go to court and let the judge decide.

If an agreement can be reached, you will need to formalize your agreement with the court by completing and filing the **Joint Petition to Modify Judgment Dissolving Marriage (Form 17)**, in Appendix B of this book. To complete Form 17:

1) Complete the top portion according to the instructions in Chapter 3.
2) In paragraph 1, fill in the date of your divorce judgment.
3) In paragraph 2, check the box or boxes for the items that you have agreed to change, and fill in the blanks as needed. You can check more than one box. For example, if you are changing custody, you may also want to change the child support and visitation. If you are changing alimony or child support, you will need to check the line for either an increase or decrease, and fill in the new alimony or support amount. If you are changing custody, you will need to check the line for who will be getting custody. For all three of these there is a line to indicate how long the change will continue. If the change is to be permanent, simply type in "N/A" on this line (for "not applicable"). If you are changing visitation, you will need to type in a description of the new visitation arrangement. There is also a space on the second page to type in any details of your agreement which can't be included elsewhere. Be sure to see the later chapters of this book relating to the specific things you are changing.
4) You and your ex-spouse must each date and sign the form where indicated, and type in your names, addresses, and telephone numbers.

5) After you make enough copies of the Petition (see Chapter 3 for information on how many copies to make), attach a copy of your original divorce judgment to each copy of the Petition.

If you are changing child support or alimony, you and your ex-spouse should each complete a **Family Law Financial Affidavit (Form 24** or **Form 25)**. Which of these forms each of you use will depend upon your income. See Chapter 5 for more information about how to determine which of these forms to use, and how to complete them. The purpose for filing these forms is to establish your financial conditions at this point in time. If either of you seek to modify child support or alimony in the future, these forms can be used to determine whether there has been a sufficient change in circumstances to justify a change in the amount of child support or alimony.

You will also need to complete the **Order Modifying Judgment Dissolving Marriage (Form 18)**. This will be done by filling in the items with the exact same information from the **Joint Petition (Form 17)**. Leave the date and signature space for the judge to complete but type in the name, address, and telephone information for yourself and your ex-spouse.

Once these forms are prepared, call the judge's secretary. Tell her that you and your ex-spouse have agreed to modify your divorce judgment, that you have prepared a petition and order, and ask her if you can bring it in to leave for the judge to review. Then follow her instructions. You may be able to bring it to the secretary, who will have the judge review the petition and sign the order while you wait; or you may need to file the petition with the court clerk first; or you may need to make an appointment with the judge. Because you and your ex-spouse agree, it should not be necessary for the judge to hold a hearing. Once the judge has signed the order, be sure that both the petition and the order get filed with the court clerk.

Chapter 3
Basic Procedures

This chapter concerns matters which are common to all modifications of divorce judgments. Rather than repeat this information in each part of this book, you will simply be referred back to this chapter when necessary.

Legal Forms

NOTE: You may need to combine two forms from Appendix B to create a single form for filing. In order to save space, and keep the price of this book low, standard signature spaces have not been repeated on each form if it would have required an extra page. For example, Form 24 is a Family Law Financial Affidavit, which must be signed before a notary public. If you look at Form 24 you will see that there is no signature page. To complete Form 24 you would need to attach Form 30 to it and sign it before a notary. When you need to do this is explained in the instructions for those forms.

There is nothing magical about legal forms. They are simply a way of communicating information to the court. Many of the forms in this book were developed by The Florida Bar, as ordered by the Florida Supreme Court. Other forms were prepared by the author. You will note that most of the forms begin as follows:

IN THE CIRCUIT COURT OF THE _____ JUDICIAL CIRCUIT, IN AND

FOR _____ COUNTY, FLORIDA

_____,
Petitioner,

AND

Case No.: _____

Division: _____

_____,
Respondent.

This section of a legal form is called the "case style." The case style tells which court the case is filed in, the case number, and the names of the parties. One of the first things you need to do is get a copy of your divorce judgment (this may be titled "Final Judgment Dissolving Marriage," "Judgment of Dissolution of Marriage," "Divorce Decree," or some similar name). If you can't find a copy, one can be obtained from the court clerk in the county where your divorce judgment was entered. Any forms you complete should have the same case style as your divorce judgment. On the first blank line will be the number of the judicial circuit, which will be spelled out. The second blank is for the name of the county where the court is located.

Next are the names of yourself and your ex-spouse, and the case number and division. Use the names, case number, and division that are on your judgment. If you or your spouse have remarried and have a new name, it is not necessary to use the new married name, although you may add it if you wish. For example, suppose your name was Mary Smith when you were divorced, and you have remarried and are now Mary Jones. Your papers should read either "Mary Smith," or "Mary Smith, nka Mary Jones." The letters "nka" mean "now known as."

For example, a completed case style will look something like this:

IN THE CIRCUIT COURT OF THE __THIRTEENTH__ JUDICIAL CIRCUIT, IN AND

FOR__HILLSBOROUGH__ COUNTY, FLORIDA

Rhett Butler _____ ,
            Petitioner,

                                Case No.: ____96-4857____

AND

                                Division: ____D____

Scarlett O'Hara Butler ____ ,
            Respondent.

It is not absolutely necessary that you use a typewriter to fill in the forms, although typing is preferred by the judges and gives a much more professional appearance than handwriting. If you don't own a typewriter, borrow one from a friend, rent one for a day, or ask if one is available at your local library. If typing is not possible, print the information and be sure that your writing can be easily read.

Filing With the Court Clerk

You will need to file your Petition in the same county where your divorce judgment was entered. For any petition you file, you will need to prepare a **Civil Cover Sheet (Form 20)**. This form is required by all courts for administrative purposes. Complete Form 20 as follows:

1) Under the heading "**I. CASE STYLE**," type in the case style according to the instrucions in the previous section of this chapter (i.e., exactly as it appears on your divorce judgment).
2) Items II and III have already been filled in for you. (Jury trials are not available in divorce or divorce modification cases.)
3) Fill in the date on the line indicated, sign your name on the line above the words "SIGNATURE OF ATTORNEY OR PARTY INITIATING ACTION," and type in your address and phone number on the lines indicated.

Make at least three copies of your petition and any of the other papers you prepared. This will give you the original to file with the clerk, one copy for your ex-spouse, and one copy for yourself, plus one extra copy just in case the clerk asks for two copies or you decide to hire an attorney and need a copy for him or her. Filing is actually about as simple as making a bank deposit, although the following information will help things go smoothly. Call the court clerk's office. You can find the phone number under the county government section of your phone directory. Ask the clerk the following questions (along with any other questions that come to mind, such as where the clerk's office is located and what their hours are):

  ✪ How much is the filing fee for a petition to modify a divorce judgment?
  ✪ Does the court have any special local forms that need to be filed with the petition. (If there are special forms which don't appear in Appendix B of this book, you will need to go down to the clerk's office and pick them up.)
  ✪ How many copies of the petition and other forms do you need to file with the clerk?

Next, take your Petition and any other papers to be filed to the clerk's office. The clerk handles many different types of cases, so be sure to look for signs telling you which office or window to go to. You should be looking for signs that say such things as "Family Court," "Family Division," "Filing," etc. If it's too confusing, ask someone where you file a petition for modifying a divorce judgment.

Once you've found the right place, simply hand the papers to the clerk and say, "I'd like to file this." The clerk will examine the papers, then do one of two things: either say "Thank you" (and collect the filing fee or direct you to where to pay it), or tell you that something is not correct. If you're told something is wrong, ask the clerk to explain to you what is wrong and how to correct the problem. Although clerks are not permitted to give legal advice, the types of problems they spot are usually very minor things that they can tell you how to correct. Often it is possible to figure out how to correct it from the way they explain what is wrong.

Notifying Your Ex-Spouse

Personal Service

The best way to notify your ex-spouse that you have filed a petition to modify your divorce judgment is by personal service. This means the sheriff delivers a copy of your Petition to your ex-spouse. If you are seeking to change rehabilitative alimony to permanent alimony, or are seeking to get child support when none was awarded in your divorce judgment, you MUST have your ex-spouse personally served by the sheriff. Even if personal service is not required, it is the best way to prove to the judge that your ex-spouse received notice of your Petition. The judge may refuse to modify your divorce judgment if he thinks your ex-spouse has not been notified.

The Petition will be delivered along with a Summons. Check with your court clerk to see if the clerk will prepare the Summons or if you need to prepare one. If you need to prepare it, you will need to complete a **Summons: Personal Service on an Individual (Form 1)**. To complete Form 1:
1) Complete the top portion according to the instructions in the first section of this chapter.
2) Type your ex-spouse's name and an address where he or she can be found (preferably during the day) on the lines after the word "TO:" The address you give is where the sheriff will try to find your ex-spouse, so be as certain as possible that it is a good address.
3) Type in your name and mailing address on the lines indicated at the bottom of the second page.
4) Go to the court clerk's office and have the clerk date and sign the Summons.

After the clerk signs the Summons, you will need to deliver or mail to the sheriff the original and one copy of the Summons, and a copy of your Petition and whatever papers you filed with the Petition (such as your Family Law Financial Affidavit, Affidavit Regarding Alimony, Uniform Child Custody Jurisdiction Act Affidavit, etc.). The sheriff will then deliver these papers to your ex-spouse and file a paper with the court verifying the date and time the papers were "served" (delivered). To assist the sheriff, you should also complete the **Process Service Memorandum (Form 2)**. On Form 2 you will note that there is a space to give any special instructions, such as the hours of the day your ex-spouse will most likely be at the place you intend for him or her to be served, or alternate addresses such as his or her work address.

Service by Mail

If you are not seeking to change rehabilitative alimony to permanent alimony, or to get child support when none was awarded in your divorce judgment, you may notify your ex-spouse by mail. You should use "certified mail, return receipt requested," where the mailman has your ex-spouse, or someone in his or her home, sign a green card showing the date the mail was received. This will be your proof to the judge that your ex-spouse was notified of your Petition. This is probably the best method of service if your ex-spouse lives in another state, although you could contact the sheriff where your ex-spouse lives and arrange for personal service. You will need to mail a copy of the Petition and any other papers being filed with it. After mailing the Petition, or any later papers, to your ex-spouse, you will need to file a **Certificate of Service (Form 10)** with the court clerk. To complete the **Certificate of Service (Form 10)**:
1) Complete the top portion according to the instructions in the first section of this chapter.
2) Type in the name of each form you sent to your ex-spouse on the line in the main paragraph which begins "I CERTIFY THAT THE." (Such as "Petition to Change Child Support and Financial Affidavit.")

3) Check the appropriate line for the manner in which you sent or delivered the forms. For service by mail, you will check the line for "mailed." Notice that you may also personally hand deliver the forms, but this won't give you any proof your ex-spouse received them as a green certified mail return receipt card will (but you could always take a friend to be a witness, or have the friend deliver the papers and complete the Certificate of Service).

4) Type in the date the papers were mailed or delivered.

5) The person mailing or delivering the papers must sign on the line marked "Signature of party," and that person's name, address, and telephone number must be typed in below that line. Once completed, this form is to be filed with the court clerk.

6) Type in the name, address and telephone information for your ex-spouse or his or her attorney, whichever you mailed the papers to, on the lines below the words "Party or their attorney (if represented)."

CAUTION: If you are mailing your Petition, you must send it to your ex-spouse, *not* to your ex-spouse's attorney. You cannot assume that the lawyer who represented you ex-spouse in the divorce is still representing him or her. You can only send papers to the lawyer *after* your ex-spouse has received the Petition *and* advised you that he or she has a lawyer.

Service by Publication

This is used if you don't know where your ex-spouse is and can't find him or her. As a practical matter, this will probably not be used to seek an increase in alimony or child support. If you don't know where your ex-spouse is, you probably aren't receiving the alimony or child support ordered in the divorce judgment. In such a case you would probably be better off trying to go through your local Child Support Enforcement office to locate your ex-spouse, and worry about an increase later. However, if you are no longer financially able to pay the amount ordered in your divorce judgment, you need to file a Petition immediately. Even if you haven't been paying because there is no address to send the payments to, alimony and child support arrearages will keep growing, so don't wait!

Service by publication is one of the more complicated procedures in the legal system. You will need to follow the steps listed below very carefully.

Step 1: The Diligent Search

The court will only permit publication when you can't locate your ex-spouse. This also includes the situation where the sheriff has tried several times to personally serve your ex-spouse, but it appears that your ex-spouse is hiding to avoid being served. First, you'll have to show that you can't locate your ex-spouse by letting the court know what you've done to try to find him or her. In making this search you may want to try the following:

- Check the phone book and directory assistance in the area where you live.
- Check directory assistance in the area where you last knew your ex-spouse to be.
- Ask friends and relatives who might know where your ex-spouse might be.
- Check with the post office where he or she last lived to see if there is a current or forwarding address. (You can ask by mail if the post office is too far away.)
- Check records of the tax collector and property assessor to see if your ex-spouse owns property.
- Write to the Department of Motor Vehicles to see if your ex-spouse has any car registrations.
- Check with your ex-spouse's last known employer. You can ask for any address to which W-2 Forms were mailed. If there is a pension or profit-sharing plan, ask to what address any information or checks are mailed.
- Check with any unions to which your ex-spouse may have belonged.
- Check with any regulartory agencies, or professional, occupational, or business licensing.
- Check with law enforcement and correctional (prison) agencies.
- Check with utility companies.
- Check with the armed forces (see the following section on the "Memorandum for Certificate of Military Service").

If you do come up with a current address in Florida, go back to personal service by the sheriff, or service by mail. If not, continue with this procedure.

Step 2: Preparing and Filing Court Papers

Once you have made your search you need to notify the court. This is done by filing the **Affidavit for Service by Publication (Form 11)**. This form tells the court what you've done to try to find your ex-spouse and asks permission to publish your notice. To complete Form 11:
1) Complete the top portion according to the instructions in the first section of this chapter.
2) Type your name in the blank at the beginning of the first, unnumbered paragraph.
3) On the lines in paragraph 1, type in what you have done to try to locate your ex-spouse. (See the items listed in *Step 1* above.)
4) Check the appropriate lines in paragraphs 2 through 4 and fill in any requested information.
5) Complete the certificate of service paragraph that begins "I CERTIFY THAT," including your ex-spouse's last known address below the words "Party or their attorney (if represented)."
6) Complete and attach the **Standard signature page with notary (Form 30)**, then take the affidavit to a notary public and sign your name before the notary on the line marked "Signature of party signing certificate and pleading/affidavit."

You will also prepare a **Notice of Action (Form 12)**. To complete Form 12:
1) Type your ex-spouse's name after the word "TO:"
2) Type your name and address in the blanks in the first paragraph. Leave the other spaces blank, as they are for the clerk to complete.
3) Take the original **Affidavit for Service by Publication (Form 11)**, and the original and two copies of the **Notice of Action (Form 12)**, to the court clerk.

The clerk will fill in the remaining blanks on the **Notice of Action** and return two copies to you. If the clerk finds any errors in your papers, he will notify you as to what needs to be corrected. You may need to provide the clerk with a self-addressed, stamped envelope when you deliver your notice.

Step 3: Publishing

After the clerk completes it, you need to have a newspaper publish the **Notice of Action (Form 12)**. Check the Yellow Pages listings under "Newspapers" and call several of the smaller ones in your county (making sure it is in the same county as the court) to ask if they are approved for legal announcements. If they are, ask how much they charge to publish a **Notice of Action** not involving property. What you want is the cheapest paper. Most areas have a paper that specializes in publishing legal announcements at a much cheaper rate than the regular daily newspapers. If you look around the courthouse you may be able to find a copy or newsstand for this paper.

Once you find the paper you want, send them a copy of the **Notice of Action** along with a check for the publication fee and a cover letter stating:

> Enclosed is a Notice of Action for publication as required by law. Please take notice of the return date in the Notice of Action, and ensure that the dates of publication meet the legal requirement that the return date be "not less than 28 nor more than 60 days after the first publication." If you cannot comply with this requirement, please notify me immediately so I can obtain an amended Notice of Action.

The **Notice of Action** will be published once a week for four weeks. Get a copy of the newspaper the first time it will appear and check to be sure it was printed correctly. If you find an error, notify the newspaper immediately.

Look at the date the clerk put in the blank space in the main paragraph of the **Notice of Action**. You must make sure that this date is at least 28 days after the date the newspaper first published the **Notice of Action**. Also make sure it is no more than 60 days after the date of the first publication. If these requirements are not met, notify the newspaper of THEIR mistake. Remind them of your cover letter if necessary. You will also need to prepare a new **Notice of Action** for the clerk to sign, and go through this procedure again. If the newspaper made the mistake, they should not charge you for the second publication.

As indicated in the **Notice of Action**, your ex-spouse has until a certain date to respond. If your ex-spouse responds to the notice published in the newspaper, proceed with setting a hearing date (see the section in this chapter on "Setting a Court Date.") If your ex-spouse does not respond by the date indicated in the **Notice of Action**, proceed with seeking a default as described below.

Memorandum for Certificate of Military Service (Form 8)

If you don't know whether your ex-spouse is in the military service, you will need to complete the **Memorandum for Certificate of Military Service (Form 8)**. To complete Form 8:
1) Complete the top portion according to the instructions in the first section of this chapter.
2) Type your spouse's name and social security number on the lines marked "[Party]" and "[Soc. Sec.#]."
3) Complete the **Standard signature page without notary (Form 29)** and attach it as the second page of the **Memorandum for Certificate of Military Service (Form 8)**.

You will then need to make seven copies of this form, and mail one to each of the seven addresses listed on the form (one to each branch of the U.S. Government considered "military" service). Be sure to enclose a stamped envelope, addressed to yourself with each one. Each service branch will then check its records and mail you a notice as to whether your spouse is in that branch (these notices may then be filed with the court clerk). If your spouse is in one of the service branches, his or her address will be provided. A fee may be charged by the military branch. Try checking on this with your closest military base, the court clerk, or the child support enforcement office. Otherwise, the branch of the military will let you know if a fee is required when it receives the form. If your spouse *is* in the military, but will not cooperate in reaching an agreement, you should contact an attorney.

Nonmilitary Affidavit (Form 9)

If your spouse is *not* in the military service (and won't quickly reach an agreement with you), you will need to complete the **Nonmilitary Affidavit (Form 9)**. To complete Form 9 you need to:
1) Complete the top portion according to the instructions in the first section of this chapter.
2) Type in the name of the county where you will be signing the form after the words "COUNTY OF."
3) Type your name in the blank space in the first (unnumbered) paragraph.
4) Check either paragraph 1 or 2, whichever applies.
5) Complete the certificate of service section.
6) Complete the **Standard signature page with notary (Form 30)** and attach it as the last page of the **Nonmilitary Affidavit (Form 9)**.
7) Sign before a notary public on the line marked "Signature of party signing certificate and affidavit."

Call the court clerk to ask when the **Nonmilitary Affidavit** needs to be filed. Some courts require that it not be signed too far in advance, because they want the information to be reasonably current. Some courts require that the notary public's date on the **Nonmilitary Affidavit** be within a certain number of days before filing a **Request to Enter Default (Form 6)**, or before the final hearing. If your spouse is not willing to reach an agreement with you, and *is* in the military service, you do not need to complete this form and should consult a lawyer. Federal laws designed to protect service personnel while overseas can create special problems in these situations and you will need a lawyer to help you.

Default

You must give your ex-spouse at least 20 days to respond to your Petition. The response must be in writing and must be filed with the court. If you receive a response but your ex-spouse doesn't file a copy with the court clerk, then you need to make a copy and file it. You may set a hearing date once your ex-spouse files a response or after the 20-day period, whichever comes first. Depending upon which method of service you use, count 20 days from the date your ex-spouse is personally served by the sheriff (check the sheriff's affidavit of service for the date), or from the date your ex-spouse signed the green return receipt card for certified mail. For service by publication, use the date filled in on the **Notice of Action**.

Request to Enter Default (Form 6)

If your ex-spouse does not respond to your Petition within 20 days after the sheriff delivers it (or the date it was received according to the green return receipt card), your spouse is "in default." You will need to notify the court clerk that your spouse has not filed an answer, and ask the clerk to formally enter the default in your court file. To accomplish this you need to complete a **Request to Enter Default (Form 6)**, and deliver it to the clerk. To complete the **Request to Enter Default (Form 6)** you need to:

1) Complete the top portion according to the instructions in the first section of this chapter.
2) Fill in the certificate of service section to show how, and to whom, you sent a copy of the form (this should be to your spouse's last known address, which will probably be the address where he or she was served by the sheriff with the Petition).
3) Fill in the date, sign your name on the line marked "Signature of party signing certificate and pleading," and type in your name, address, and phone numbers on the lines below your signature.

Default (Form 7)

The **Default (Form 7)** is the form the court clerk will sign to officially declare that your spouse is in default. Complete the top portion according to the instructions in the first section of this chapter. On the second page, type in your name, address, and phone numbers on the lines indicated. Take this form to the clerk along with the **Request to Enter Default (Form 6)**. The clerk will review these forms, check the court file to be sure that the required time has expired and that no response has been filed by your spouse, and will date and sign the **Default (Form 7)**. Complete the **Standard signature page without notary (Form 29)** and attach it as the second page of the **Default**.

Setting a Court Date

Once your ex-spouse files a response, or fails to respond within the time period discussed above, you need to get a hearing date. Getting a hearing date set is a simple matter. Call the secretary of the judge assigned to your case. (If you don't know which judge, call the court clerk, give the clerk your case number, and ask for the name and phone number of the judge assigned to your case.) Usually the judge's phone number can be found in the government section of your phone book. Tell the secretary that you've filed a petition to modify your divorce judgment and that you need to set a hearing date.

The secretary may ask you how long the hearing will take. The answer will depend upon the type of modification you are seeking. For changes in child support, a ten minute hearing should be enough, provided you have all of the income information you need for yourself and your ex-spouse. For changes in alimony or visitation, the time needed will depend upon how complicated the change in circumstances are. Somewhere between 15 and 30 minutes should be enough. For custody disputes, there are frequently several witnesses for both parties, which can result in a hearing anywhere from an hour to two or three days! It's a good idea to ask for the most amount of time you think it will take, because if you don't finish the hearing in the time allowed, it may be several weeks before you can get another hearing date to finish. Figure on about 20 to 30 minutes for each witness, and don't forget to figure in the number of witnesses your ex-spouse may bring. The secretary will then give you a date and time for the hearing, but you will also need to know where the hearing will be. Ask the secretary for the location. You'll need the street address of the courthouse, as well as the room number, floor or other location within the building. The next section will explain why you need this information.

Hearing Notices

Depending upon the procedure used in your county, there are various types of hearing notices you may need to use. In some counties you will simply get a hearing date and time from the judge's secretary, and send your ex-spouse a **Notice of Hearing (Form 3)**. In other counties you will first need to file a **Motion to Set Final Hearing/ Trial (Form 4)** and submit an **Order Setting Matter for Final Hearing or for Status Conference (Form 5)**. The judge will then complete the order and return it to you; then you can send your ex-spouse the **Notice of Hearing (Form 3)**. In other counties your case may be referred to a General Master, who is an attorney that will hear your case and make a recommendation to the judge. If a General Master will be used, the court will notify you either by sending you an order or asking you to prepare and submit an order. If you need to prepare the order, you will complete the **Order of Referral to General Master (Form 22).** You will then arrange a hearing date and time with the General Master's office and send your ex-spouse a **Notice of Hearing Before General Master (Form 23).** Following are instructions to help you complete each of these forms.

Notice of Hearing (Form 3)

To complete the **Notice of Hearing (Form 3):**
1) Complete the top portion according to the instructions in the first section of this chapter.
2) Type in your ex-spouse's name and address after the word "TO:"
3) Complete the main paragraph by typing in the information asked for, relating to where and when the hearing will be held. For example:

> There will be a hearing before Judge *{name of judge}*
> ___Barry D. Hatchett___, on *{date}*___October 23___, 19__96__,
> at *{time}*___9:00 a.m.___, in Room ___245___ of the
> ___Hillsborough County___ Courthouse, on the following matter:
> ___Petition to Modify Child Support___.

5) After you have talked with the judge's secretary about a hearing date, fill in the amount of time the secretary has reserved for the hearing.
6) Call the court clerk to obtain the information you need to complete the section relating to the Americans with Disabilities Act.
7) Complete the certificate of service section on the second page, including your ex-spouse's name, address, and phone information.
8) Sign your name on the line marked "Signature of party signing certificate and pleading," and type in your name, address, and telephone number information on the lines indicated. Make three copies of the **Notice of Hearing** and mail one copy to your ex-spouse (along with a blank **Family Law Financial Affidavit (Form 24** or **Form 25)** if you are seeking to modify alimony or child support). File the original **Notice of Hearing** with the court clerk and keep two copies for yourself.

Motion to Set Final Hearing/Trial (Form 4)

To complete the **Motion to Set Final Hearing/Trial (Form 4),** fill in the top portion according to the instructions in the first section of this chapter, then check the appropriate boxes, type in how long you expect the hearing will take in paragraph "2," complete the Certificate of Service section and fill in your name, address, and phone information. Then sign the form and file it with the clerk.

Order Setting Matter for Final Hearing or Status Conference (Form 5)

When you file the **Motion to Set Final Hearing/Trial (Form 4),** you will also need to complete the top portion of Form 5 and leave it with the court clerk (along with two extra copies to be returned to you). The clerk or judge will then fill in the rest, and return a copy of Form 5 to you. Form 5 is a modified version of the Supreme Court-approved form. The Supreme Court-approved form did not have any provision for a contested case, so this form has been changed to allow for its use in more situations. If your case is contested, the judge may go ahead and set it for trial, or may first schedule a status conference where you and your spouse will sit down with the judge for a few minutes to make it clear to everyone what issues the judge needs to determine at the trial. Your next step will be to notify your spouse of the hearing or status conference by sending him or her a copy of the **Order Setting Matter for Final Hearing of Status Conference (Form 5),** and file a **Certificate of Service (Form 10)** listing the "Order Setting Matter for Final Hearing or Status Conference" as the document served (see the subsection of this chapter on "Notice of Hearing").

Order of Referral to General Master (Form 22)

If the judge refers your case to a General Master, you will need to complete the **Order of Referral to General Master (Form 22)**, and submit it to the judge for his or her signature. Read this entire form carefully, because it spells out your rights and provides other important information regarding referrals to general masters. To complete Form 22, complete the top portion according to the instructions in Chapter 3, and fill in the name, address, and phone number information for you and your ex-spouse on the second page of the form. Check with the judge's secretary or the court clerk to find out if you need to complete more of this form. If so, you will need to list the matters being referred to the General Master in items 1 through 4 at the top of the form, type in the name of the General Master in the first paragraph, and fill in any other information as instructed. Or, the judge may fill in these items. Once signed by the judge, a copy of this form will be sent to you, your ex-spouse, and the General Master. The General Master will then schedule a hearing date.

Notice of Hearing Before General Master (Form 23)

Once the General Master sets a hearing date, you will need to notify your ex-spouse by sending him or her a **Notice of Hearing Before General Master (Form 23)**. This is very similar to the **Notice of Hearing (Form 3)**, so see the instructions for that form on page 20.

Preparing Your Case

Subpoenas

To prepare for your hearing, you may need to have subpoenas issued. There are several types of subpoenas, so be sure you use the correct form.

Subpoenas to Get Information Before Hearing

If you are seeking to modify alimony or child support, the judge will require a **Family Law Financial Affidavit (Form 24** or **Form 25)** from you, and also one from your ex-spouse. If your ex-spouse has indicated that he or she will not cooperate at all and will not provide a **Family Law Financial Affidavit**, you may have to try to get the information yourself. You can go to the hearing and tell the judge that your ex-spouse won't cooperate, but the judge may just issue an order requiring your ex-spouse to provide information (or be held in contempt of court) and continue the hearing to another date. It may help to speed things up if you are able to get the information yourself and have it available at the hearing. This will require you to get a subpoena issued.

> **CAUTION:** Before you send a subpoena to your ex-spouse's employer, bank, or accountant, you need to let your ex-spouse know what you are about to do. The thought that you are about to get these other people involved in your case may be enough to get your ex-spouse to cooperate. If your ex-spouse calls and says "I'll give you the information," give him or her a few days to follow through. Ask when you can expect to receive the **Family Law Financial Affidavit** and offer to send your ex-spouse a blank copy if he or she needs one. If your ex-spouse sends a completed **Family Law Financial Affidavit** as promised, don't send the subpoena. If your ex-spouse doesn't follow through, go ahead with the subpoena. You can send out subpoenas to as many people or organizations as you need, but you'll need to use the following procedure for each subpoena.

The advance notice to your ex-spouse is called a **Notice of Production From Non-Party (Form 13)**. To complete Form 13:

1) Complete the top portion according to the instructions in the first section of this chapter.
2) Type your ex-spouse's name and address after the words "TO: [all parties]"
3) On the line in the main paragraph, type in the name of the person or company, bank, etc., where the subpoena will be sent. If at all possible, use a person's name or title so that the subpoena is directed to a specific person. For example: "Jim Jackson, Payroll Director," or "Records Clerk."
4) Complete the certificate of service section, including your ex-spouse's name, address, and phone information.
5) Complete and attach a **Standard signature page without notary (Form 29)**.

Next, you will complete a form called **Subpoena for Production of Documents (Form 14)**. This form will eventually be sent to whomever you want to get information from. Look at the **Family Law Financial Affidavit (Form 24 or Form 25)** and see what type of information is asked for. Your ex-spouse's income information can be obtained from his or her employer. Stock and bond information can be obtained from his or her stock broker, bank account balances from the bank, auto loan balances from the lender, etc. You can have subpoenas issued to any or all of these places, but don't overdo it. Concentrate on income information.

To complete the **Subpoena for Production of Documents (Form 14)**:
1) Complete the top portion according to the instructions in the first section of this chapter.
2) Type your ex-spouse's employer's (or broker's, bank's, etc.) name and address after the word "TO:" Again, try to use a person's name or title.
3) Complete the first paragraph by filling in the information on the appropriate lines as to where and when the person is to appear with the requested information. This could be your home or place of business, the office of a court reporter (they will charge you a fee), or any other appropriate place where you will have access to a copy machine.
4) In the space after the first paragraph (after the words "and place the following:") type in a description of the documents or other items you want produced. Be as specific as possible, such as including your ex-spouse's Social Security number, an account number, or any other information that will help the person receiving the subpoena to know what you are asking for.)
5) Call the court clerk to get the information needed to complete the Americans with Disabilities Act section at the top of the second page.
6) Leave the rest of the spaces blank.

Next, mail a copy of the **Notice of Production From Non-Party (Form 13)** along with a copy of the **Subpoena for Production of Documents (Form 14)** and a blank **Family Law Financial Affidavit (Form 24 or Form 25)** to your ex-spouse. Make sure that you actually mail it on the date you filled in on the certificate of service section of the **Notice of Production From Non-Party**. If your ex-spouse doesn't file a **Family Law Financial Affidavit** within 15 days, you will complete the **Subpoena for Production of Documents** and have it issued by the clerk. To complete the **Subpoena for Production of Documents**, below the paragraph that begins "I HEREBY CERTIFY," type in the date and your name, address and telephone information on the appropriate lines, and sign your name on the line marked "Signature of party signing certificate and pleading."

Subpoenas for Hearing

These are subpoenas which require a person to appear at the hearing and either give testimony (a Subpoena), or give testimony and produce documents or other items (a Subpoena Duces Tecum). Before using the forms that appear in Appendix B, check with the court clerk to see if they have subpoena forms. If the clerk has a form, use it. If not, you can use the forms in Appendix B. The instructions below will still help you to complete the clerk's forms.

In order to force someone to appear at the hearing and testify, you will need to have the person served by the sheriff with a **Subpoena (Form 15)**. Even if your witness is a friend who wants to appear to testify for you, it is a good idea to have him or her served with a subpoena. The subpoena will enable your friend to get off of work to come to the hearing and will enable you to have the hearing continued to a later date if your friend has car trouble, or becomes ill, so that he or she can't make it to the hearing. To complete the **Subpoena (Form 15)**:
1) Complete the top portion according to the instructions in the first section of this chapter.
2) Type in the name and address of the person to be served with the **Subpoena** after the word "TO:" Use an address where the person can be found by the sheriff during the day. You can also complete the **Process Service Memorandum (Form 2)** and deliver it to the sheriff along with the subpoena.
3) In the main paragraph, fill in the information for the place and time of the hearing [see the instructions for the **Hearing Notice (Form 3)**, on page 20].
4) Type in your name, address and telephone number under the heading "Attorney or Party Requesting Subpoena." This will allow the witness or the sheriff to contact you if the witness has any questions or if the sheriff has any trouble serving the subpoena.
5) Take the **Subpoena** to the court clerk for the clerk to issue (how to have subpoenas issued and served is discussed below).

A **Subpoena Duces Tecum (Form 16)** is simply a subpoena which also requires the witness to bring something with him. Usually it will be documents or records, but it might also be objects which are relevant to the issues to be decided by the judge (such as a paddle used to spank your child which you are claiming constitutes abuse). To complete a **Subpoena Duces Tecum (Form 16)** you need to:

1) Complete the top portion according to the instructions in the first section of this chapter.
2) Complete the other portions of the form the same as for a **Subpoena (Form 15)**.
3) In the space after the words "AND to bring the following items with you:" type in a description of whatever it is you want the witness to bring. This might be such things as "Your police report relating to... [give the date and names of the persons the report relates to]" or "Medical records relating to... [give the person's name]" or "Payroll records relating to . . . [give the person's name and social security number]."
4) Type in your name, address and telephone number under the heading "Attorney or Party Requesting Subpoena." This will allow the witness or the sheriff to contact you if the witness has any questions or if the sheriff has any trouble serving the subpoena.
5) Have the Subpoena Duces Tecum issued and served by the sheriff.

Getting a Subpoena Issued and Served

To get any type of subpoena issued, take the subpoena to the court clerk. The clerk will sign and date the subpoena and return it to you. Next, have the sheriff personally serve the subpoena to the person or place named in the subpoena. The sheriff will need at least one extra copy of the subpoena and a check for the service fee. You should also provide the sheriff with a **Process Service Memorandum (Form 2)**, filled in with information to help the sheriff find the person to be served. Call the sheriff's office for more information on having a subpoena served. The sheriff will have also filed an affidavit verifying when the subpoena was served.

For the **Subpoena for Production of Documents (Form 14)**, the employer, bank, etc., should send you the requested information. If the employer calls you and says you must pay for copies, ask him how much they will cost and send a check or money order. If the employer doesn't provide the information, tell the judge this at the hearing and show him the subpoena. There are more procedures you could go through to force the employer to give the information, but it probably isn't worth the hassle and you'd probably need an attorney to help you with it. Let the judge order your ex-spouse to provide the information.

For subpoenas for hearing, the person served must appear and testify. Anyone failing to appear is subject to contempt of court penalties.

Witnesses

See the section on "Preparing And Presenting Your Proof" in Chapter 7 for a discussion of witnesses. Chapter 7 refers mostly to custody cases, but can easily be applied to witnesses for other types of cases as well.

Rules of Evidence

As stated in the Introduction, this book cannot make you a lawyer. However, you should be aware of a few basic rules of evidence.

✪ *Relevancy.* The documents you present to the judge and questions that you ask any witnesses should be related to the facts you need to prove. For example, if you are trying to have your child support lowered because you have been laid off from your job, the fact that your ex-spouse gives you a hard time when you come to pick up the child for visitation has no relevancy to the child support issue. You need to determine what information you need to give the judge for the type of change you are seeking, and stick to that information.

✪ *Hearsay.* Generally, a witness cannot testify to what someone else told him. For example, suppose you are trying to change custody due to physical abuse, and your ex-spouse's neighbor actually saw your ex-spouse beat your child with an electric cord. You need the neighbor in court to testify to what she saw. You cannot have your cousin testify that the neighbor told him she saw the beating. This can also apply to documents which contain statements made by someone who is not in court to testify. (There are numerous exceptions to the hearsay rule, and many lawyers and judges don't fully understand this area of law. One important exception is that you can use any statements your ex-spouse made to the person testifying.)

○ *Documents.* Generally, documents must be introduced at the hearing by someone's testimony. You need someone (it can even be you) who can identify the paper, say who prepared the paper, and how they know who prepared the paper. For example, to introduce documents you received from your ex-spouse's employer, you can testify as to how you got the documents.

○ *Examining Witnesses.* This refers to asking questions of your witnesses (direct examination) and of your ex-spouse's witnesses (cross-examination). One problem most non-lawyers have with this is that they tend to start testifying instead of asking questions. This is not the time for you to explain anything. You need to ask simple questions, and wait for the witness to answer. You should be particularly careful in cross-examining your ex-spouse's witnesses. If you aren't *very* sure what their answer will be, don't ask the question. Don't feel that you must ask questions of each witness. Often it is best to let the witness go without further damaging your case.

Preparing for the Hearing

To prepare for the hearing you need to decide what you are going to say, what documents and witnesses (if any) you will present, and the order in which you will present them. You should make a list of each fact you intend to prove, and next to each fact write down how you will prove it. For example:

(1)	My income at time of judgment	Original Financial Affidavit.
(2)	Ex-wife's income at time of judgment	Original Financial Affidavit.
(3)	My current income	My Financial Affidavit and pay stub.
(4)	Ex-wife's current income	Her Financial Affidavit.
(5)	Decreased special needs of child	Testimony of doctor that child no longer needs costly medication.

You will want to have your notes ready to keep you on track at the hearing and have your documents arranged in the order you will present them. If you have witnesses, you will want to have a **Witness Testimony Worksheet (Form 31)** filled out for each witness and have these arranged in the order in which the witnesses will testify (see Chapter 7 for more information on the use of the **Witness Testimony Worksheet**).

The Hearing

Courtroom Manners

There are certain rules of procedure that are used in a court. These are really the rules of good conduct, or good manners, and are designed to keep things orderly. Many of the rules are written down, although some are unwritten customs that have just developed over many years. They aren't difficult, and they do make sense.

Show respect for the judge. This basically means, don't do anything to make the judge angry at you, such as arguing with him. Be polite, and call the judge "Your Honor" when you speak to him, such as "Yes, Your Honor," or "Your Honor, I brought proof of my income." Although many lawyers address judges as "Judge," this is not proper. Showing respect also means wearing appropriate clothing, such as a coat and tie for men and a dress for women. This especially means no T-shirts, blue jeans, shorts, or "revealing" clothing. Many of the following rules also relate to showing respect for the court.

Whenever the judge talks, you listen. Even if the judge interrupts you, stop talking immediately and listen.

Only one person can talk at a time. Each person is allotted his or her own time to talk in court. The judge can only listen to one person at a time, so don't interrupt your ex-spouse when it's his or her turn. And as difficult as it may be, stop talking if your ex-spouse interrupts you. (Let the judge tell your ex-spouse to keep quiet and let you have your say.)

Talk to the judge, not to your ex-spouse. Many people get in front of a judge and begin arguing with each other. They actually turn away from the judge, face each other, and begin arguing as if they are in the room alone. This generally has several negative results: The judge can't understand what either one is saying since they both start talking at once, they both look like fools for losing control, and the judge gets angry with both of them. So whenever you speak in a courtroom, look only at the judge. Try to pretend that your ex-spouse isn't there. Remember, you are there to convince the judge that you should have your divorce judgment changed. You don't need to convince your ex-spouse.

Talk only when it's your turn. The usual procedure is for you to present your case first. When you are done saying all you came to say, your ex-spouse will have a chance to say whatever he or she came to say. Let your ex-spouse have his or her say. When he or she is finished you will get another chance to respond to what has been said.

Keep calm. Judges like things to go smoothly in their courtrooms. They don't like shouting, name calling, crying, or other displays of emotion. Generally, judges don't like family law cases because they get too emotionally charged. So give your judge a pleasant surprise by keeping calm and focusing on the issues.

Show respect for your ex-spouse. Even if you don't respect your ex-spouse, act like you do. All you have to do is refer to your ex-spouse as "Mr. Smith" or "Ms. Smith" (using his or her correct name, of course).

Following these suggestions will make the judge respect you for your maturity and professional manner and possibly even make him forget for a moment that you are not a lawyer. It will also increase the likelihood that you will get the change you request.

Presenting Your Case

The judge will know that you don't have a lawyer, and he may help you through the hearing by asking you what he needs to know or even telling you what you need to do to present your case. When you first meet the judge, smile and say "Good morning, your Honor," or "Good afternoon, your Honor." Then just follow his lead. If he starts guiding you, or asking questions, just let him control the hearing. Otherwise, be ready to give your brief opening statement, telling the judge what type of petition you filed, the basic reason you filed the petition, and what change you want in the divorce judgment.

The judge may stop you before you have the chance to complete your opening statement and just ask you to present your proof. This is usually done to save time. If this happens just present your proof (which may simply be the **Family Law Financial Affidavits** filed by you and your ex-spouse). The judge will probably swear you in, then tell you to proceed. What you do to proceed will depend upon what change you are asking for. Presenting your case will be discussed more in later chapters of this book.

The Modified Order

After you and your ex-spouse have presented your information to the judge, he will make a decision. You will then need to prepare an order for the judge to sign. There are different orders for each type of change that might be requested, and they will be discussed in detail in later chapters. Along with the order you will need to prepare a **Final Disposition Form (Form 21)**. Like the **Civil Cover Sheet (Form 20)**, this is another form required by the courts for their administrative purposes. Part I of the form should be completed exactly the same as the **Civil Cover Sheet**. Under the heading "II. MEANS OF FINAL DISPOSITION," check the box marked "Disposed by Judge." This form also needs to be dated and signed by you, but be sure to use the date of the final hearing. Take this form with you to the final hearing and give it to the judge at the hearing, along with the order.

When You Can't Afford Court Costs

If you do not have the financial ability to pay for filing fees, having your ex-spouse and any witnesses served, or for guardian ad litem, drug testing or psychological evaluation fees, you will need to prepare and file an **Affidavit of Insolvency (Form 19)**. This is referred to in some of the other forms as an "indigency affidavit," "affidavit for suspension of fees and costs," or "request for suspension of fees and costs." (This is another example of how inconsistent The Florida Bar was when it drafted the standardized forms. It prepared motions which referred to a document by one name, then called that document by another name.) In order to qualify for a waiver of the filing fee, you must be "indigent." If you are indigent, your income is probably low enough for you to qualify for public assistance (welfare).

> **CAUTION:** If you decide to use the **Affidavit of Insolvency (Form 19)**, you will probably be asked for more information to prove that you meet the requirements for being declared indigent, and therefore eligible to have the filing and service fees waived. Before you file this form, you may want to see if the court clerk will give you any information on what is required to be declared indigent. You should also be aware that you can be held in contempt of court for giving false information on this form.

To complete the **Affidavit of Insolvency (Form 19)**:
1) Complete the top portion according to the instructions in the first section of this chapter.
2) After the words "COUNTY OF {name}," type in the name of the county in which you live.
3) In the first paragraph, type in your name.
4) In the second paragraph, if you are on public assistance, place an "x" on the line before paragraph "a." Then type in the amount of assistance you receive, the period it represents ("week," "month," etc.), and your public assistance case number. If you are on public assistance you do not need to complete paragraph "b" and you can skip down to number 7 of these instructions.
6) If you are *not* on public assistance, you will need to check paragraph "b." You will then need to complete all of the items under paragraph "b." Type in the name and address of your employer, and the length of time you have been employed there. Type in your average gross pay, your average net pay, and check the space for the payroll period which applies to you. Under the heading "ASSETS," list all of the property you own and the value of each item. Under the heading "DEBTS/BILLS," list all your monthly bills .
7) Complete and attach a **Standard signature page with notary (Form 30)**, but do not sign this form yet.
8) Take this form to a notary, and sign it before the notary on the line marked "Signature of party signing certificate and pleading/affidavit." The notary will then date and sign the form. This form is now ready for filing.

Good Things to Know

Mediation. In any case where child custody, visitation, or support are in dispute, the court may order you and your ex-spouse into mediation. The mediator will try to help you reach an agreement, which will then be put in writing and approved by the judge.

Tax Effects. A change in your divorce judgment may also result in a change in your tax situation. Alimony is income to the person who receives it, and is a tax deduction for the person who pays it. Child support is neither income, nor a deduction. Only the person with whom the child resides may claim the tax exemption for the child, unless you and your ex-spouse file a special IRS form each year. In setting a child support amount the judge may consider the tax effect and may order the custodial parent to sign the necessary paper to waive the exemption. If your ex-spouse is ordered to sign this tax paper and refuses to do so, he or she may then be held in contempt of court.

Chapter 4
Lawyers

Whether you *need* an attorney will depend upon many factors, such as how comfortable you feel handling the matter yourself, whether your situation is more complicated than usual, how much opposition you get from your ex-spouse, and whether your ex-spouse has an attorney. It may also be advisable to hire an attorney if you encounter a judge with a hostile attitude. There are no court appointed lawyers in divorce cases, so if you want an attorney you will have to hire one. A very general rule is that you should consider hiring an attorney whenever you reach a point where you no longer feel comfortable representing yourself. This point will vary greatly with each person, so there is no easy way to be more definite. A more appropriate question is "Do you *want* a lawyer?"

Do You Want a Lawyer?

One of the first questions you will want to consider, and most likely the reason you are reading this book, is: How much will an attorney cost? Lawyers usually charge an hourly rate ranging from about $75 to $300 per hour, and a hotly contested custody fight can cost from $2,000 to $15,000! Most new (and therefore less expensive) attorneys would be quite capable of handling a simple modification, but, if your situation became more complicated, you would probably prefer a more experienced lawyer.

Some Advantages to Having a Lawyer

- ✪ Judges and other attorneys may take you more seriously. Most judges prefer both parties to have attorneys. They feel this helps the case move in a more orderly fashion. Persons representing themselves very often waste a lot of time on matters which have absolutely no bearing on the outcome of the case.
- ✪ A lawyer will serve as a "buffer" between you and your ex-spouse. This can speed things up by reducing the chance for emotions to take control.
- ✪ Attorneys prefer to deal with other attorneys for the same reasons listed above.
- ✪ You can let your lawyer worry about all of the details. By having an attorney you need only become generally familiar with the contents of this book.
- ✪ Lawyers provide professional assistance with problems. In the event your case is complicated, or suddenly becomes complicated, it is an advantage to have an attorney who is familiar with your case. It can also be comforting to have a lawyer to turn to for advice and to get your questions answered.

Some Advantage to Representing Yourself

○ You save the cost of a lawyer.
○ Sometimes judges feel more sympathetic toward a person not represented by an attorney. This may result in the unrepresented person being allowed a certain amount of leeway with the procedure rules (but not with poor conduct).
○ The procedure may be faster. Two of the most frequent complaints about lawyers received by the bar association involve delay in completing the case and failure to return phone calls. Most lawyers have a heavy caseload, which sometimes results in cases being neglected for various periods of time. If you are following the progress of your own case you'll be able to push it along the system diligently.
○ Selecting any attorney is not easy. As the next section shows, it is hard to know whether you are selecting an attorney you will be happy with. There are numerous "horror stories" of attorneys getting $1,000 in advance, using it up without any significant progress being made, and demanding more money to continue. This problem will be discussed in more detail later in this chapter.

Middle Ground

You may want to look for an attorney who will be willing to accept an hourly fee to answer your questions and give you help as you need it. This way you will save some legal costs, but still get some professional assistance.

Selecting a Lawyer

Selecting a lawyer is a two-step process. First you need to decide which attorney to make an appointment with, then you need to decide if you want to hire that attorney.

Finding Possible Lawyers

○ Check with the attorney who handled your divorce. If you were happy with the lawyer who handled your original divorce case, you may want to use him or her for a modification.
○ Ask a friend. A common, and frequently the best, way to find a lawyer is to ask someone you know to recommend one to you. This is especially helpful if the lawyer represented your friend in a divorce or other family law matter.
○ Call a lawyer referral service. You can find one by looking in the Yellow Pages phone directory under "Attorney Referral Services" or "Attorneys." This is a service, usually operated by a bar association, which is designed to match a client with an attorney handling cases in the area of law the client needs. The referral service does not guarantee the quality or work, nor the level of experience or ability, of the attorney. Finding a lawyer this way will at least connect you with one who is interested in divorce and family law matters and probably has some experience in this area.
○ Check the Yellow Pages. Check under the heading for "Attorneys" in the Yellow Pages phone directory. Many of the lawyers and law firms will place display ads here indicating their areas of practice and educational backgrounds. Look for firms or lawyers which indicate they practice in areas such as "divorce," "family law," or "domestic relations."
○ Ask another lawyer. If you have used the services of an attorney in the past for some other matter (for example, a real estate closing, traffic ticket or a will), you may want to call and ask if he or she could refer you to an attorney whose ability in the area of family law is respected.

Evaluating a Lawyer

From your search you should select three to five lawyers worthy of further consideration. Your first step will be to call each attorney's office, explain that you are interested in modifying your divorce judgment, and ask the following questions:
1) Does the attorney (or firm) handle modifications of divorce judgments?
2) How much can you expect it to cost?
3) Is there any charge for the initial consultation?
4) How soon can you get an appointment?

If you like the answers you get, ask if you can speak to the attorney. Some offices will permit this, but others will require you to make an appointment. Make the appointment if that is what is required. Once you get in contact with the attorney (either on the phone or at the appointment), ask the following questions:

1) How much will it cost?
2) How will the fee be paid?
3) Does the lawyer use a written fee agreement? (Make sure he or she does).
4) How long has the attorney been in practice?
5) How long has the attorney been in practice in Florida?
6) What percentage of the attorney's cases involve divorce cases or other family law matters? (Don't expect an exact answer, but you should get a rough estimate that is at least 20%.)
7) How long will it take? (Again, don't expect an exact answer, but the attorney should be able to give you an average range and discuss things which may make a difference.)

If you get acceptable answers to these questions, it's time to ask *yourself* the following questions about the lawyer:

1) Do you feel comfortable talking to the lawyer?
2) Is the lawyer friendly toward you?
3) Does the lawyer seem confident in himself or herself?
4) Does the lawyer seem to be straightforward with you, and able to explain things so that you understand?

If you get satisfactory answers to all of these questions you probably have a lawyer you'll be able to work with. Most clients are happiest with an attorney they feel comfortable with.

Working With a Lawyer

In general, you will work best with your attorney if you keep an open, honest and friendly attitude. You should also consider the following suggestions.

Get a fee agreement. Lawyers are usually the first to tell you: "Get it in writing." This should especially apply to your agreement with your lawyer! Many lawyers do have a standard fee agreement which includes such things as the hourly fee to be charged, what is included in the fee and what is extra, and how the fee is to be billed and paid. Your fee agreement should also have a statement as to exactly what the lawyer is to do and when. For example, suppose that you are to give the lawyer $1,000 in advance. At the very least, your agreement should provide that the initial $1,000 includes the preparation and filing of a petition to modify your divorce judgment and proper service of the papers upon your ex-spouse. This will avoid the situation, which is all too common, where the lawyer makes several phone calls to your ex-spouse in order to try to get him or her to agree to a modification, then tells you that he has used up the $1,000 and wants another $1,000 before he will file the petition.

Ask questions. If you want to know something or if you don't understand something, ask your attorney. If you don't understand the answer, tell your attorney and ask him or her to explain it again. There are many points of law that many lawyers don't fully understand, so you shouldn't be embarrassed to ask questions. Many people who say they had a bad experience with a lawyer either didn't ask enough questions or had a lawyer who wouldn't take the time to explain things to them. If your lawyer isn't taking the time to explain what he's doing, it may be time to look for a new lawyer.

Give your lawyer complete information. Anything you tell your attorney is confidential. An attorney can lose his license to practice if he reveals information without your permission. So don't hold back. Tell your lawyer everything, even if it doesn't seem important to you. There are many things which seem unimportant to the average person but can change the outcome of a case. Also, don't hold something back because you are afraid it will hurt your case. It will definitely hurt your case if your lawyer doesn't find out about it until he hears it in court from your ex-spouse's attorney! But if he knows in advance, he can plan to eliminate or reduce damage to your case.

Accept reality. Listen to what your lawyer tells you about the law and the system, and accept it. It will do you no good to argue because the law or the system doesn't work the way you think it should. For example, if your lawyer tells you that the judge can't hear your case for two weeks, don't try demanding that he set a hearing tomorrow. By refusing to accept reality, you are only setting yourself up for disappointment. And remember: It's not your attorney's fault that the system isn't perfect or that the law doesn't say what you'd like it to say.

Be patient. This applies to being patient with the system (which is often slow, as we discussed earlier), as well as with your attorney. Don't expect your lawyer to return your phone call within an hour. He may not be able to return it the same day either. Most lawyers are very busy and overworked, and can't make each client feel as if he or she is the only client.

Talk to the secretary. Your lawyer's secretary can be a valuable source of information. So be friendly and get to know her. Often she will be able to answer your questions, and you won't get a bill for the time you talk to her.

Let your attorney deal with your ex-spouse. It is your lawyer's job to communicate with your ex-spouse, or with your ex-spouse's lawyer. Let him do his job. Many lawyers have had clients lose or damage their cases when the client decides to say or do something on their own.

Be on time. Be sure to be on time for appointments with your lawyer and to court hearings. Plan on getting to court hearings at least 15 minutes early.

Keep your case moving. Many lawyers operate on the old principle of "The squeaking wheel gets the oil." Work on a case tends to get put off until a deadline is near, an emergency develops, or the client calls. There is a very good reason for this. After many years of education (and the expense of that education), lawyers hope to earn the income due a professional. This is difficult with a great many attorneys competing for clients, and the high cost of office overhead. Many lawyers find it necessary to take more cases than can be effectively handled in order to make an acceptable living. That is why many attorneys work 65 hours a week or more. Your task is to become a squeaking wheel that doesn't squeak *too* much. Whenever you talk to your lawyer ask the following questions:

    1) What is the next step?
    2) When do you expect it to be done?
    3) When should I talk to you next?

If you don't hear from the lawyer when you expect, call him the following day. Don't remind him that he didn't call; just ask how things are going.

Learn to save money. Of course you don't want to spend unnecessary money for an attorney. Here are a few things you can do to avoid excess legal fees:

    1) Don't make unnecessary phone calls to your lawyer.
    2) Give information to the secretary whenever possible.
    3) Direct your question to the secretary first. She'll refer it to the attorney if she can't answer it.
    4) Plan your phone calls so you can get to the point, and take less of your attorney's time.
    5) Do some of the "leg work" yourself. Pick up and deliver papers yourself, for example. Ask your attorney what you can do to assist with your case.
    6) Be prepared for appointments. Have all related papers with you, plan your visit to get to the point, and make an outline of what you want to discuss and what questions you want to ask.

Pay your attorney bill when it's due. No client gets prompt attention like a client who pays his lawyer on time.

Firing your lawyer. If you don't think your lawyer is doing a good job or you lose faith in your lawyer, it is time to fire your lawyer. It is a good idea to discuss your feelings with the lawyer and give him or her a chance to make you a happy client again; but if this doesn't help, fire the bum! This is as simple as sending your attorney a letter saying: "This is to notify you that I am discharging you as my attorney." You should expect to pay for the services that have been provided (unless you are disputing that your attorney is entitled to payment). Your attorney should give you his file on your case, or a copy of that file, so you can take it to another lawyer or use it yourself. If the lawyer refuses to give you the file for any reason, threaten to complain to the judge and to The Florida Bar. If the lawyer still refuses, send a written complaint to the judge and file a grievance with The Florida Bar .

Chapter 5
Alimony

How Alimony is Determined

In General

There are three types of alimony:

1) **Rehabilitative**. This is for a limited period of time and is to enable one of the spouses to get the education or training necessary to find a job. This is usually awarded where one of the parties has not been working during the marriage.
2) **Permanent**. This continues for a long period of time, usually until the death or remarriage of the party receiving the alimony. This is typically awarded where one of the parties is unable to work due to a physical or mental illness.
3) **Lump Sum**. This is usually used as a way to equalize an otherwise unequal distribution of property. Generally, such lump sum alimony may not be modified, so it will not be discussed further.

Alimony may be subject to modification in several ways, including reducing or eliminating it, increasing it, converting rehabilitative alimony to permanent alimony, converting permanent alimony to rehabilitative, or extending the period of time during which alimony is to be paid. In order to modify alimony, it is necessary to show a change in the parties' financial situation since the divorce judgment was entered.

Your Divorce Judgment

Take a look at your divorce judgment and find the alimony section. Which type of alimony is ordered? Does the judgment discuss the reasons that alimony was awarded? Florida law now requires the judgment to give the reasons, but it didn't always. If there is such a statement, it may give you an idea of what circumstances may need to have changed in order to justify a change in alimony now. You should also look at the financial affidavits, or similar documents, which may have been filed before the divorce judgment. This will show the financial situations of you and your ex-spouse at the time of your divorce, so you can look for significant changes in the current circumstances.

If the alimony was the result of an agreement between you and your ex-spouse, it may be more difficult to get a modification. This is especially true if the settlement agreement is unclear as to whether the payment is for support or is actually part of the property settlement. You will want to read your settlement agreement to see if it clearly states that the payment is for "alimony" and that it is not attached to the wife giving up any property rights. If the "alimony" is really part of the property division, it may not be modified.

If you decide that it is alimony, you must now determine if the alimony may be modified. Generally, alimony may not be modified if it is lump sum alimony or if the settlement agreement or divorce judgment says it may not be modified. Also look to see if the settlement agreement or judgment limits modification in any way.

Evaluating Your Situation

Be sure to read both of the following sections, which will help you understand how the courts look at changes in alimony. These sections will refer to the person receiving alimony as the "wife" and the person paying alimony as the "husband," as this is more often the case.

Increasing Alimony

To justify an increase in alimony, you will generally need to show that your needs have increased since the divorce judgment was entered. The change in circumstances must be substantial, involuntary, and permanent. The change must also be one that was not expected at the time of the divorce judgment. Also, your ex-spouse must be financially able to pay the increased amount. However, the mere fact that your husband has had an increase in his income is not enough to justify an increase in alimony (unless he did not have enough income to meet your needs at the time of the divorce, and does now). More common situations which justify an increase are where the wife becomes completely and permanently disabled or when the children have reached the age of majority, resulting in the termination of child support so that the wife has insufficient income to meet fixed living expenses.

An increase in the cost of living may justify an increase (or a decrease for that matter). However, it will be necessary for you to show how the cost of living increase has affected you. This can be done by producing copies of your bills and testifying at the hearing about how certain bills (such as rent, property taxes and insurance, food. and utility costs) have increased.

Whether an increase will be granted may also depend upon the type of alimony awarded in the judgment. The examples listed above may justify an increase in permanent alimony. Rehabilitative alimony may only be modified before the rehabilitative period specified in the judgment ends. Justification for an increase in rehabilitative alimony might be a serious illness which interrupted the wife's school attendance (if the alimony was to permit her to obtain education for a particular profession), a substantial and unexpected increase in the cost of school, or any other change which would increase the time or amount of money needed for rehabilitation. Permanent disability may also be a reason for changing rehabilitative alimony to permanent alimony.

These are all just examples of the types of changes which could justify an increase. As you will see when you begin filling out forms, you will basically need to explain what circumstances have changed that have increased your needs. You will also need to show that your ex-spouse has the ability to pay more.

Decreasing Alimony

A decrease in alimony can either be a decrease in the amount or a total elimination of alimony. To justify a decrease in alimony, you will need to show either that your income has substantially decreased since the divorce judgment was issued, so that you are no longer able to pay the amount ordered in the divorce judgment; or that your wife's needs have been substantially reduced. For permanent alimony, this might be where your wife's disabling medical condition is relieved by surgery or new drugs so that she is able to return to work. For rehabilitative alimony, a decrease might be allowed if your wife voluntarily quits school and is no longer pursuing "rehabilitation." For either type of alimony, the wife receiving a substantial gift, inheritance, or lottery winnings may justify modification (the Florida courts have held that $31,000 did not justify a decrease, but $100,000 did).

A reduction in income alone will not justify a decrease. You will also need to show that your reduced income leaves you unable to pay the current amount. Also, your reduction in income must be involuntary. If it appears that you quit your job in order to avoid paying further alimony, the court may deny your request for a decrease. Similarly, if you are laid-off or fired, your conduct in seeking new income must be in good faith. This does not necessarily require you to seek the same type of job at the same pay. For example, in one case the court considered the husband's age, history of problems with employers, and job stress, and found it appropriate for him to start his own business rather than seek another job with an employer.

Other changes which have justified a decrease in alimony include losses or reductions in income due to participating in a legal labor strike, tax changes which significantly affected the husband's business, and a verified significant increase in business expenses. Although a reduction in income due to voluntary retirement may be considered by the court, the Florida appellate courts are not in agreement as to whether this justifies a decrease in alimony. This determination may be made based on the husband's age and health. For example, a decrease may not be allowed for a person in good health who is seeking to retire voluntarily at age 55. However, there may be a different result if he is seeking to retire at age 70 or is in poor health due to the nature of his job.

REMARRIAGE, etc. The remarriage of the spouse receiving alimony does not usually justify a reduction in rehabilitative alimony unless this is provided for in the divorce judgment. However, it is a factor which the court may consider. In a case of permanent alimony, the spouse's remarriage will usually justify terminating alimony. If the spouse receiving alimony begins living with someone, without marriage, this will not usually justify a change in alimony. However, if this situation changes her "rehabilitation" (for example, if she drops out of school and allows her boyfriend to support her) or otherwise affects her need for support, a decrease may be granted. It is not the change in her living arrangement itself, but how the marriage or living-together arrangement affects her needs that will determine if a decrease will be allowed.

An increase in the cost of living may justify a decrease (or an increase for that matter). However, it will be necessary for you to show how the cost of living increase has affected you. This can be done by producing copies of your bills and testifying at the hearing about how certain bills (such as rent, property taxes and insurance, food and utility costs) have increased, causing your ability to pay alimony to decrease. However, don't try arguing that your expenses have increased because you have remarried and now have a new family to support!

> **CAUTION:** Do not stop or reduce alimony payments unless you get an order signed by the judge allowing you to do so. If you do this without a court order, you risk accumulating alimony arrearages and contempt of court proceedings.

The procedure to modify alimony is simple. There are basically four steps:
1) File a petition with the court clerk.
2) Notify your spouse.
3) Get a hearing date.
4) Go to the hearing and present the information required.

This chapter will discuss these steps in detail, along with other key points relating to preparing for the hearing and special circumstances.

Petition to Modify Alimony (Form 32)

The **Petition to Modify Alimony (Form 32)** is the basic form used to ask for an increase or decrease in alimony. To complete the **Petition to Modify Alimony (Form 32)**:
1) Complete the top portion according to the instructions in Chapter 3.
2) In the first paragraph, check the line for "Husband" or "Wife," whichever applies to you; fill in the date of your divorce judgment; check the line for "Husband" or "Wife," whichever is paying alimony; the current amount of alimony; and the payment period (such as "week" or "month").
3) Check the appropriate box or boxes for the kind of changes you desire in the alimony. For example, if you want the alimony terminated altogether, you will also want to ask for a decrease. This will give the judge a choice to reduce the alimony even if he refuses to terminate it altogether. Generally, the

judge will only consider what you have asked for in your petition, so it's a good idea to check all of the boxes you may want to apply.

5) Complete and attach a **Standard signature page with notary (Form 30)**, and sign before a notary.

Affidavit Regarding Alimony (Form 33)

Use the **Affidavit Regarding Alimony (Form 33)** to explain what circumstances have changed that justify modifying the alimony. To complete the **Affidavit Regarding Alimony (Form 33)**:

1) Complete the top portion according to the instructions in Chapter 3.
2) Type in the name of the county where you will have this form notarized after the words "COUNTY OF."
3) Type in your name on the line in the first unnumbered paragraph.
4) In the blank space after paragraph 2, type in the reasons you want the alimony changed. Refer to the earlier sections of this chapter for information on the kinds of circumstances which may justify a change. Remember, for an increase you need to concentrate on information showing that your needs have increased and that your spouse has the financial ability to pay more. For a decrease, you need to show either that your income has gone down so that you can no longer afford to pay the current amount, or that your spouse's needs have gone down so that he she no longer needs as much alimony.
5) Take this form to a notary public and sign it before the notary on the line marked "AFFIANT." The notary will complete the notary section.

Family Law Financial Affidavit (Form 24 and Form 25)

Rule 12.105(c) of the *Florida Family Law Rules* requires both parties to complete and file a **Family Law Financial Affidavit (Form 24 or Form 25)**. Be sure to make an extra copy of the appropriate **Family Law Financial Affidavit** form for your spouse to complete.

If you (or your spouse) have annual income and expenses of less than $50,000, you will use the **Family Law Financial Affidavit (Short Form) (Form 24)**. If annual income or expenses are $50,000 or more, you will use the **Family Law Financial Affidavit (Long Form) (Form 25)**. The form to be used is determined by each of you separately. For example, if your income is less than $50,000 and your spouse's is more than $50,000, you will file Form 24 and your spouse will file Form 25. Form 25 is a little more detailed than Form 24, but both require the same type of information about the following four areas: your income, expenses, assets, and debts. Since the support guidelines use monthly income figures, the **Family Law Financial Affidavit** is also on a monthly basis. If you are paid weekly, or every two weeks, you will need to convert your income to a monthly figure. The same conversion will be required for any of your expenses that are not paid monthly. To convert weekly amounts to monthly amounts, just take the weekly figure and multiply it by 4.3. (There are roughly 4.3 weeks to a month.) To convert from every two weeks, divide by 2 and then multiply by 4.3.

Fill in all of the blank spaces on the **Family Law Financial Affidavit** forms, then take them to a notary public before you sign them. You will sign them before the notary, then file them along with your **Petition** (after you have made three copies). Most of the blanks in both versions of the **Family Law Financial Affidavit** clearly indicate what information is to be filled in there; however, the following may answer some questions:

1) Complete the top portion according to the instructions in Chapter 3.
2) After the words "COUNTY OF {name}," type in the name of the county in which **Family Law Financial Affidavit** will be signed.
3) Type in your name in the blank in the first paragraph.
4) Fill in the information on your employment and income. "PAY PERIOD" refers to how often you receive your paycheck, such as "weekly," "every two weeks," "twice a month," etc. "RATE OF PAY" refers to your hourly rate, or weekly, monthly, or yearly salary, whichever applies to your situation.
5) If you are unemployed or expect to be unemployed soon, read the last paragraph on the first page of the form and fill in the information requested.
6) Be sure to read the paragraph at the top of the second page of the form, and follow the instructions given there. You and your spouse may agree to waive these disclosure requirements. Check the appropriate line to indicate whether you are in agreement about such a waiver.
7) For the section on "**LAST YEAR'S INCOME**," use the figures from last year's W-2 and tax return.

8) For each item listed for current income (This is designated "**AVERAGE GROSS MONTHLY IN-COME FROM EMPLOYMENT**" on Form 24, and "**PRESENT INCOME; AVERAGED ON A MONTHLY BASIS**" in Form 25), fill in the monthly amount (before taxes) that you receive. Total the amounts you listed, then complete the deductions section(marked "LESS MONTHLY DEDUCTIONS" o Form 24, and "**LESS DEDUCTIONS ALLOWABLE UNDER SECTION 61.30, FLORIDA STAT-UTES**" on Form 25). Total the deductions, then subtract that amount from the total monthly income and type is the answer on the line marked "TOTAL NET INCOME" on Form 23 and "**AVERAGE NET MONTHLY INCOME**" on Form 25. Form 25 also has spaces to deduct court ordered payments for child support from a prior marriage, alimony, and attorneys fees.

9) For the section on "**AVERAGE MONTHLY EXPENSES**," simply refer to each item listed and estimate as best you can the amount you spend on that item in a month. If a particular item is an annual expense, such as auto insurance, convert it to a monthly amount.

10) To complete the sections on "**ASSETS**" and "**DEBTS**" by filling in the value for each item in the column marked "Petitioner." If you know your spouse's assets and debts, list them in the column marked "Respondent." Form 24 also requires you to fill in other information about your assets and debts.

11) Complete the **Standard signature page with notary (Form 30)** and attach it as the last page of the **Family Law Financial Affidavit**. Take the form to a notary and sign it before the notary on the line designated "Signature of party signing certificate and affidavit." The notary will complete the part of the form directly below your signature. Staple your **Family Law Financial Affidavit** (and your spouse's) to the **Petition** and file it with the court clerk.

Interrogatories and Financial Disclosure

Be sure to read Rule 12.285 of the Family Law Rules of Procedure (found in Appendix A of this book), particularly subsections (c) and (d). This rule describes the financial disclosure requirements you must satisfy. However, if you and your ex-spouse agree, all of these requirements, except the **Family Law Financial Affidavit**, can be waived (this will be discussed in more detail below).

If you or your ex-spouse has an annual income or annual expenses of $50,000 or more, you (or your ex-spouse) are required to file answers to the **Standard Family Law Interrogatories (Form 27)**. Of course, if you earn $50,000 or more per year, you may have enough at stake to justify hiring a lawyer to represent you. The following information will discuss the forms you will need to file in connection with these disclosure requirements.

Standard Family Law Interrogatories (Form 27)

You only need to file this form if you have an annual income or expenses of $50,000 or more. (You will also need to file it if your ex-spouse requests it, regardless of your income.) To complete Form 27:

1) Complete the top portion according to the instructions in Chapter 3. Because you are answering the interrogatories, you will need to change the title of this form by adding the words "ANSWERS TO" just before the title "STANDARD FAMILY LAW INTERROGATORIES."

2) For each question, type in the information requested. If an item is not applicable to you, type in "not applicable." Form 27 was prepared in a manner so as to save space, therefore, there may not be enough space below each item for you to fill in your answer. If this happens, you can either re-type Form 27 and leave enough space for your answer, or type in "see attached sheet" and type your answer on a separate sheet of paper with the questions number clearly indicated. If an item is clearly answered by information in your **Family Law Financial Affidavit (Form 24 or Form 25)**, you can type in "see Family Law Financial Statement."

3) Fill in the date on the last page, and complete the certificate of service section, including your ex-spouse's name, address, and phone information.

4) Complete and attach the **Standard signature page without notary (Form 29)**.

Certificate of Compliance with Family Law Rule 12.285 (Form 28)

Once you have met the financial disclosure requirements of Rule 12.285, you need to prepare and file a **Certificate of Compliance with Family Law Rule 12.285 (Form 28)**, to show the judge that you have met the requirements. To complete Form 28:

1) Complete the top portion according to the instructions in Chapter 3.
2) In the main paragraph, check the box for either "Petitioner" or "Respondent," whichever applies to your ex-spouse.
3) Check the box for each item you "served on" (delivered or maile to) your ex-spouse, and fill in the date of service. There are spaces provided for you to fill in other items required by Rule 12.285. If you and your ex-spouse agree to waive the disclosure requirements (except for the **Family Law Financial Affidavit** which may not be waived), you can check the box for "Delivery of all other documents referred to in Family Law Rule 12.285 has been waived." In order to be able to check this box, your ex-spouse must date and sign the section on the second page of the form marked "**WAIVER OF RECEIPT OF DOCUMENTS.**" If you are going to waive the receipt of documents from your ex-spouse, you will need to make a copy of Form 28 and prepare it for your spouse to sign (with you signing the waiver section on the second page of the form). Generally, this will be done if you are satisfied that your ex-spouse has provided sufficient information in his or her **Family Law Financial Affidavit**, and you want to avoid the hassle of providing each other with a lot of unnecessary information and documents.
4) Fill in the date, sign your name on the line marked "Signature of party," and type in your name, address, and phone informtion. Also, type in your ex-spouse's information at the top of the second page.

Notice of Service of Standard Family Law Interrogatories (Form 26)

If you want your ex-spouse to file answers to the **Standard Family Law Interrogatories (Form 27)**, you will need to file a **Notice of Service of Standard Family Law Interrogatories (Form 26)** and send a copy to your ex-spouse along with a copy of the **Standard Family Law Interrogatories**. You should do this either because your ex-spouse is required to file the answers because he or she meets the $50,000 limit, and has failed to do so; or just because you want him or her to provide you with the information, even if he or she doesn't meet the $50,000 limit. To complete the **Notice of Service of Standard Family Law Interrogatories (Form 26)**:
1) Complete the top portion according to the instructions in Chapter 3.
2) On the lines in the main paragraph, type in your name, the date you served your ex-spouse with a copy of the **Standard Family Law Interrogatories (Form 27)**, and your ex-spouse's name, respectively.
3) Complete the certificate of service section, including your ex-spouse's name, address, and phone information.
4) Sign you name on the line marked "Signature of party signing certificate and pleading," and type in your name, address, and phone information.

Filing With the Court Clerk, Etc.

See Chapter 3 for information on how to file your Petition with the court, and how to notify your ex-spouse. Remember, if you are asking to change rehabilitative alimony to permanent alimony, you MUST use personal service to notify your ex-spouse that you have filed a Petition. To modify alimony, you should be filing a **Civil Cover Sheet (Form 20)**, **Petition to Modify Alimony (Form 32)**, an **Affidavit Regarding Alimony (Form 33)**, and a **Family Law Financial Affidavit (Form 24** or **Form 25)**. These should be stapled together, with the Petition first. If you are having your ex-spouse personally served, the sheriff will prepare and file an affidavit of service. If you used certified mail to notify your ex-spouse, you will need to file a **Certificate of Service (Form 10)**, indicating that the Petition sas served. Staple the green return receipt card to a sheet of paper, and attach it to Form 10. See Chapter 3 for information on how to get a court date set.

Preparing and Presenting Your Proof

Much of your proof will be found in your **Affidavit Regarding Alimony (Form 32)** and the **Financial Affidavit (Form 24** or **Form 25** each of you will file. See Chapter 3 for information on how to obtain financial information about your ex-spouse. You should have the following forms available for the hearing:
1) Your **Petition to Modify Alimony (Form 32)**, **Affidavit Regarding Alimony (Form 33)**, and **Family Law Financial Affidavit (Form 24** or **Form 25)**. Also, copies of bills, receipts, bank statements, etc., to verify the information you put in your papers.
2) Any response your ex-spouse may have filed, or the **Default (Form 7)**.
3) Your ex-spouse's **Family Law Financial Affidavit** and any other information you may have received from your ex-spouse's employer, bank, etc., regarding your ex-spouse's financial situation.

4) Any written information you may have received regarding your or your ex-spouse's needs, if it relates to the reasons you are asking for a change in alimony.

You may also need to issue subpoenas to people you will need to testify at the hearing. See Chapter 3 regarding subpoenas to testify. These might be doctors to testify to a change in your or your ex-spouse's medical condition, administrators to verify that your ex-spouse is no longer in school, employers to verify income, etc.

Because you are asking for the change, you will go first in presenting your case. You will basically want to tell the judge three things: why you are in court (to ask for an increase or decrease in alimony), why you are asking for a change, and what the new alimony order should be. First you will make a short opening statement, then you will present whatever proof you have.

The following is an example of an opening statement:

"Your Honor, we are here on a petition to decrease alimony. The divorce judgment ordered me to pay rehabilitative alimony in the amount of $700 per month, for a period of two years, in order to allow my ex-wife to finish her bachelor's degree in finance. Since the entry of the divorce judgment, I have been laid-off from my job and have been forced to take a new job at only one-half of my former pay. Therefore, I am asking for a decrease in alimony to $350 per month."

Next, you need to present your proof. The judge will probably swear you in, then tell you to proceed. For the situation above, you might present the judge with a letter from your former employer indicating the date of your lay-off, and a paystub or letter from your new employer showing your current income. You would also want to refer the judge to your **Family Law Financial Affidavit**, which should be in the court file. Simply tell the judge what each document is. Your statement might be like this:

"I have filed a current Financial Affidavit showing my current income. I have with me a copy of the Financial Affidavit I filed just before the judgment was issued, a copy of my lay-off notice from my last employer, and a copy of my most recent paystub from my current employer showing my current weekly pay."

The judge may ask you a few questions, then give your ex-spouse an opportunity to make a statement and ask you questions. He will give you a chance to respond to what your ex-spouse says, and may ask you more questions. Just answer the judge's questions honestly, as best you can. After the judge has heard all of the facts, he will announce his decision.

Order Modifying Alimony (Form 34)

Whatever changes the judge approves will need to be put into an order. An **Order Modifying Alimony (Form 34)** may be found in Appendix B. You will not be able to complete the second paragraph of this form until the judge announces what changes in alimony he or she approves. You can simply check the appropriate box or boxes and fill in any necessary amounts at the hearing. To complete Form 34:

1) Complete the top portion according to the instructions in Chapter 3.
2) Fill in the date of the hearing in the first paragraph.
3) In the second paragraph, check the appropriate box or boxes for the type of change the judge orders. Then fill in the information required for each box you check. The first box is for an increase or decrease in alimony. This will be the most common change in most cases. The second box is for the complete termination of all alimony. Fill in either the date of termination, or the word "immediately," or the phrase "as of the date of the Petition." The third box is for a change from rehabilitative to permanent alimony, and the new amount will need to be filled in, as well as checking the line for the husband or wife, whichever will be receiving alimony. The fourth box is for a change from permanent to rehabilitative alimony, and the last box is for any additional changes or provisions not covered by the first four boxes.
4) Once all of the appropriate information has been filled in, the order needs to be presented to the judge for him to fill in the date and sign the order. You can either present it to the judge at the hearing or deliver or mail it to his or her office later. If you decide to deliver or mail it, you will need to mail a copy to your ex-spouse at the same time. You will also need a completed **Final Disposition Form (Form 21)**.

Order Requiring Payment Through Central Depository (Form 38)

See Chapter 6 for information about why and how to complete this form.

Child Support Income Deduction Order (Form 39)

Even though we are only dealing with alimony here, the form is still titled "Child Support Income Deduction Order" (you'll have to ask the Florida Supreme Court if you want to know why they used this misleading title). See Chapter 6 for information about why and how to complete this form.

Final Disposition Form (Form 21)

See the section in Chapter 3 on "The Modified Order," for instructions on completing this form. The only additional instruction is that if your spouse did not respond and a default was issued, you will check the box in Part II for "Disposed by Default."

Chapter 6
Child Support

How Child Support is Determined

Two factors are used to determine the amount of support: (1) the needs of the child, and (2) the financial ability of each parent to meet those needs. Florida has established a formula to be used in calculating both the needs of the child and each parent's ability to meet those needs. The following steps are used in determining the proper amount of support:

1) You and your ex-spouse each provide proof of your "gross" incomes.
2) Taxes and other deductions are allowed to determine each of your "net" incomes.
3) Your net incomes are added together to arrive at your "combined income."
4) The combined income and the number of children you have are used to establish the children's needs. (This is done by reading a chart.)
5) The net income of the parent without custody is divided by the combined income. This gives that parent's percentage of the combined income.
6) That percentage is multiplied by the needs of the children, to arrive at the amount of support to be paid by the parent without custody.

This procedure can be used by most people. However, if you and your spouse's combined income is less than $650 per month these guidelines can't be used. If your combined income is over $10,000 per month, you will need to add a percentage of the amount over $10,000, depending upon the number of children. Also, the judge may depart from the guidelines by up to five percent (a written reason must be given in the judgment if the judge departs by more than 5%). These guidelines will be discussed more below, and their text can be found in Appendix A, Section 61.30, Florida Statutes. An increase or decrease in child support will only be allowed if this calculation results in a significantly different amount than what is currently ordered.

The judge may depart slightly from the guidelines after considering the needs of the child and each parent's age, station in life, standard of living, and financial status. The judge can also adjust the amount of child support in consideration of the following factors:

○ The impact of IRS dependency exemption or waiver of the exemption (the judge may also order the custodial parent to sign a waiver of the exemption).
○ Whether the guidelines would require the payment of more than 55% of the payor's gross income.

✪ Whether the noncustodial parent has visitation for more than 28 consecutive days (in which case support may be reduced by up to 50% during such visitation periods).

Evaluating Your Situation

In order to modify child support you will need to show that one or more of the following have occurred:
1) Your income has gone down significantly.
2) Your ex-spouse's income has gone up significantly.
3) Your child's "special needs" have changed.
4) The current guidelines would justify a change of 15% or $50, whichever is greater.

As the child's needs are generally determined by the parents' incomes, most cases will be determined by the parents' incomes, using the child support tables in the Florida Statutes. The only exception is where your child has some special needs, such as for medical treatment for a disability, that exceed the needs presumed by your incomes. These special needs will be discussed more later in this chapter.

Because needs and ability to pay must have changed, it is important for you to get any information you can regarding your and your ex-spouse's financial situation at the time the divorce judgment was entered. The best source would be the Financial Affidavits you both filed with your divorce case. If you don't have copies, go to the court clerk's office and get copies of the Financial Affidavits from your divorce file. Compare your current incomes with the incomes in the original Financial Affidavits to see how things have changed. A change of a few dollars won't justify a change in child support. The change must be substantial.

The **Child Support Guidelines Worksheet (Form 36)** is used to calculate the proper amount of child support. The rest of this chapter will guide you in completing this form. It is important to get the most accurate income information about yourself and your ex-spouse. Completing this form will give you a good idea of how much of a child support change is called for, if any, so that you can decide whether you should file a Petition.

Because you may need to file Form 36 with the court, make a copy of it to use now. Here you are only trying to get a rough idea of the amount of child support to expect so that you can compare it to the current child support amount and decide if it is worth your time and effort to ask for an increase or decrease. Later, after you have more accurate income information, you will complete the final copy to file along with your Petition. As you prepare your form to file, you will refer back to this section for instructions on completing it.

The **Child Support Guidelines Worksheet (Form 36)**, is a bit unusual, in that you don't start with the first page. The first page of this form is used to fill in totals from later sections of the form. In filling out Form 35, be sure to convert everything to monthly amounts. The following subsections relate to Form 34.

Income Determination

Gross Income. As stated above, you do not start with the first page of the **Child Support Guidelines Worksheet (Form 36)**. The first thing you will need to do is determine your "gross income," which is done by filling in "SECTION III — INCOME." This is basically your income before any deductions for taxes, social security, etc. Sources that are considered part of gross income are listed in this section. Florida law specifically provides that Aid to Families with Dependent Children (AFDC) benefits are not included as income. Fill in the amounts for yourself and your spouse in "SECTION III," add up these amounts to get the total gross monthly income for each of you, then write the totals on the first page, where it states: "Total actual income (Section III)."

The line on the first page for "Imputed income" is rarely used. If you voluntarily reduce your income, or quit your job, the judge can refuse to recognize the reduction or loss of income. This is "imputed income." The only exception is where you are required to take such an action to stay home and care for your child. If this question comes up, the judge will decide whether you need to stay home, so be ready to explain your reasons.

Net Income. The allowed deductions from gross income (to arrive at net income) are listed in the part designated "SECTION IV — DEDUCTIONS." Total the deductions for you and your spouse, then write in the totals on the first page, where it states: "Less total deductions (Section IV)." The gross income minus these deductions will give you the "net income." Now subtract the total deductions from the gross incomes, and write the answers on the lines on the first page, marked: "**Total Net Monthly Income**. "

Combined Income. "Combined Income" is your net income added to your spouse's net income. For example: Your net income is $1,200 per month. Your spouse's net income is $1,800 per month. Your combined income is $3,000 (1,200 + 1,800). Add your net income and your spouses's total net monthly incomes. This is your combined income, which should be written in on the line on the first page, marked: "**COMBINED NET MONTHLY INCOME**."

Calculating Child Support

Once you determine your combined income, turn to the child support guidelines table in Appendix A, pages 63 and 64 of this book, which comes from Section 61.30(6), Florida Statutes. Read down the first column to your combined income, then read across to the column for the number of children for which support is owed. This figure will give you the needs of your children. Write in the needs indicated by the support table on the first page, on the lines marked "Basic obligation (from chart)." You will note that there are two columns, one for the "FATHER" and one for the "MOTHER." The same amount from the chart goes in each column.

Again using our example: We've established that your combined income is $3,000 per month. Find the figure "3,000" in the left column of the child support guidelines table, then read across for the number of children. For one child the needs are $644 per month; for two children the needs are $1,001; for three children the needs are $1,252, etc. For our example, let's assume you have two children, so their monthly needs are $1,001.

The next step is to determine each parent's percentage share of their combined income. To get your share, divide your net income by the combined income ($1,200 divided by $3,000). The answer is .4. Next divide your spouse's net income by the combined income ($1,800 divided by $3,000). The answer is .6. Write in these percentages on the lines on the first page, marked: "Pro rate financial responsibility." (You will note that this line of the form calls for a percentage, which requires dropping the decimal point. Using our example, ".4" would be shown here as " _4_ %;" not as " _.4_ %."

Next, multiply the needs (or "basic obligation") by your percentage share ($1,001 x .4 = $400.40). This gives you the amount of your children's needs you will be expected to contribute. Now multiply the needs by your spouse's percentage share ($1,001 x .6 = $600.60). This is the amount your spouse will be expected to contribute. Write in the contributions of you and your spouse on the lines marked "Pro rate share of basic obligation." Whichever parent does not have custody will be ordered to pay support according to this calculation. In our example, if you have custody your spouse will be ordered to pay $600.60 per month. If your spouse has custody, you will be ordered to pay $400.40 per month. (If you and your spouse are each going to have custody of one child, the support will be offset, so that your spouse would pay $200.20 per month ($600.60 - $400.40).

There are some factors which may change the amount of support ordered according to the guidelines explained above. In all cases the judge has the right to adjust the amount by up to five percent without stating a reason in writing. Also, other factors are covered in "SECTION II — ADDITIONS TO BASIC OBLIGATION" and "SECTION V — ADJUSTMENTS." Review these sections to see if any of the items listed apply to your situation. SECTION II concerns what either of you are paying for child care costs or health insurance premiums. If there are child care costs for your child, note that only 75% of these costs can be used. This 75 % of child care costs and any health insurance premiums should be totalled in SECTION II. Each party's share of these expenses should be written in on the appropriate line on the first page (apply the same percentage as you did to the basic obligation amount). Next, total the amounts to get the "Statutory child support obligation." Note that Section VI states: "Insert applicable section of child support guidelines table." For filing, make a copy of either page 63 or page 64 from this book, whichever has the part of the child support table that applies to your situation, and attach it to Form 36.

Now, review SECTION V to see if any of these adjustments are applicable to your situation. If so, fill in the appropriate amounts in SECTION V, and fill in the amounts on the appropriate lines on the first and second pages of Form 36. For further explanation of these factors, see Section 61.30, Florida Statutes, in Appendix A.

Finally, add up the amounts for you and your spouse. This is the total amount each of you are expected to contribute to the support of your children.

> **CAUTION:** Do not stop or reduce child support payments unless you get an order signed by the judge allowing you to do so. If you do this without a court order, you will accumulate a child support arrearage, and will risk contempt of court proceedings.

Petition for Modification of Child Support (Form 35)

The **Petition/Request for Modification/Change of Child Support and Other Relief (Form 35)** is the basic form used to ask for an increase or decrease in child support. To complete Form 35:
1) Complete the top portion according to the instructions in Chapter 3.
2) Check the line for "Petitioner" or "Respondent," whichever applies to you.
3) In paragraph 1, fill in the date of your divorce judgment or the most recent child support order if one has been entered since your divorce judgment.
4) Check the appropriate lines and fill in the required information in paragraphs 2 through 3.d.
5) Paragraph 3.e. indicates that a "guideline worksheet" is attached. This refers to the **Child Support Guidelines Worksheet (Form 36)**. On the line after the words "Please explain," type in what change is called for. For example: "Guidelines support change from $250 per month to $325 per month." Paragraph 3.f. is to add anything not covered above to show a change in circumstances.
6) On the second page, in the paragraph beginning with the word "WHEREFORE," check the line for "Petitioner" or "Respondent," whichever applies to you.
7) Complete the certificate of service section.
8) Type your name, address, and telephone information where indicated below the line marked "Signature of party signing certificate and pleading."
9) Attach the completed **Child Support Guidelines Worksheet (Form 36)**. (See below for instructions for completing Form 36.)
10) Take this form to a notary and sign before the notary.

Family Law Financial Affidavit (Form 24 and Form 25)

Before completing the **Family Law Financial Affidavit**, make a copy of the form to send to your ex-spouse along with your **Petition**. See Chapter 5 for instructions on completing the **Family Law Financial Affidavit**.

Child Support Guidelines Worksheet (Form 36)

See the section on page 40 on "Evaluating Your Situation" for basic instruction on preparing the **Child Support Guidelines Worksheet**. In addition to filling the form as instructed above, you will need to:
1) Complete "SECTION I — CHILDREN," by typing in each minor child's name, date of birth, and age.
2) Type in your and your ex-spouse's name, address, and telephone information on the appropriate lines after SECTION VI.
3) Make a copy of either page 63 or page 64 of this book, whichever one contains the portion of the child support schedule showing your calculations. (If your combined income is more than $10,000 per month you will need to complete SECTION VI, although with that much money at stake you may want to consult an attorney.)
4) Attach the completed form to your **Petition (Form 35)**.

Interrogatories and Financial Disclosure

See the section on "Interrogatories and Financial Disclosure" in Chapter 5.

Filing With the Court Clerk, Etc.

See Chapter 3 for information on filing your court papers. To modify child support, you should be filing a **Civil Cover Sheet (Form 20)**, **Petition/Request for Modification/Change of Child Support and Other Relief (Form 35)** with a **Child Support Guidelines Worksheet (Form 36)** attached, and **Family Law Financial Affidavit (Form 24 or Form 25)**. See Chapter 3 for information on setting a court date.

See Chapter 3 also for information on notifying your ex-spouse that you have filed a Petition and notifying him or her of the court hearing. When you send your ex-spouse a **Notice of Hearing (Form 3)**, you will need to enclose a blank **Family Law Financial Affidavit (Form 24 or Form 25)** for your ex-spouse to complete and file. A copy of your **Notice of Hearing (Form 3)** should also be filed with the court clerk.

Preparing and Presenting Your Proof

Your proof will mostly be the information in your **Petition (Form 35)** and **Family Law Financial Affidavit**. If your ex-spouse fails to file a **Family Law Financial Affidavit** and you obtained information from his or her employer through a **Subpoena for Production of Documents (Form 14)**, this information will also be part of your proof. See Chapter 3 for more information on preparing your case for hearing.

Be sure to review Chapter 3 for more information on presenting your case to the judge. You will basically want to tell the judge three things: why you are in court (to ask for an increase or decrease in child support), why you are asking for a change, and what the new child support order should be. First you will make a short opening statement, then you will present whatever proof you have.

The following is an example of an opening statement:

"Your Honor, we are here on a petition to increase child support. The divorce judgment ordered my ex-spouse to pay child support in the amount of $583.20 per month for our two children. Since the entry of the divorce judgment, my ex-husband's net income has increased from $1,800 per month to $2,300 per month, and I have lost my job due to an illness and am without income. These changes are reflected in the **Family Law Financial Affidavits** filed by my ex-husband and myself. Therefore, considering the minimum support schedule, I am asking for an increase in child support to $768 per month."

Next, you will present your proof (which may simply be the **Family Law Financial Affidavits** filed by you and your ex-spouse). The judge will probably swear you in, then tell you to proceed. For the situation above, you might present the judge with a letter from your former employer indicating the last day you worked; and a letter from your doctor verifying your illness and how it affects your ability to work. You would also want to refer the judge to your **Family Law Financial Affidavit**, which should be in the court file. Simply tell the judge what each document is. Your statement might be like this:

"I have filed a current **Family Law Financial Affidavit** showing my current expenses and lack of income and a **Child Support Guidelines Worksheet** calculating the proper amount of support under the minimum support schedule. My ex-husband has filed a **Family Law Financial Affidavit** verifying his income. I have with me a copy of the **Family Law Financial Affidavit** I filed just before the judgment was issued, a letter from my last employer verifying my last day of work, and a letter from my doctor regarding my medical condition."

The judge will then ask you any questions he or she may have, then give your ex-spouse an opportunity to make a statement or to ask you questions. He may then give you a chance to respond to what your ex-spouse says, and ask you more questions. Just answer the judge's questions honestly, as best you can. Be prepared to guide the judge through the calculations in your **Child Support Guidelines Worksheet** to show him how you arrived at the support amount you are asking for. After the judge has heard all of the facts, he will announce his decision.

Final Judgment Modifying Child Support (Form 37)

The **Final Judgment Modifying Child Support (Form 37)** will be filled in by you *according to what the judge decides*. If you aren't sure how to fill in an item, ask the judge how he or she wants you to fill it in. Keep in mind that you are completing this form according to what the judge finds and orders. To complete the **Final Judgment Modifying Child Support (Form 37)**:

1) Complete the top portion according to the instructions in Chapter 3.
2) Type in the date of the hearing on the line in the first paragraph, and check either "Petitioner's" or "Respondent's," whichever applies to you.
3) Paragraph 3: check the appropriate boxes. This paragraph states that your ex-spouse was properly notified of the Petition and hearing, and indicates whether a default was entered. Check the box for "Petitioner" or "Respondent," whichever applies to your ex-spouse. You should check the line for "was...duly served. If a default was entered, check the box before "Family Law Form 12.922(b)," and the line for "was."
4) Paragraph 4: Type in the date of the last support order, which may be the date of your original divorce judgment if this is the first change that has been made.
5) Paragraph 5: Check the line before the word "has" if the judge is ordering a change in child support, and check the line before the words "has not" if the judge is not ordering a change. If a change is ordered, you will need to fill in a description of what change in circumstances justifies the change in child support. For example: "The Respondent's income has increased by 35% since the entry of the last child support order." Ask the judge if he or she wants any particular language here.
6) Paragraph 6: Check the line before the word "is" if the judge is ordering a change in support, and check the line before the words "is not" if no change is ordered. You will also need to fill in a brief explanation of why a change is in the child's best interest.
7) Paragraph 7: Fill in your and your ex-spouse's incomes on the appropriate lines in subsections "a" and "b." Check subsection "c" if the judge is ordering support according to the child support guidelines.

   If the judge agrees that child support should be set according to the **Child Support Guidelines Worksheet (Form 36)** that either you or your ex-spouse filed, check the line for subsection "d," and the line for either "petitioner" or "respondent," whichever worksheet the judge follows. If the judge decides that the child support guidelines should not be followed, subsection "e" will have to be completed. This requires the judge to state why he or she is not following the guidelines, so you will have to ask the judge how he wants this subsection completed. Subsection "f" needs to be completed if there are arrearages in child support. Subsections "g" and "h" relate to medical and dental insurance, and should be filled in the same as in your divorce judgment or last support order, unless the judge orders something different.
8) Paragraph 8: If attorneys' fees are requested by either party you will need to complete this paragraph. Of course, if you are asking for attorneys' fees then you have hired an attorney and he or she will be the one preparing this form. If attorneys' fees and court costs have been requested by either party, the judge must state why he or she grants or denies such a request, so you will have to ask the judge how he or she wants this section completed.
9) So far, we have discussed the portion of this form relating to what the judge finds the facts to be. Now we will discuss the portion of the form where the judge actually orders the changes. This portion of the form begins with the phrase: "Therefore, upon consideration of the above findings, it is hereby ORDERED AND ADJUDGED that:" In Paragraph A, check the line for "GRANTED" if the judge is ordering a change, or the line for "DENIED" if the judge refuses to change the support order. If you check "DENIED," you can skip down to instruction 11 below.
10) Paragraph B: Complete subsections 1 through 5 in basically the same manner as you completed paragraph 7 above. Complete subsection 6 if the judge orders one of you to maintain life insurance to benefit the children. Subsection 7 concerns how the child support is to be paid. Under most circumstances, you will *not* check the line for payment "Directly to the person the court has ordered will be paid the support." Usually the judge will order payments through the Central Depository by way of an income deduction order, so you will complete the second and third lines in subsection 7. If the judge orders payment through the Central Depository, you will need to complete and attach Form 37. If income deduction is ordered, you will also need to complete Form 38.
11) Paragraph C: Complete this section in basically the same manner as you did for paragraph 8 above. Paragraph D is to fill in any orders of the judge that are not covered in the other parts of this form.

12) In the paragraph beginning "DONE and ORDERED," type in the name of the county. Leave the rest of this paragraph blank for the judge to fill in the date.
13) Type in your and your ex-spouse's names, addresses, and telephone information on the lines for the petitioner and respondent.

Order Requiring Payment Through Central Depository (Form 38)

If child support or alimony is to be paid to the Central Depository (which will almost always be the case), the **Order Requiring Payment Through Central Depository (Form 38)** should be completed. Although the law does not require that child support be paid through the Central Depository, it is a good idea in most cases. The Central Depository will keep track of what has been paid, and its records will be very helpful in the event of any payment dispute. This form gives the Central Depository important information about how to handle your account. Some terminology may be helpful. The "obligor" is the person who ultimately owes the child support (either you or your spouse). The "payor" is who will actually be sending the payments to the Central Depository (this may be the obligor, or the obligor's employer if there is an income deduction order. The "payee" is the person who will receive the child support (again, either you or your spouse). In subsection D, you will need to check the appropriate line and fill in the requested information about how much is to be paid, the frequency of payment (per week, per month, etc.), the number of children, address and phone numbers of the Central Depository, etc. This form will then be submitted to the judge for his or her signature, along with the **Final Judgment Modifying Child Support (Form 37)** at the final hearing. You will then need to fill in the names and addresses of all who are to be sent a copy of the order. Usually this will just be you and your spouse (or his or her attorney).

Child Support Income Deduction Order (Form 39)

The **Child Support Income Deduction Order (Form 39)** must be completed in most cases where child support or alimony is to be paid. This is an order to the employer of the person required to make the payment (the "obligor"), requiring the employer to deduct the payment from the obligor's paycheck and send it to the Central Depository (usually the court clerk serves as the Central Depository). This form is to be prepared before the final hearing and presented to the judge at the hearing. Some items on this form may need to be filled in at the hearing, depending upon what the judge orders.

Generally, to complete the **Child Support Income Deduction Order (Form 39)**:
1) Complete the top portion according to the instructions in Chapter 3.
2) In the first paragraph, type in the date of the final hearing, the obligor's name, and the obligor's social security number on the appropriate lines.
3) Type in the obligor's name on the line in the paragraph that begins: "INCOME DEDUCTION:"
4) Check the appropriate lines, and fill in the requested information indicated in items "A" through "G."
5) In item "G," type in the name, address, and phone numbers of the Central Depository (call the Central Depository or the court clerk for this information).
6) Item "J" is to indicate when the Income Deduction Order will take effect. Check either the line for it to become effective immediately, or the line for it to become effective only after a one-month delinquency (if so, type in the amount of a one-month delinquency on the line provided.
7) Complete the section headed "NOTICE TO PAYOR" by filling in the required information. In item 6, check the line for "___ notice to **payor OR**." In item 7, check the line for "payee" if payments will be made directly to the payee without going through the Central Depository. If payment are going through the Central Depository, check the line for "___ depository."
8) Complete the section headed "STATEMENT OF RIGHTS, REMEDIES, AND DUTIES IN REGARD TO INCOME DEDUCTION ORDER" by filling in the required information. In item A, fill in the amounts of fees and interest to be imposed, if any. Item B is to fill in the information about what and when the employer is to deduct, and whether there will be any automatic change once any arrearage is paid off.

Motion for Health Insurance Coverage (Form 40)

If you already have a child support order that requires your ex-spouse to provide health insurance to the children, but you haven't been able to secure the health insurance, you need to file a **Motion for Health Insurance**

Coverage (Form 40). To complete Form 40:
1) Complete the top portion according to the instructions in Chapter 3.
2) In paragraph 1, type in the date of the order requiring health insurance, and check the line for which parent was ordered to provide the coverage. Fill in each child's name, date of birth, age, and social security number on the appropriate lines.
3) In paragraph 2, check the line for "Petitioner" or "Respondent," whichever applies to your ex-spouse. The purpose of paragraph 2 is to show that your ex-spouse has received notice of your motion. In most cases you will check item "a" and fill in the date notice was given and your ex-spouse's name on the two lines, and check either "certified mail" or "personal service," depending on how notice was given. You should only check item "b" if your ex-spouse has filed a written waiver of notice, or if you are certain that your ex-spouse will appear at the hearing (sometimes this is done when the ex-spouse is willing to provide insurance but his or her employer is refusing to do so).
4) Complete the certificate of service section, including your ex-spouse's name, address, and phone information.
5) Attach a **Standard signature page with notary (Form 30)**, and sign it before a notary.

Either send a copy of Form 40 to your ex-spouse by certified mail with return receipt requested, or have him or her served by the sheriff. Call the judge's secretary and ask if you need a hearing for a motion for health insurance coverage. If so, see the section in Chapter 3 on "Setting a Court Hearing." If a hearing has been set, you will also need to send your ex-spouse a **Notice of Hearing (Form 3)**.

Order for Health Insurance Coverage (Form 41)

You will also need to prepare an **Order for Health Insurance Coverage (Form 41)** to present to the judge. If no hearing is required, you can provide the Order along with your Motion. Otherwise, present it to the judge at the end of the hearing. To complete Form 41:
1) Complete the top portion according to the instructions in Chapter 3.
2) Type in your ex-spouse's name on the lines at the end of the paragraph beginning with the word "TO," and at the end of paragraph 2 .
3) On the second page of the form, type in your and your ex-spouse's names, addresses, and phone information on the appropriate lines.

Instructions to Employer or Other Person Providing Health Insurance (Form 42)

You will also need to complete the Instructions to **Employer or Other Person Providing Health Insurance (Form 42)**. To complete Form 42 you just need to complete the top portion of the form according to the instructions in Chapter 3. The remainder of Form 42 is for the employer to complete if no health insurance is available.

Chapter 7
Custody

How a Change in Custody is Determined

Florida law distiquishes between "primary residence" (where the child lives) and "parental responsibility" (who makes major decisions regarding the child, such as medical care, educational needs, etc.). Many judges and lawyers still refer to parental responsibility as "custody," and we will too. If your situation has come to the point where you are reading this book, you probably want your child to live with you, and you want the sole parental responsibility for making major decisions about your child's welfare. Your first step is to read your divorce judgment to see how it describes your custody/parental responsibility situation. Most divorce judgments award custody to one parent, but provide for "joint parental responsibility." Florida law favors joint parental responsibility (see Appendix A).

In awarding custody in a contested divorce case, the judge will consider the following factors:

1) Which parent is most likely to allow the other to visit with the child. (If your ex-spouse is denying you visitation or is causing serious problems with visitation or your relationship with your child, this may justify a change in custody. Just be ready to assure the judge that you will do a better job of fostering a good relationship between the children and your ex-spouse.)

2) The love, affection and other emotional ties existing between the child and each parent.

3) The ability and willingness of each parent to provide the child with food, clothing, medical care, and other material needs.

4) The length of time the child has lived with either parent in a stable environment. (This may be the most significant factor in a custody fight because the courts are reluctant to remove a child from such a stable environment unless there is a very good reason.)

5) The permanence, as a family unit, of the proposed custodial home. (An example is where you have remarried, your new spouse and you have developed a stable household, possibly with other children about the same age as the child involved in the custody case, and your ex-spouse is single, working outside the home, and the child is left home alone for long periods of time. Or maybe you have the situation described, but your ex-spouse, who has also remarried, is in the midst of a divorce or involved in a physically abusive marriage.)

6) The moral fitness of each parent.

7) The mental and physical health of each parent.

8) The home, school and community record of the child.

9) The preference of the child, providing the child is of sufficient intelligence and understanding. (Especially if your child is older, you may want to give a lot of consideration to where the child wants to live.)

10) Any other fact the judge decides is relevant.

However, these are not necessarily the same factors the judge will consider in a request to *change* custody.

To justify a change in custody you will need to show either that the child's needs and the parents' circumstances have changed since the divorce judgment was entered, or that the current custody arrangement has failed (such as where your ex-spouse is not following the current custody or visitation order). If the child is in a stable environment, it will be difficult to get the judge to upset things by changing custody. Generally, you will need to prove that the child is in some kind of danger by staying in your ex-spouse's custody. Other factors which have been considered in change of custody cases include the the sex of the child; the relocation of one of the parents; and the morals, race, religion, and social views of the parents which have an effect on the child's welfare. These things may be considered, but they do not necessarily decide the question. The primary concern is the best interest of the child, with a strong presumption in favor of maintaining a stable home environment. You will need to look at your divorce judgment and see if there are any statements about why custody was awarded to your ex-spouse. If custody was based upon your agreement, there will probably be no such statement.

Factors to Consider

Financial Inability. It is almost impossible to justify a change of custody on the grounds that your ex-spouse lacks the ability to provide for your child. This is because your ex-spouse's difficulty can be fixed by you paying child support! However, while financial *inability* won't get you a change of custody, financial *unwillingness* may. This is where you can prove that your ex-spouse is not using the child support and other available financial resources to care for the child. In other words, your ex-spouse has the money, but isn't using it to provide for the child. This may also constitute neglect, which is covered below. You will need to show an actual negative effect on the child. Mere speculation will not be enough.

Health of the Parents. This relates to both physical and mental health. To obtain a change of custody you will need to prove that your ex-spouse has a mental or physical condition which renders him or her unable to adequately take care of the child. This will require testimony of expert witnesses, especially doctors or psychologists who have examined or treated your ex-spouse. It may also require you to show that your child is actually not receiving proper care. If you believe your ex-spouse suffers from a mental problem, you can file a motion for a psychological evaluation (this is discussed more in the next chapter).

Lifestyle and Beliefs of the Parents. Generally, a custodial parent is allowed to have his or her own beliefs, morals and lifestyle as long as it doesn't affect his or her ability to be a parent and raise the child. Here again you will probably need expert witness testimony to prove a negative effect on the child. One of the big issues today is drug abuse. If you believe your ex-spouse is a drug abuser, you can file a motion to have your ex-spouse tested for drugs (this is discussed more in the next chapter). A word of caution: Drug abuse is a charge that is frequently made in custody disputes, often without any real proof. Don't make such a charge lightly.

Abuse and Neglect. If you suspect that your ex-spouse is physically abusing your child, you are required by law to call the Department of Health and Rehabilitative Services (HRS) (their toll-free number is 1-800-962-2873). HRS will investigate, and if they find abuse you may be able to use their investigators as witnesses to justify a change in custody. In most cases, if HRS can't prove abuse (and they often can't), you won't be able to either. Also, be aware that it is a criminal offense to make a false abuse report to HRS, so don't do it simply to harass your ex-spouse.

If HRS does find abuse or neglect, it may remove the child from your ex-spouse's home, temporarily place the child with you or another relative, and file a petition in juvenile court to get a court order permanently removing the child from your ex-spouse's home. However, if HRS believes that the child would not be any better off in your custody, the child may end up with other relatives or in a foster home for a long period of time, while you or your ex-spouse take parenting courses and see psychologists.

An HRS investigation may result in an administrative hearing that is similar to a trial, and may involve your child being called to testify, which can be traumatic. It could also trigger a criminal investigation by the police, criminal abuse or neglect charges against your ex-spouse, and your child being interviewed by police officers, State Attorney Office investigators and lawyers, and being called to testify at depositions and in a criminal trial. These things can take months to complete, with no guarantee that anything will be sufficiently proven. This should not discourage you from pursuing the matter if you really believe your ex-spouse is abusing or neglecting your child, but you should be aware of what you may be getting yourself and your child involved in.

Physical Abuse. In order to make a physical abuse charge hold up, you will generally need to show some kind of an injury and how the injury occurred. This may require you to decide if you want to drag your child into court to testify about what happened. It may also require bringing doctors to court to testify.

Sexual Abuse. This is usually even more difficult to prove than physical abuse, especially if it involves a young child and no physical evidence of abuse (as determined by a doctor). You will also need to consider whether you want to have your child testify, which will probably be unavoidable if you want to pursue the matter. As with physical abuse, you also need to be aware that children sometimes make up stories of abuse in an attempt to manipulate their parents. HRS social workers and psychologists may tell you that young children don't make up sexual abuse stories, but they are wrong. Even a physician's conclusion that there has been sexual abuse cannot be relied upon, as many other medical problems can create symptoms similar to those caused by sexual abuse.

Emotional Abuse. Emotional abuse is impossible to prove unless you can get a psychologist or psychiatrist to testify that something your ex-spouse did caused serious psychological damage to your child. This must clearly be different than the problems caused by the divorce itself.

Neglect. Neglect can mean failing to provide adequate housing, food, clothing, medical care, or education.

The "Special Needs" Child

If your child has "special needs," the ability of you and your ex-spouse to meet these needs may also be considered. Special needs involve the gifted child who has special educational needs, as well as the child with physical or mental problems and handicaps. This will probably involve expert testimony to verify the child's condition and needs, and show which parent is best able to meet those needs. For example, if your handicapped child needs frequent at-home physical therapy, the judge may not change custody if you work full time and your ex-spouse stays at home with the children.

Relationship to Support and Visitation

A change in child custody will also result in a change in child support and visitation. If you get custody of your child, your ex-spouse may be required to pay child support. If you don't want child support, the judge will probably go along with no support as long as you can satisfy the judge that you have the financial ability to take care of your child. Otherwise, see Chapter 7 for more information on how to determine child support.

If you will have custody, you need to consider your ex-spouse's visitation rights. If you and your ex-spouse got along all right with whatever visitation arrangement is in your divorce judgment, you can simply reverse the situation now that you have custody. But if your petition to change custody has led to bitter disputes with your ex-spouse, it is a good idea to get a detailed visitation order to minimize problems in the future. See Chapter 8 for more information on changing visitation.

Petition to Modify Custody (Form 43)

The basic form used to ask for a change in custody is the **Petition/Request to Modify/Change Primary Residency/Custody of Children (Form 43)**. You will see that there are also provisions in this form to ask for child support, as a change in child support usually goes with a change in custody. To complete Form 43:
  1) Complete the top portion according to the instructions in Chapter 3.
  2) In the first, unnumbered paragraph, check the line for "Petitioner" or "Respondent," whichever applies to you.

3) In paragraph 1, check the line for "Petitioner" or "Respondent," whomever has custody now. Also fill in the date of the last custody order, which will be the date of your divorce judgment if this is the first modification. You will need to attach a copy of the judgment or other more recent custody order.
4) In the space below paragraph 3, you will need to type in a brief explanation of the reasons you want to change custody.
5) In the space after paragraph 4, type in why a change in custody is in the best interest of the children.
6) In paragraph 5, check the line for "Petitioner" or "Respondent," whichever does *not* apply to you.
7) For each item after the phrase "WHEREFORE, I am asking that the court enter and order:," check the approriate lines and fill in the required information to indicate what changes you are requesting.
8) Complete the certificate of service provisions at the top of the third page, including the name, address, and phone information for your ex-spouse.
9) Take this form to a notary public and sign it before the notary.

Financial Disclosure Documents

Although it is not always necessary, it is probably a good idea to complete and file a **Family Law Financial Affidavit (Form 24** or **Form 25)**. This will at least assure the judge that you can financially take care of your child. If you are arguing that a change in custody is necessary because your ex-spouse no longer has the financial ability to take care of the child or if you also want to change child support, you *must* file a **Family Law Financial Affidavit**. To complete this form, see the instructions in Chapter 5. Be sure to read Chapters 6 and 8 if you also want child support and visitation covered in your request to change custody.

Uniform Child Custody Jurisdiction Act (UCCJA) Affidavit (Form 44)

The **Uniform Child Custody Jurisdiction Act (UCCJA) Affidavit (Form 44)** must be completed in all cases involving custody or visitation. To complete Form 44:
1) Complete the top portion according to the instructions in Chapter 3.
2) In paragraph 1, type in the name and current address of each of your children.
3) In paragraph 2, type in the addresses where each child has lived during the past five years. If a child is not yet five years old, type in the places the child has lived since birth.
4) In paragraph 3, type in the names and *current* addresses of persons with whom each child has lived during the past five years.
5) Paragraph 4 requires you to list any other court cases involving the custody of, or visitation with, your children. Do not include the divorce case which you are seeking to modify.
6) Similarly, paragraph 5 requires you to tell if you know of any court case involving custody of, or visitation with, the children (even if you weren't involved in the case). If there are no such cases, you don't need to do anything with paragraphs 4 or 5. If there are such cases, you need to check the appropriate lines to indicate whether the other case is continuing or has been "stayed" (temporarily stopped) by the other court and whether you want the judge in your case to take some action to protect the children from abuse or neglect.
7) You will only complete paragraph 6 if there is any person other than you or your ex-spouse who has custody of your child or who claims custody or visitation rights.
8) Complete the certificate of service section at the bottom of the second page, including your ex-spouse's name, address, and phone information.
9) Attach a **Standard signature page with notary (Form 30)**, and sign it before a notary. This form should be filed with the court clerk along with your **Petition**.

Guardian Ad Litem (Form 45 and Form 46)

If charges of child abuse or neglect are raised, the judge is required to appoint a "guardian ad litem." You may also ask the judge to appoint a guardian ad litem in any case. The guardian ad litem will either be an attorney or a person certified by the State Guardian Ad Litem Program. The guardian ad litem has the authority to conduct an investigation to determine whether a change of custody is in the child's best interest. Unless you and your ex-spouse are financially unable to pay for the services of the guardian ad litem, either or both of you will be assessed the costs. If your ex-spouse poses a danger to your child, but you can't get the necessary proof, you may want to ask for the appointment of a guardian ad litem. This will require you to prepare two forms.

First is a **Motion for Appointment of Guardian Ad Litem (Form 45)**. To complete Form 45 you need to:
1) Complete the top portion according to the instructions in Chapter 3.
2) In the first (unnumbered) paragraph, check "Petitioner" or "Respondent," whichever applies to you.
4) In paragraph 1, check the matters that are to be determined by the judge. "Primary residential parent" refers to the question of where the child should live. "Primary responsibility" refers to who should have responsibility for making major decisions regarding the child.
5) In paragraph 2, type in each child's name, date of birth, age, sex, and who they are currently living with, under the appropriate headings.
6) In paragraph 4, check the line to show if you and your spouse have a history of domestic violence.
7) In paragrah 5, indicate if there are any other court-ordered social investigations pending.
8) Complete the certificate of service section, including your ex-spouse's name, address, and phone information.
9) Attach a **Signature page with notary (Form 30)**, and sign it before a notary.

It is a good idea to check with the guardian ad litem program in the county where your child lives to find out what type of costs to expect. THIS CAN BECOME EXPENSIVE. If you can't afford to pay the fees, you will need to complete and file an **Affidavit of Insolvency (Form 19)** (see Chapter 3 for instructions for completing this form).

The other form is the **Order Appointing Guardian Ad Litem, (Form 46)**. To complete Form 65 you need to:
1) Complete the top portion according to the instructions in Chapter 3.
2) On the third page of the form, type in the name, address, and telephone number information at the end of the form for yourself and your spouse. The judge or his secretary will have to complete the other portions of the form or tell you what information to fill in. (In the first, unnumbered paragraph and in paragraph 2 the judge or you will need to fill in the information for the judicial circuit in which the guardian ad litem will be appointed. This will usually be the judicial circuit for the county where the child lives, which may or may not be the same circuit that is hearing your case.)

File the motion with the court clerk, and deliver a copy of the motion and proposed order to the judge's secretary. Ask the secretary if you need to set a hearing, or if the judge will consider the motion without a hearing. If a hearing is required, get a hearing date from the secretary (see Chapter 3 about setting hearing dates). Mail your ex-spouse a copy of your motion, and a **Notice of Hearing (Form 3)** if a hearing is necessary.

Filing with the Court Clerk, Etc.

See Chapter 3 for information about filing your papers with the court. To modify custody you should file a **Civil Cover Sheet (Form 20)**, **Petition/Request to Change Primary Parental Responsibility/Custody of Children (Form 43)**, and **Uniform Child Custody Jurisdiction Act (UCCJA) Affidavit (Form 44)**. Depending upon the circumstances, you may also need to file the other forms discussed in this chapter. See Chapter 3 for information about setting a court date and about notifying your ex-spouse.

Preparing and Presenting Your Proof

Selecting and Interviewing Witnesses

The witnesses you choose to have testify will depend upon what you are trying to prove at the hearing. Witnesses may include relatives, friends, neighbors, police officers, HRS investigators, doctors and psychologists, and your child's school teachers and counselors. You will need to decide who you think would be a witness to help your position, and who your ex-spouse might use to hurt your position. First, make a list of each fact you want to prove at the hearing. Again, this will depend upon the reasons you are asking for a change in custody. Beside each fact, write down the name of the witness or witnesses you believe will be able to testify to that fact. Next, make a list of each potential witness, their address and telephone number, what fact they will prove for you, and what you expect each would say in court. You can use the **Witness Testimony Worksheet (Form 31)** to help you. See the "Questioning Witnesses" section of this chapter regarding Form 31.

Your next step is to talk to each potential witness to be sure of what they would say at the hearing. Never assume what a witness will say at the hearing! Many cases have been lost by a witness giving surprise testimony at a hearing. Regarding questioning witnesses at hearings, one of the first lessons law students are taught is: "Never ask a question unless you know what the answer will be." For each witness you interview, you want to ask the specific questions you might ask at the hearing and also allow the witness to describe what he or she saw, heard, and "knows." This will allow you to find out new information and will possibly lead you to other witnesses.

There is a big danger of a witness telling you one thing before the hearing, then changing his or her testimony at the hearing. The best way to reduce this danger is to take the witness' deposition. This is where you have the sheriff serve a notice on the witness to appear at a specific place and time to answer questions before a court reporter. Unfortunately, this can be very expensive. You will have to pay for the court reporter to show up and record the testimony and pay for the reporter to type up a record or "transcript" of the deposition. You can expect to pay about $45 for the court reporter, plus at least $100 per hour of testimony transcribed. The advantage to having a transcript is that you can use it to contradict the witness if he or she says something different at the hearing. Most lawyers only take depositions of the witnesses for the opposing parent. They do extensive questioning of their own witnesses and tell them that they will be expected to give the same testimony at the hearing.

One alternative is to ask the witness to give you a written, signed statement of what they saw, heard, and know. It may also help to have someone with you when you interview the witness, so that person can testify to the original statements if the witness changes his or her story at the hearing. The important message here is to be as sure as possible what your witnesses will say before you put them on the witness stand.

Private Investigators. If you are basing your change of custody on abuse or the lifestyle of your ex-spouse, you may want to hire a private investigator to help you prove it (if you can afford the fee). You do not necessarily want to rely on HRS investigators, who are frequently inexperienced and undertrained, and always underpaid and overworked.

Expert Witnesses. Sometimes, especially in custody and alimony cases, it is necessary to have an expert witness testify. An expert witness is someone you are having testify because of his or her special education, training or experience, such as a doctor or psychologist. An expert witness will testify to something that requires special training to be able to evaluate, and where a professional opinion is given. At the hearing, it is first necessary to have the judge determine that the witness is qualified as an expert. This is usually done by asking the witness to tell his or her profession and to describe his or her training and job experience. Once this is done, you say to the judge, "I would like this witness qualified as an expert."

Notifying Witnesses

The best way to notify witnesses of your hearing date is by having the sheriff serve them with a subpoena. It's a good idea to call your witnesses to let them know of the hearing date, and that they will be receiving a subpoena. It is not absolutely necessary to serve a subpoena on witnesses who are willing to come and help you out. But if they have car trouble or are ill on the hearing date, the judge will probably not continue the hearing so they can testify at a later date unless they were served with a subpoena. For doctors, psychologists, school teachers, police officers, HRS investigators, etc., it is absolutely necessary that you serve them with subpoenas. This should be done at least five days before the hearing, but no earlier than about two weeks before. Police officers must be served at least five days before, or they do not need to appear. If you just need the person to testify, use a regular **Subpoena (Form15)**. If you need the person to bring records or other evidence (such as a police report, medical records, etc.), you need to use the **Subpoena Duces Tecum (Form 16)**. See Chapter 3 for information on how to prepare and serve subpoenas.

Questioning Witnesses

In questioning witnesses at the hearing, you want to show three basic things: who the witness is, what the witness knows, and how the witness knows it. The **Witness Testimony Worksheet (Form 31)** will help you prepare for questioning your witnesses at the hearing. Make a copy of the Witness Testimony Worksheet for each witness you will be calling (including yourself) and fill it in as follows:
1) Type in a short reminder of what you expect this witness to prove by his or her testimony, in the box marked "PURPOSE OF WITNESS."

2) For questions in Part I, type in the answers you expect from the witness.

3) If your witness is a relative, friend, neighbor, HRS investigator, police officer, or other non-expert witness, skip Part II. If the witness is an expert, complete Part II by typing in the expected answers.

4) Part III is for you to type in the questions you want to ask the witness to prove your position, and the expected answer to each question. Refer back to what you put in the "PURPOSE OF WITNESS" section when deciding on your questions.

Keep in mind that most judges try to finish hearings as soon as possible. So you don't want your witnesses to get off the track of what they need to say to prove your case. To prepare your witnesses, you should go over the questions you will ask with the witness a day or two before the hearing. This will reassure you that the witness will give the testimony you want and will understand your questions. Use the **Witness Testimony Worksheet** to prepare your questions and review them with the witness. (See Chapter 3 on "Preparing Your Case," and Chapter 10 on "Preparing And Presenting Your Proof," for more information on witnesses.) You will also want to decide the order in which the witnesses will testify. Generally, you will want to have them testify in an order that will make sense, so the judge can understand the facts you are trying to present. However, to accommodate the doctor, police officer, etc., you may want to have them testify first so you don't keep them from their business longer than necessary.

Documents

Have copies of all documents you may want to present to the judge, and arrange them in the order you will present them. Generally, a document must be introduced by the person who prepared it. For example, if you are going to present a doctor's medical records about an injury your child was treated for, you will need to have the doctor talk about the records during his testimony. So keep in mind the order in which your witnesses will testify when you are arranging your documents. See Chapter 3 on "Preparing Your Case," and Chapter 10 on "Preparing And Presenting Your Proof," for more information about presenting testimony of witnesses and documents.

Final Judgment of Modification of Parental Responsibility and Visitation (Form 47)

At the hearing you will need to present the judge with a **Final Judgment of Modification of Parental Responsibility and Visitation (Form 47)**. To complete Form 47:

1) Complete the top portion according to the instructions in Chapter 3.

2) Type in the hearing date in the first, unnumbered paragraph.

3) In paragraph 3, check the line to indicate your ex-spouse was served, and the appropriate line to indicate whether a default was entered.

4) In paragraph 4, type in the date of the most recent custody order. This may be your divorce judgment.

5) In paragraph 5, check the line to indicate whether the judge determines there has been a substantial change in circumstances to justify a change in custody. Type in a brief description of what circumstances the judge determines have changed.

6) In paragraph 6, check the line to indicate whether the judge determines that a change in custody is in the child's best interest, and type in a brief statement of why the judge made that decision.

7) For the rest of the form, fill in the information that applies to your case. If child support is also being changed, refer to the section in Chapter 6 on the "Final Judgment Modifying Child Support."

8) On the last page of Form 47, type in the name, address, and phone information for you and your ex-spouse.

If you are also changing child support, you may need to complete a new **Order Requiring Payment Through Central Depository (Form 38)**, and **Child Support Income Deduction Order (Form 39)**. Form 38 will need to be completed if there is not already such an order. Form 39 will need to be completed if the amount of child support is changed.

Chapter 8
Visitation

Of all the provisions in a divorce judgment, visitation is the easiest to get modified. All you generally need to show is that the current arrangement is not working. This may be due to a change in circumstances (such as one party moving farther away), or because the current order is too general and a more rigid schedule is needed. In such cases you want to be specific, so there is no room for your ex-spouse to be uncertain about what is required. If the current order is already specific, but your ex-spouse isn't following it, you need to file a motion to enforce the order rather than to modify the order.

If you have custody and you are seeking to completely terminate visitation between your child and your ex-spouse, you will need to show that your ex-spouse poses a serious danger to the child. This will be very similar to asking for a change in custody, so be sure to read Chapter 7 of this book. If your judgment or current court order denies you all visitation and you are asking the judge to start giving you visitation, you will need to show a significant change in the circumstances which made the judge deny visitation in the first place. Legally, there is no relationship between child support and visitation. If your ex-spouse fails to pay child support, you cannot refuse visitation. If your ex-spouse denies visitation, you cannot refuse to pay child support.

Supplemental Petition to Modify Visitation (Form 48)

The **Supplemental Petition/Request to Modify/Change Visitation (Form 48)** is the basic form used to ask the court for a change in visitation. To complete Form 48:
1) Complete the top portion according to the instructions in Chapter 3.
2) In the first, unnumbered paragraph, check "Petitioner" or "Respondent," whichever applies to you.
3) In paragraph 1, type in the date of the last visitation order. You will also need to attach a copy of the last visitation order, which may be your divorce judgment.
4) In paragraph 2, type in the number of the paragraphs from the last order that sets forth the current visitation order.
5) In paragraph 3, type in a brief statement about why you want the visitation order changed.
6) In paragraph 4, type in an explanation of why a change would be in the child's best interest.
7) In the space after the paragraph begining with the word "WHEREFORE," type in a description of the visitation arrangement you would like. Be as specific as possible.
8) Complete the certificate of service section, including your ex-spouse's name, address, and phone information.

9) Attach a **Standard signature page with notary (Form 30)**, and sign it before a notary. (Be sure to also attach a copy of the last visitation order.)

Other Forms

Although not legally necessary, filing a **Uniform Child Custody Jurisdiction Act (UCCJA) Affidavit (Form 44)** may make the judge feel more comfortable about going ahead with a hearing and issuing a new visitation order. See Chapter 6 for information about completing this form. If you also want a change in the child support amount, you *must* file a **Family Law Financial Affidavit (Form 24** or **Form 25)** (see the instructions in Chapter 5). Also see the section on "Interrogatories and Financial Disclosure" in Chapter 5.

Filing With the Court Clerk, Etc.

See Chapter 3 for information about filing your papers with the court. To modify visitation, you should be file a **Civil Cover Sheet (Form 20)**, **Supplemental Petition/Request to Modify/Change Visitation (Form 48)**, and **Uniform Child Custody Jurisdiction Act (UCCJA) Affidavit (Form 44)**. If you are seeking to terminate your ex-spouse's visitation altogether, you may also need to file some of the forms discussed in the section in Chapter 7 on "Guardian Ad Litem." See Chapter 3 about setting a court date and notifying your ex-spouse.

Preparing and Presenting Your Proof

In most cases, it will not be necessary to have any witnesses testify. (The only exception is if you want to severely limit or terminate visitation because your ex-spouse poses a threat to the child. In such cases, review Chapter 3 on "Preparing and Presenting Your Proof," and all of Chapter 7, which discuss some of the factors for custody that may also be used in a visitation case.) Generally, your statements to the judge that the current visitation arrangement is not working will be enough.

Again, in most cases, this will simply involve thinking about what you want to tell the judge. Basically, you want to point out the visitation provision in your judgment or any more recent visitation order, briefly explain some of the problems you have had with your ex-spouse regarding visitation, and tell the judge what kind of visitation order you would like to end these problems. The following is an example of such an opening statement:

"Your Honor, we are here on a Petition to Modify Visitation. The judgment currently provides for "reasonable and liberal visitation." This arrangement has not been working. My ex-husband never brings the children home at the agreed upon time, frequently arrives an hour late to pick them up or forgets to pick them up at all, and last Christmas Eve he was to have them home by 8:00 P.M., but kept them until 3:00 P.M. on Christmas Day. I would like an order specifying alternate weekend visitation from 7:00 P.M. Friday until 5:00 P.M. Sunday. If he doesn't arrive to pick up the children or call to advise me of a delay by 7:20 P.M., visitation may be cancelled for that weekend. I would also like the order to provide for visitation on alternate holidays from 9:00 A.M. to 8:00 P.M., and that the holidays be designated as New Year's Day, Easter Day, Memorial Day, Fourth of July, Labor Day, Thanksgiving Day, Christmas Eve, and Christmas Day."

You are telling the judge three things: What the current order is, why you want it changed, and what you want it changed to. The judge will then hear your ex-spouse's story. You may get a chance to respond to your ex-spouse, then the judge will make a decision. Have paper and pen ready, so you can write down what the judge orders and can prepare the new visitation order.

Final Judgment of Modification of Parental Responsibility and Visitation (Form 47)

At the hearing you will need to present the judge with a **Final Judgment of Modification of Parental Responsibility and Visitation (Form 47)**, which is the same form used for changes in custody. Refer to the instructions in Chapter 7. If you are also changing child support, you may need to prepare a new **Order Requiring Payment Through Central Depository (Form 38)** and **Child Support Income Deduction Order (Form 39)**.

Appendix A: Florida Statutes and Court Rules

The following are excerpts from the Florida Statutes and the Family Law Rules of Procedure. These are not the only provisions relating to this subject, it is strongly recommended that you read the most current version of Chapter 61 of the Florida Statutes, as well as the family law rules.

Chapter 61, Florida Statutes

61.08 Alimony.—

(1) In a proceeding for dissolution of marriage, the court may grant alimony to either party, which alimony may be rehabilitative or permanent in nature. In any award of alimony, the court may order periodic payments or payments in lump sum or both. The court may consider the adultery of either spouse and the circumstances thereof in determining the amount of alimony, if any, to be awarded. In all dissolution actions, the court shall include findings of fact relative to the factors enumerated in subsection (2) supporting an award or denial of alimony.

(2) In determining a proper award of alimony or maintenance, the court shall consider all relevant economic factors, including but not limited to:

(a) The standard of living established during the marriage.

(b) The duration of the marriage.

(c) The age and the physical and emotional condition of each party.

(d) The financial resources of each party, the nonmarital and the marital assets and liabilities distributed to each.

(e) When applicable, the time necessary for either party to acquire sufficient education or training to enable such party to find appropriate employment.

(f) The contribution of each party to the marriage, including, but not limited to, services rendered in homemaking, child care, education, and career building of the other party.

(g) All sources of income available to either party.

The court may consider any other factor necessary to do equity and justice between the parties.

(3) To the extent necessary to protect an award of alimony, the court may order any party who is ordered to pay alimony to purchase or maintain a life insurance policy or a bond, or to otherwise secure such alimony award with any other assets which may be suitable for that purpose.

(4)(a) With respect to any order requiring the payment of alimony entered on or after January 1, 1985, unless the provisions of paragraph (c) or paragraph (d) apply, the court shall direct in the order that the payments of alimony be made through the appropriate depository as provided in s. 61.181.

* * * * *

(c) If there is no minor child, alimony payments need not be directed through the depository.

(d)1. If there is a minor child of the parties and both parties so request, the court may order that alimony payments need not be directed through the depository. In this case, the order of support shall provide, or be deemed to provide, that either party may subsequently apply to the depository to require that payments be made through the depository. The court shall provide a copy of the order to the depository.

2. If the provisions of subparagraph 1. apply, either party may subsequently file with the depository an affidavit alleging default or arrearages in payment and stating that the party wishes to initiate participation in the depository program. The party shall provide copies of the affidavit to the court and the other party or parties. Fifteen days after receipt of the affidavit, the depository shall notify all parties that future payments shall be directed to the depository.

61.13 Custody and support of children; visitation rights; power of court in making orders.—

(2)(a) The court shall have jurisdiction to determine custody, notwithstanding that the child is not physically present in this state at the time of filing any proceeding under this chapter, if it appears to the court that the child was removed from this state for the primary purpose of removing the child from the jurisdiction of the court in an attempt to avoid a determination or modification of custody.

(b)1. The court shall determine all matters relating to custody of each minor child of the parties in accordance with the best interests of the child and in accordance with the Uniform Child Custody Jurisdiction Act. . . .

2. The court shall order that the parental responsibility for a minor child be shared by both parents unless the court finds that shared parental responsibility would be detrimental to the child. The court shall consider evidence of spouse or child abuse as evidence of detriment of the child. The court shall consider evidence that a parent has been convicted of a felony of the second degree or higher involving domestic violence as defined in s. 741.28 and chapter 775, as a rebuttable presumption of detriment to the child. If the presumption is not rebutted, shared parental responsibility, including visitation, residence of the child, and decisions made regarding the child, shall not be granted to the convicted parent. However, the convicted parent shall not be relieved of any obligation to provide financial support. If the court determines that shared parental responsibility would be detrimental to the child, it may order sole parental responsibility and make such arrangements for visitation as will best protect the child or abused spouse from further harm.

a. In ordering shared parental responsibility, the court may consider the expressed desires of the parents and may grant to one party the ultimate responsibility over specific aspects of the child's welfare or may divide those responsibilities between the parties based on the best interests of the child. Areas of responsibility may include primary residence, education, medical and dental care, and any other responsibilities which the court finds unique to a particular family.

b. The court shall order "sole parental responsibility, with or without visitations rights, to the other parent when it is in the best interests of" the minor child.

(4)(c) When a custodial parent refuses to honor a noncustodial parent's visitation rights without proper cause, the court may:

2. Award custody or primary residence to the noncustodial parent, upon the request of the noncustodial parent, if the award is in the best interests of the child.

(8) If the court orders that parental responsibility, including visitation, be shared by both parents, the court may not deny the noncustodial parent overnight contact and access to or visitation with the child solely because of the age or sex of the child.

61.30 Child support guidelines.—

(1)(a) The child support guideline amount as determined by this section presumptively establishes the amount the trier of fact shall order as child support in an initial proceeding for such support or in a proceeding for modification of an existing order for such support, whether the proceeding arises under this or another chapter. The trier of fact may order payment of child support which varies, plus or minus 5 percent, from the guideline amount, after considering all relevant factors, including the needs of the child or children, age, station in life, standard of living, and the financial status and ability of each parent. The trier of fact may order payment of child support in an amount which varies more than 5 percent from such guideline amount only upon a written finding, or a specific finding on the record, explaining why ordering payment of such guideline amount would be unjust or inappropriate.

(b) The guidelines may provide the basis for proving a substantial change in circumstances upon which a modification of an existing order may be granted. However, the difference between the existing order and the amount provided for under the guidelines shall be at least 15 percent or $50, whichever amount is greater, before the court may find that the guidelines provide a substantial change in circumstances.

(2) Income shall be determined for the obligor and for the obligee as follows:

(a) Gross income shall include, but is not limited to, the following items:

1. Salary or wages.
2. Bonuses, commissions, allowances, overtime, tips, and other similar payments.
3. Business income from sources such as self-employment, partnership, close corporations, and independent contracts. "Business income" means gross receipts minus ordinary and necessary expenses required to produce income.
4. Disability benefits.
5. Worker's compensation.
6. Unemployment compensation.
7. Pension, retirement, or annuity payments.
8. Social security benefits.
9. Spousal support received from a previous marriage or court ordered in the marriage before the court.
10. Interest and dividends.
11. Rental income, which is gross receipts minus ordinary and necessary expenses required to produce the income.
12. Income from royalties, trusts, or estates.
13. Reimbursed expenses or in kind payments to the extent that they reduce living expenses.
14. Gains derived from dealings in property, unless the gain is nonrecurring.

(b) Income shall be imputed to an unemployed or underemployed parent when such employment or underemployment is found to be voluntary on that parent's part, absent physical or mental incapacity or other circumstances over which the parent has no control. In the event of such voluntary unemployment or underemployment, the employment potential and probable earnings level of the parent shall be determined based upon his or her recent work history, occupational qualifications, and prevailing earnings level in the community; however, the court may refuse to impute income to a primary residential parent if the court finds it necessary for the parent to stay home with the child.

(c) Temporary assistance under the WAGES Program shall be excluded from gross income.

(3) Allowable deductions from gross income shall include:

(a) Federal, state, and local income tax deductions, adjusted for actual filing status and allowable dependents and income tax liabilities.

(b) Federal insurance contributions or self-employment tax.

(c) Mandatory union dues.

(d) Mandatory retirement payments.

(e) Health insurance payments, excluding payments for coverage of the minor child.

(f) Court-ordered support payments for other children which is actually paid.

(g) Spousal support paid pursuant to a court order from a previous marriage or the marriage before the court.

(4) Net income for the obligor and net income for the obligee shall be computed by subtracting allowable deductions from gross income.

(5) Net income for the obligor and net income for the obligee shall be added together for a combined net income.

(6) The following schedules shall be applied to the combined net income to determine the minimum child support need:

[See Child support Schedule on page 63]

For combined monthly available income less than the amount set out on the above schedules, the parent should be ordered to pay a child support amount, determined on a case-by-case basis, to establish the principle of payment and lay the basis for increased orders should the parent's income increase in the future. For combined monthly available income greater than the amount set out in the above schedules, the obligation shall be the minimum amount of support provided by the guidelines plus the following percentages multiplied by the amount of income over $10,000:

Child or Children

One	Two	Three	Four	Five	Six
5.0%	7.5%	9.5%	11.0%	12.0%	12.5%

(7) Child care costs incurred on behalf of the children due to employment, job search, or education calculated to result in employment or to enhance income of current employment of either parent shall be reduced by 25 percent and then shall be added to the basic obligation. Child care costs shall not exceed the level required to provide quality care from a licensed source for the children.

(8) Health insurance costs resulting from coverage ordered pursuant to s. 61.13(1)(b) shall be added to the basic obligation.

(9) Each parent's percentage share of the child support need shall be determined by dividing each parent's net income by the combined net income.

(10) Each parent's actual dollar share of the child support need shall be determined by multiplying the minimum child support need by each parent's percentage share.

(11) The court may adjust the minimum child support award, or either or both parent's share of the minimum child support award, based upon the following considerations:

(a) Extraordinary medical, psychological, educational, or dental expenses.

(b) Independent income of the child.

(c) The payment of support for a parent which regularly has been paid and for which there is a demonstrated need.

(d) Seasonal variations in one or both parents' incomes or expenses.

(e) The age of the child, taking into account the greater needs of older children.

(f) Special needs that have traditionally been met within the family budget even though the fulfilling of those needs will cause the support to exceed the proposed guidelines.

(g) The particular shared parental arrangement, such as where the children spend a substantial amount of their time with the secondary residential parent, thereby reducing the financial expenditures incurred by the primary residential parent, or the refusal of the secondary residential parent to become involved in the activities of the child, or giving due consideration to the primary residential parent's homemaking services. If a child has visitation with a noncustodial parent for more than 28 consecutive days the court may reduce the amount of support paid to the custodial parent during the time of visitation not to exceed 50 percent of the amount awarded.

(h) Total available assets of the obligee, obligor, and the child.

(i) The impact of the Internal Revenue Service dependency exemption and waiver of that exemption. The court may order the primary residential parent to execute a waiver of the Internal Revenue Service dependency exemption if the noncustodial parent is current in support payments.

(j) When application of the child support guidelines requires a person to pay another person more than 55 percent of his gross income for a child support obligation for current support resulting from a single support order.

(k) Any other adjustment which is needed to achieve an equitable result which may include, but not be limited to, a reasonable and necessary existing expense or debt. Such expense or debt may include, but is not limited to, a reason-able and necessary expense or debt which the parties jointly incurred during the marriage.

(12) A parent with a support obligation may have other children living with him or her who were born or adopted after the support obligation arose. The existence of such subsequent children should not as a general rule be considered by the court as a basis for disregarding the amount provided in the guidelines. The parent with a support obligation for subsequent children may raise the existence of such subsequent children as a justification for deviation from the guidelines. However, if the existence of such subsequent children is raised, the income of the other parent of the subsequent children shall be considered by the court in determining whether or not there is a basis for deviation from the guideline amount. The issue of subsequent children may only be raised in a proceeding for an upward modification of an existing award and may not be applied to justify a decrease in an existing award.

(13) If the recurring income is not sufficient to meet the needs of the child, the court may order child support to be paid from nonrecurring income or assets.

(14) Every petition for child support or for modification of child support shall be accompanied by an affidavit which shows the party's income, allowable deductions, and net income computed in accordance with this section. The affidavit shall be served at the same time that the petition is served. The respondent, whether or not a stipulation is entered, shall make an affidavit which shows the party's income, allowable deductions, and net income computed in accordance with this section. The respondent shall include his affidavit with the answer to the petition, or as soon thereafter as is practicable, but in any case at least 72 hours prior to any hearing on the finances of either party.

(15) For purposes of establishing an obligation for support in accordance with this section, if a person who is receiving public assistance is found to be noncooperative as defined in s. 409.2572, the IV-D agency is authorized to submit to the court an affidavit attesting to the income of the custodial parent based upon information available to the IV-D agency.

(16) The Legislature shall review the guidelines established in this section at least every 4 years, and shall review the guidelines in 1997.

Family Law Rules of Procedure

The following is one of the more significant rules of the new Family Law Rules of Procedure. You would be well advised to review both the Florida Rules of Civil Procedure and the full Family Law Rules of Procedure.

RULE 12.285. MANDATORY DISCLOSURE

(a) **Application.**

(1) **Scope.** This rule shall apply to all proceedings within the scope of these rules except proceedings involving adoption, simplified dissolution, enforcement, contempt, and injunctions for domestic or repeat violence. Additionally, no financial affidavit or other documents shall be required under this rule from a party seeking attorneys' fees, suit money, or costs, if the basis for the request is solely under section 57.105, Florida Statutes, or any successor statute. Except for the provisions as to financial affidavits, any portion of this rule may be modified by order of the court or agreement of the parties.

(2) **Original and Duplicate Copies.** Unless otherwise agreed by the parties or ordered by the court, copies of documents required under this rule may be produced in lieu of originals. Originals, when available, shall be produced for inspection upon request. Parties shall not be required to serve duplicates of documents previously served.

(b) **Time for Production of Documents.**

(1) **Temporary Financial Hearings.** Any document required under this rule in any temporary financial relief proceeding shall be served on the other party for inspection and copying as follows.

(A) The party seeking relief shall serve the required documents on the other party with the notice of temporary financial hearing, unless the documents have been served under subdivision (b)(2) of this rule.

(B) The responding party shall serve the required documents on the party seeking relief on or before 5:00 p.m., 2 business days before the day of the temporary financial hearing if served by delivery or 7 days before the day of the temporary financial hearing if served by mail, unless the documents have been received previously by the party seeking relief under subdivision (b)(2) of this rule. A responding party shall be given no less than 12 days to serve the documents required under this rule, unless otherwise ordered by the court. If the 45-day period for exchange of documents provided for in subdivision (b)(2) of this rule will occur before the expiration of the 12 days, the provisions of subdivision (b)(2) control.

(2) **Initial and Supplemental Proceedings.** Any document required under this rule for any initial or supplemental proceeding shall be served on the other party for inspection and copying within 45 days of service of the initial pleading on the respondent.

(c) **Parties Whose Annual Income and Expenses Are Less Than $50,000.** Any party whose gross annual income from all sources is less than $50,000 and whose total annual expenses are less than $50,000 shall be required to serve the following documents in any proceeding for an initial or supplemental request for temporary or permanent financial relief, including, but not limited to, a request for child support, alimony, equitable distribution of assets or debts, or attorneys' fees, suit money, or costs:

(1) A financial affidavit in substantial conformity with Family Law Form 12.901(d), which requirement cannot be waived by the parties.

(2) All federal and state income tax returns, gift tax returns, and intangible personal property tax returns filed by the party or on the party's behalf for the past three years.

(3) IRS forms W-2, 1099, and K-1 for the past year, if the income tax return for that year has not been prepared.

(4) Pay stubs or other evidence of earned income for the 3 months prior to service of the financial affidavit.

(5) A statement by the producing party identifying the amount and source of all income received from any source during the 3 months preceding the service of the financial affidavit required by this rule if not reflected on the pay stubs produced.

(6) All loan applications and financial statements prepared or used within the 3 years preceding service of that party's financial affidavit required by this rule, whether for the purpose of obtaining or attempting to obtain credit or for any other purpose.

(d) **Parties Whose Annual Income or Expenses Are Equal To or Exceed $50,000.** Any party whose gross annual income from all sources is equal to or exceeds $50,000 or whose total annual expenses are equal to or exceed $50,000 shall be required to serve the documents on the other party as follows.

(1) **Temporary Financial Relief.** In any proceeding for temporary financial relief, the following documents shall be served on the other party:

(A) A financial affidavit in substantial conformity with Family Law Form 12.901(e), which requirement cannot be waived by the parties.

(B) All federal and state income tax returns, gift tax returns, and intangible personal property tax returns filed by the party or on the party's behalf for the past 3 years.

(C) IRS forms W-2, 1099, and K-1 for the past year, if the income tax return for that year has not been prepared.

(D) Pay stubs or other evidence of earned income for the 3 months prior to service of the financial affidavit.

(E) A statement by the producing party identifying the amount and source of all income received from any source during the 3 months preceding the service of the financial affidavit required by this rule if not reflected on the pay stubs produced.

(F) All loan applications and financial statements prepared or used within the 3 years preceding service of that party's financial affidavit required by this rule, whether for the purpose of obtaining or attempting to obtain credit or for any other purpose.

(G) Corporate, partnership, and trust tax returns for the last tax year, if the producing party has an interest in a corporation, partnership, or trust greater than or equal to 30%.

(2) **Initial Proceedings.** In any initial proceeding for permanent financial relief, including, but not limited to, a request for child support, alimony, equitable distribution of assets or debts, or attorneys' fees, suit money, or costs, the following documents shall be served on the other party:

(A) All documents listed in subdivision (d)(1).

(B) The answers to interrogatories found in Family Law Form 12.930(b).

(C) All documents showing reimbursed expenses and in-kind payments that reduce the party's personal living expenses that were received by or made available to the party for the last 3 years.

(D) All deeds, mortgages, promissory notes, and closing statements pertaining to real estate in which the party owns or owned an interest within the last 3 years, whether held in the party's name individually, in the party's name jointly with any other person, in the party's name as trustee or guardian for any other person, or in someone else's name on the party's behalf.

(E) All periodic statements and passbooks from the last 3 years for all checking accounts, savings accounts, money market funds, certificates of deposit, and credit union accounts (regardless of whether or not the account has been closed), including those held in the party's name individually, in the party's name jointly with any other person or entity, in the party's name as trustee or guardian for any other person, or in someone else's name on the party's behalf.

(F) All brokerage account statements in which either party to this action held within the last 3 years or holds an interest including those held in the party's name individually, in the party's name jointly with any person or entity, in the party's name as trustee or guardian for any other person, or in someone else's name on the party's behalf.

(G) All title certificates, lease agreements, and registration certificates for all motor vehicles, boats, airplanes, and any other vehicle requiring registration that the party regularly uses, owns, or owned in the last 3 years.

(H) The most recent statement for any profit sharing, retirement, or pension plan in which the party is a participant or alternate payee and the summary plan description for any retirement, profit sharing, or pension plan in which the party is a participant or an alternate payee (The summary plan description must be furnished to the party on request by the plan administrator as required by 29 U.S.C. § 1024(b)(4).)

(I) All documents pertaining to any money owed to the party or spouse.

(J) All life insurance policies insuring the party's life or the life of the party's spouse.

(K) Corporate, partnership, and trust tax returns for the last 3 years if the party has an ownership or interest in a corporation, partnership, or trust greater than or equal to 30%.

(L) Periodic statements, amortization schedules, or other records showing the party's indebtedness as of the date of the filing of this action and for the last 3 years.

(M) All written premarital or marital agreements entered into at any time between the parties to this marriage, whether before or during the marriage.

(N) All documents and tangible evidence supporting the producing party's claim of special equity or nonmarital status of an asset or debt for the time period from the date of acquisition of the asset or debt to the date of production or from the date of marriage, if based on premarital acquisition.

(O) Any court orders directing a party to pay or receive spousal or child support.

(3) **Supplemental Proceedings.** In any temporary or permanent supplemental proceeding regarding financial relief, documents shall be produced as set forth in subdivisions (d)(1) and (d)(2), respectively and shall be served as set forth in subdivision (b)(1). Additionally, in any modification proceeding, each party shall serve on the opposing party all written agreements entered into between them at any time since the order to be modified was entered.

(e) **Duty to Supplement Disclosure; Amended Financial Affidavit.**

(1) Parties have a continuing duty to supplement documents described in this rule, including financial affidavits, whenever a material change in their financial status occurs.

(2) If an amended financial affidavit or an amendment to a financial affidavit is served, the amending party also shall serve any subsequently discovered or acquired documents supporting the amendments to the financial affidavit if the party falls within the provisions of subdivision (d).

(f) **Sanctions.** Any document to be produced under this rule that is served on the opposing party fewer than 24 hours before a nonfinal hearing or in violation of the court's pretrial order shall not be admissible in evidence at that hearing unless the court finds good cause for the delay. In addition, the court may impose other sanctions authorized by rule 12.380 as may be equitable under the circumstances. The court may also impose sanctions upon the offending lawyer in lieu of imposing sanctions on a party.

(g) **Objections to Mandatory Automatic Disclosure.** Objections to the mandatory automatic disclosure required by this rule shall be served in writing at least 5 days prior to the due date for the disclosure or the objections shall be deemed waived. For good cause shown, the court may extend the time for the filing of an objection or permit the filing of an otherwise untimely objection.

(h) **Certificate of Compliance.** All parties subject to automatic mandatory disclosure shall file with the court a certificate of compliance identifying with particularity the documents which have been delivered and certifying the date of service of the financial affidavit and documents by that party.

(i) **Place of Production.**

(1) Unless otherwise agreed by the parties or ordered by the court, all production required by this rule shall take place in the county where the action is pending and in the office of the attorney for the party receiving production. Unless

otherwise agreed by the parties or ordered by the court, if a party does not have an attorney or if the attorney does not have an office in the county where the action is pending, production shall take place in the county where the action is pending at a place designated in writing by the party receiving production, served at least 5 days before the due date for production.

(2) If venue is contested, on motion by a party the court shall designate the place where production will occur pending determination of the venue issue.

Child Support Schedule

[from Section 61.30(6), Florida Statutes]

Combined Monthly Available Income	One	Two	Three	Four	Five	Six
$650	74	75	75	76	77	78
700	119	120	121	123	124	125
750	164	166	167	169	171	173
800	190	211	213	218	218	220
850	202	257	259	262	265	268
900	213	302	305	309	312	315
950	224	347	351	355	359	363
1000	235	365	397	402	406	410
1050	246	382	443	448	453	458
1100	258	400	489	495	500	505
1150	269	417	522	541	547	553
1200	280	435	544	588	594	600
1250	290	451	565	634	641	648
1300	300	467	584	659	688	695
1350	310	482	603	681	735	743
1400	320	498	623	702	765	790
1450	330	513	642	724	789	838
1500	340	529	662	746	813	869
1550	350	544	681	768	836	895
1600	360	560	701	790	860	920
1650	370	575	720	812	884	945
1700	380	591	740	833	907	971
1750	390	606	759	855	931	996
1800	400	622	779	877	955	1022
1850	410	638	798	900	979	1048
1900	421	654	818	923	1004	1074
1950	431	670	839	946	1029	1101
2000	442	686	859	968	1054	1128
2050	452	702	879	991	1079	1154
2100	463	718	899	1014	1104	1181
2150	473	734	919	1037	1129	1207
2200	484	751	940	1060	1154	1234
2250	494	767	960	1082	1179	1261
2300	505	783	980	1105	1204	1287
2350	515	799	1000	1128	1229	1314
2400	526	815	1020	1151	1254	1340
2450	536	831	1041	1174	1279	1367
2500	547	847	1061	1196	1304	1394
2550	557	864	1081	1219	1329	1420
2600	568	880	1101	1242	1354	1447
2650	578	896	1121	1265	1379	1473
2700	588	912	1141	1287	1403	1500
2750	597	927	1160	1308	1426	1524
2800	607	941	1178	1328	1448	1549
2850	616	956	1197	1349	1471	1573
2900	626	971	1215	1370	1494	1598
2950	635	986	1234	1391	1517	1622
3000	644	1001	1252	1412	1540	1647
3050	654	1016	1271	1433	1563	1671
3100	663	1031	1289	1453	1586	1695
3150	673	1045	1308	1474	1608	1720
3200	682	1060	1327	1495	1631	1744
3250	691	1075	1345	1516	1654	1769
3300	701	1090	1364	1537	1677	1793
3350	710	1105	1382	1558	1700	1818
3400	720	1120	1401	1579	1723	1842
3450	729	1135	1419	1599	1745	1867
3500	738	1149	1438	1620	1768	1891
3550	748	1164	1456	1641	1791	1915
3600	757	1179	1475	1662	1814	1940
3650	767	1194	1493	1683	1837	1964
3700	776	1208	1503	1702	1857	1987
3750	784	1221	1520	1721	1878	2009
3800	793	1234	1536	1740	1899	2031
3850	802	1248	1759	1920	1920	2053
3900	811	1261	1570	1778	1940	2075
3950	819	1275	1587	1797	1961	2097
4000	828	1288	1603	1816	1982	2119
4050	837	1302	1620	1835	2002	2141
4100	846	1315	1637	1854	2023	2163
4150	854	1329	1654	1873	2044	2185
4200	863	1342	1670	1892	2064	2207
4250	872	1355	1687	1911	2085	2229
4300	881	1369	1704	1930	2106	2251
4350	889	1382	1721	1949	2127	2273
4400	898	1396	1737	1968	2147	2295
4450	907	1409	1754	1987	2168	2317
4500	916	1423	1771	2006	2189	2339
4550	924	1436	1788	2024	2209	2361
4600	933	1450	1804	2043	2230	2384
4650	942	1463	1821	2062	2251	2406
4700	951	1477	1838	2081	2271	2428
4750	959	1490	1855	2100	2292	2450
4800	968	1503	1871	2119	2313	2472
4850	977	1517	1888	2138	2334	2494
4900	986	1530	1905	2157	2354	2516
4950	993	1542	1927	2174	2372	2535
5000	1000	1551	1939	2188	2387	2551
5050	1006	1561	1952	2202	2402	2567
5100	1013	1571	1964	2215	2417	2583
5150	1019	1580	1976	2229	2432	2599
5200	1025	1590	1988	2243	2447	2615
5250	1032	1599	2000	2256	2462	2631
5300	1038	1609	2012	2270	2477	2647
5350	1045	1619	2024	2283	2492	2663
5400	1051	1628	2037	2297	2507	2679
5450	1057	1638	2049	2311	2522	2695
5500	1064	1647	2061	2324	2537	2711
5550	1070	1657	2073	2338	2552	2727
5600	1077	1667	2085	2352	2567	2743
5650	1083	1676	2097	2365	2582	2759
5700	1089	1686	2109	2379	2597	2775
5750	1096	1695	2122	2393	2612	2791
5800	1102	1705	2134	2406	2627	2807
5850	1107	1713	2144	2418	2639	2820
5900	1111	1721	2155	2429	2651	2833

Child Support Schedule

[from Section 61.30(6), Florida Statutes]

Combined Monthly Available Income	One	Two	Three	Four	Five	Six
5950	1116	1729	2165	2440	2663	2847
6000	1121	1737	2175	2451	2676	2860
6050	1126	1746	2185	2462	2688	2874
6100	1131	1754	2196	2473	2700	2887
6150	1136	1762	2206	2484	2712	2900
6200	1141	1770	2216	2495	7243	2914
6250	1145	1778	2227	2506	2737	2927
6300	1150	1786	2237	2517	2749	2941
6350	1155	1795	2247	2529	2761	2954
6400	1160	1803	2258	2540	2773	2967
6450	1165	1811	2268	2551	2785	2981
6500	1170	1819	2278	2562	2798	2994
6550	1175	1827	2288	2573	2810	3008
6600	1179	1835	2299	2584	2822	3021
6650	1184	1843	2309	2595	2834	3034
6700	1189	1850	2317	2604	2845	3045
6750	1193	1856	2325	2613	2854	3055
6800	1196	1862	2332	2621	2863	3064
6850	1200	1868	2340	2630	2872	3074
6900	1204	1873	2347	2639	2882	3084
6950	1208	1879	2355	2647	2891	3094
7000	1212	1885	2362	2656	2900	3103
7050	1216	1891	2370	2664	2909	3113
7100	1220	1897	2378	2673	2919	3123
7150	1224	1903	2385	2681	2928	3133
7200	1228	1909	2393	2690	2937	3142
7250	1232	1915	2400	2698	2946	3152
7300	1235	1921	2408	2707	2956	3162
7350	1239	1927	2415	2716	2965	3172
7400	1243	1933	2423	2724	2974	3181
7450	1247	1939	2430	2733	2983	3191
7500	1251	1945	2438	2741	2993	3201
7550	1255	1951	2446	2750	3002	3211
7600	1259	1957	2453	2758	3011	3220
7650	1263	1963	2461	2767	3020	3230
7700	1267	1969	2468	2775	3030	3240
7750	1271	1975	2476	2784	3039	3250
7800	1274	1981	2483	2792	3048	3259
7850	1278	1987	2491	2801	3057	3269
7900	1282	1992	2498	2810	3067	3279
7950	1286	1998	2506	2818	3076	3289
8000	1290	2004	2513	2827	3085	3298
8050	1294	2010	2521	2835	3094	3308
8100	1298	2016	2529	2844	3104	3318
8150	1302	2022	2536	2852	3113	3328
8200	1306	2028	2544	2861	3122	3337
8250	1310	2034	2551	2869	3131	3347
8300	1313	2040	2559	2878	3141	3357
8350	1317	2046	2566	2887	3150	3367
8400	1321	2052	2574	2895	3159	3376
8450	1325	2058	2581	2904	3168	3386
8500	1329	2064	2589	2912	3178	3396
8550	1333	2070	2597	2921	3187	3406
8600	1337	2076	2604	2929	3196	3415
8650	1341	2082	2612	2938	3205	3425
8700	1345	2088	2619	2946	3215	3435
8750	1349	2094	2627	2955	3224	3445
8800	1352	2100	2634	2963	3233	3454
8850	1356	2106	2642	2972	3242	3464
8900	1360	2111	2649	2981	3252	3474
8950	1364	2117	2657	2989	3261	3484
9000	1368	2123	2664	2998	3270	3493
9050	1372	2129	2672	3006	3279	3503
9100	1376	2135	2680	3015	3289	3513
9150	1380	2141	2687	3023	3298	3523
9200	1384	2147	2695	3032	3307	3532
9250	1388	2153	2702	3040	3316	3542
9300	1391	2159	2710	3049	3326	3552
9350	1395	2165	2717	3058	3335	3562
9400	1399	2171	2725	3066	3344	3571
9450	1403	2177	2732	3075	3353	3581
9500	1407	2183	2740	3083	3363	3591
9550	1411	2189	2748	3092	3372	3601
9600	1415	2195	2755	3100	3381	3610
9650	1419	2201	2763	3109	3390	3620
9700	1422	2206	2767	3115	3396	3628
9750	1425	2210	2772	3121	3402	3634
9800	1427	2213	2776	3126	3408	3641
9850	1430	2217	2781	3132	3414	3647
9900	1432	2221	2786	3137	3420	3653
9950	1435	2225	2791	3143	3426	3659
10000	1437	2228	2795	3148	3432	3666

Appendix B: Forms

General Forms

Form 1	Summons: Personal Service on an Individual	66
Form 2	Process Service Memorandum	68
Form 3	Notice of Hearing	69
Form 4	Motion to Set Final Hearing/Trial	71
Form 5	Order Setting Matter for Final Hearing or Status Conference	72
Form 6	Request to Enter Default	74
Form 7	Default	75
Form 8	Memorandum for Certificate of Military Service	76
Form 9	Nonmilitary Affidavit	77
Form 10	Certificate of Service	78
Form 11	Affidavit for Service by Publication (use with Form 30)	79
Form 12	Notice of Action	80
Form 13	Notice of Production From Non-Party (use with Form 29)	81
Form 14	Subpoena for Production of Documents	82
Form 15	Subpoena	84
Form 16	Subpoena Duces Tecum	85
Form 17	Joint Petition to Modify Judgment Dissolving Marriage	86
Form 18	Order Modifying Judgment Dissolving Marriage	88
Form 19	Affidavit of Insolvency (use with Form 30)	90
Form 20	Civil Cover Sheet	91
Form 21	Final Disposition Form	92
Form 22	Order of Referral to General Master	93
Form 23	Notice of Hearing Before General Master	95
Form 24	Family Law Financial Affidavit (Short Form) (use with Form 30)	97
Form 25	Family Law Financial Affidavit (Long Form) (use with Form 30)	103
Form 26	Notice of Service of Standard Family Law Interrogatories	113
Form 27	Standard Family Law Interrogatories	114
Form 28	Certificate of Compliance with Family Law Rule 12.285	121
Form 29	Standard signature page without notary	123
Form 30	Standard signature page with notary	124
Form 31	Witness Testimony Worksheet	125

Alimony Forms

Form 32	Petition to Modify Alimony (use with Form 30)	126
Form 33	Affidavit Regarding Alimony	127
Form 34	Order Modifying Alimony	128

Child Support Forms

Form 35	Petition/Request for Modification/Change of Child Support and Other Relief	130
Form 36	Child Support Guidelines Worksheet	131
Form 37	Final Judgment Modifying Child Support	136
Form 38	Order Requiring Payment Through Central Depository	140
Form 39	Child Support Income Deduction Order	144
Form 40	Motion for Health Insurance Coverage (use with Form 30)	150
Form 41	Order for Health Insurance Coverage	151
Form 42	Instructions to Employer or Other Person Providing Health Insurance	153

Custody and Visitation Forms

Form 43	Petition/Request to Modify/Change Primary Residency/Custody of Children	155
Form 44	Uniform Child Custody Jurisdiction Act (UCCJA) Affidavit (use with Form 30)	158
Form 45	Motion for Appointment of Guardian Ad Litem (use with Form 29)	160
Form 46	Order Appointing Guardian Ad Litem	161
Form 47	Final Judgment of Modification of Parental Responsibility and Visitation	164
Form 48	Supplemental Petition/Request to Modify/Change Visitation (use with form 30)	170

IN THE CIRCUIT COURT OF THE _____ JUDICIAL CIRCUIT, IN AND

FOR _____ COUNTY, FLORIDA

_____,

Petitioner

Case No.: _____

AND

Division: _____

_____,

Respondent.

SUMMONS: PERSONAL SERVICE ON AN INDIVIDUAL

TO: _____
    (name)

_____
(address)

_____
(city, state, zip)

IMPORTANT

A lawsuit has been filed against you. You have **20 calendar days** after this summons is served on you to file a written response to the attached complaint/petition with the clerk of this circuit court. A phone call will not protect you. Your written response, including the case number given above and the names of the parties, must be filed if you want the court to hear your side of the case. If you do not file your written response on time, you may lose the case, and your wages, money, and property may thereafter be taken without further warning from the court. There are other legal requirements. You may want to call an attorney right away. If you do not know an attorney, you may call an attorney referral service or a legal aid office (listed in the phone book).

If you choose to file a written response yourself, at the same time you file your written response to the court you must also mail or take a copy of your written response to the person named below.

WARNING: Rule 12.285, Florida Family Law Rules of Procedure, requires that you provide to the other party in this lawsuit access to or copies of certain documents and information. Failure to do this can result in the court taking action against you, including dismissal (throwing out your case) or striking of pleadings (throwing out part of your case).

IMPORTANTE

Usted ha sido demandado legalmente. Tiene veinte (20) dias, contados a partir del recibo de esta notificacion, para contestar la demanda adjunta, por escrito, y presentarla ante este tribunal. Una llamada

Florida Family Law Form 12.910(a), Summons: Personal Service on an Individual

telefonica no lo protegera. Si usted desea que el tribunal considere su defensa, debe presentar su respuesta por escrito, incluyendo el numero del caso y los nombres de las partes interesadas. Si usted no contesta la demanda a tiempo, pudiese perder el caso y podria ser despojado de sus ingresos y propiedades, o privado de sus derechos, sin previo aviso del tribunal. Existen otros requisitos legales. Si lo desea, usted puede consultar a un abogado inmediatamente. Si no conoce a un abogado, puede llamar a una de las oficinas de asistencia legal que aparecen en la guia telefonica.

Si desea responder a la demanda por su cuenta, al mismo tiempo en que presente su respuesta ante el tribunal, usted debe enviar por correo o entregar una copia de su respuesta a la persona denominada abajo.

AVISO: La regla 12.285, de las reglas de procedimiento del derecho de la familia del estado de la Florida exige que se entreguen ciertos datos y documentos a la parte adversa...So Ud. no cumple con estos requisitos, se le podran aplicar sanciones, las cuales pueden dar lugar al rechazo o a la desestimacion de sus escritos.

IMPORTANT

Des poursuites judiciaries ont ete entreprises contre vous. Vous avez 20 jours consecutifs a partir de la date de l'assignation de cette citation pour deposer une response ecrite a la plainte ci-jointe aupres de ce tribunal. Un simple coup de telephone est insuffisant pour vous proteger; vous etes obliges de deposer votre reponse ecrite, avec mention du numero de dossier ci-dessus et du nom des parties nommees ici, si vous souhaitez que le tribunal entende votre cause. Si vous ne deposez pas votre reponse ecrite dans le delai requis, vous risquez de perdre la cause ainsi que votre salaire, votreargent, et vos biens peuvent etre saisis par la suite, sans aucun preavis ulterieur du tribunal. Il y a d'autres obligations juridiques et vous pouvez requerir les services immediats d'un avocat. Si vous ne connaissez pas d'avocat, vous pourriez telephoner a un service de reference d'avocats ou a un bureau d'assistance juridique (figurant a l'annuaire de telephones).

Si vous choisissez de deposer vous-meme une response ecrite, il vous faudra egalement, en meme temps que cette formalite, faire parvenir ou expedier une copie au carbone ou une photocopie de votre reponse ecrite a la personne nommee ci-dessous.

ATTENTION: La regle 12.285 des regles de procedure du droit de la famille de la Floride exige que l'on remette certains renseignements et certains documents a la partie adverse. Tout refus de les fournir pourra donner lieu a des sanctions, y compris le rejet ou la suppression d'un ou de plusieurs actes de procedure.

_____

Petitioner

_____

Mailing Address

_____

City/State/Zip Code

THE STATE OF FLORIDA
TO EACH SHERIFF OF THE STATE: You are commanded to serve this summons and a copy of the complaint in this lawsuit on the above named defendant.

DATED: _____

                       (SEAL)
                       CLERK OF THE CIRCUIT COURT

                    By: _____
                               Deputy Clerk.

Florida family Law Form 12.910(a), Summons: Personal Service on an Individual

PROCESS SERVICE MEMORANDUM

TO: Sheriff of _____ County, Florida; _____ Division

RE: _____, Petitioner

and _____, Respondent

_____Circuit Court, County of _____

Case No. _____

Please serve the Summons and Petition herein, in the above-styled cause upon:

Respondent: _____

Home Address: _____

_____

Work Address: _____

_____

Thank you.

SPECIAL INSTRUCTIONS:

_____
Signature of party

_____
Printed name

_____
Address

_____
City   State   Zip

_____
Telephone (area code and number)

_____
Telefax (area code and number)

Florida Family Law Form 12.910(b), Process Service Memorandum

IN THE CIRCUIT COURT OF THE _____ JUDICIAL CIRCUIT, IN AND

FOR _____ COUNTY, FLORIDA

_____,
Petitioner

Case No.: _____

AND

Division: _____

_____,
Respondent.

NOTICE OF HEARING (GENERAL FORM)

[Fill in **all** blanks]

TO: _____

_____

_____

There will be a hearing before Judge *{name of judge}*_____,

on *{date}*_____, 19_____, at *{time}*_____, in Room _____ of

the_____ Courthouse, on the following matter:

_____.

_____ hours/_____ minutes have been reserved for this hearing.

If you are represented by an attorney or plan to retain an attorney for this matter you should notify the attorney of this hearing.

If this matter is resolved, the moving party shall contact the judge's office to cancel this hearing.

You will need to get the information from your local courthouse to fill out this part:

In accordance with the Americans with Disabilities Act of 1990, persons needing a special accommodation to participate in this proceeding should contact_____ for proceedings in court or_____ at _____ for out of court proceedings no later than 7 days before the proceeding. Telephone _____ or_____ for assistance. If hearing impaired, telephone (TDD) _____ for proceedings in court or Florida Relay Service 1-800-955-8771 for out of court proceedings.

Florida Family Law Form 12.923, Notice of Hearing (General Form)

I CERTIFY THAT THE NOTICE OF HEARING ON *{name of motion or petition to be heard}*_____WAS:
(✔ check **one** only) _____ mailed, _____telefaxed and mailed, or _____ hand delivered to the person(s) listed below on *{date}*_____,19_____.

Party or their attorney (if represented)   Other

Name_____   Name_____

Address_____   Address_____

_____   _____
City   State   Zip   City   State   Zip

Telephone No._____   Telephone No._____

Telefax No._____   Telefax No._____

DATED:_____

_____
Signature of party signing certificate and pleading

Printed name_____

Address_____

_____
City   State   Zip

_____
Telephone (area code and number)

_____
Telefax (area code and number)

IF A NONLAWYER HELPED YOU FILL OUT THIS FORM THEY MUST FILL IN THE BLANKS BELOW: [Fill in **all** blanks]

I, *{name of nonlawyer}* _____, a nonlawyer, located at
{street} _____, *{city}* _____, *{state}* _____,
{phone} _____, helped *{name}* _____,who is the
[✔ **one** only] _____ petitioner **or**_____ respondent, fill out this form.

Florida Family Law Form 12.923, Notice of Hearing (General Form)

IN THE CIRCUIT COURT OF THE _____ JUDICIAL CIRCUIT, IN AND

FOR _____ COUNTY, FLORIDA

_____,

Petitioner

Case No.: _____

AND

Division: _____

_____,

Respondent.

MOTION TO SET FINAL HEARING / TRIAL

The ❏ Petitioner ❏ Respondent moves the court for an order setting this matter for

❏ Uncontested final hearing   ❏ Non-jury trial   ❏ Status conference

pursuant to Rule 1.440, Florida Rules of Civil Procedure, and states:

1. This matter is at issue and ready to set for final hearing/trial.

2. The estimated time necessary to conduct the final hearing/trial is:_____.

DATED:_____

_____

Signature

Printed name:_____

Address:_____

_____

City   State   Zip

_____

Telephone (area code and number)

_____

Telefax (area code and number)

IF A NONLAWYER HELPED YOU FILL OUT THIS FORM THEY MUST FILL IN THE BLANKS BELOW:
[Fill in **all** blanks]

I, {name} _____, a nonlawyer, located at
{street} _____, {city} _____, {state} _____,
{phone} _____, helped {name} _____,who is the
[✔ **one** only] _____ petitioner **or**_____ respondent, fill out this form.

IN THE CIRCUIT COURT OF THE _____ JUDICIAL CIRCUIT, IN AND

FOR _____ COUNTY, FLORIDA

_____,

Petitioner

Case No.: _____

AND

Division: _____

_____,

Respondent.

ORDER SETTING MATTER FOR FINAL HEARING
OR FOR STATUS CONFERENCE

The court having reviewed the file finds that:

_____ The time to file an answer has expired, and therefore,

IT IS ORDERED that:

This case is set for uncontested final hearing before Judge {name of judge}_____

_____, on {date}_____, 19_____, at {time}_____ in

Room _____ of the_____ Courthouse [✔ **one** only]

_____ If no answer has been filed, please bring your default order. You will also need to bring proof of residency, i.e., a residency witness, affidavit of residency, valid Florida driver's license, or valid Florida voter registration card.

_____ If an answer has been filed, this hearing will serve as a status conference.

The Petitioner, or the attorney for the Petitioner, is required to notify all other parties immediately of this hearing.

FAILURE TO APPEAR MAY RESULT IN A DISMISSAL OF THIS CASE

DATED:_____, 19_____.

_____

CIRCUIT JUDGE

This part to be filled in by court:

In accordance with the Americans with Disabilities Act of 1990, persons needing a special accommodation to participate in this proceeding should contact _____ for proceedings in court or _____ at _____ for out of court proceedings no later than 7 days before the proceeding. Telephone _____ or _____ for assistance. If hearing impaired, telephone (TDD) _____ for proceedings in court or Florida Relay Service 1-800-955-8771 for out of court proceedings.

cc:

Petitioner or their attorney (if represented)	Respondent or their attorney (if represented)
Name_____	Name_____
Address_____	Address_____
_____	_____
City State Zip	City State Zip
Telephone No._____	Telephone No._____
Telefax No._____	Telefax No._____

Other

Name_____

Address_____

_____
City   State   Zip

Telephone No._____

Telefax No._____

IF A NONLAWYER HELPED YOU FILL OUT THIS FORM TO GIVE TO THE JUDGE TO SIGN, THE NONLAWYER WHO HELPED YOU MUST FILL IN THE BLANKS BELOW:
[Fill in **all** blanks]

I, {name of nonlawyer} _____, a nonlawyer, located at {street} _____, {city} _____, {state}_____, {phone} _____, helped {name} _____,who is the [✔ **one** only] _____ petitioner **or** _____ respondent, fill out this form.

IN THE CIRCUIT COURT OF THE _____ JUDICIAL CIRCUIT, IN AND

FOR _____ COUNTY, FLORIDA

_____,

Petitioner

Case No.: _____

AND

Division: _____

_____,

Respondent.

REQUEST TO ENTER DEFAULT

TO THE CLERK OF COURT: Please enter a default against the Respondent who has failed to respond to the petition.

I CERTIFY THAT THIS REQUEST TO ENTER DEFAULT WAS:

(✔ check **one** only) ____ mailed, ____telefaxed and mailed, or ____ hand delivered to the person(s) listed below on {date}_____,19____.

<u>Party or their attorney (if represented)</u>   <u>Other</u>

Name_____   Name_____

Address_____   Address_____

_____   _____
City   State   Zip   City   State   Zip

Telephone No._____   Telephone No._____

Telefax No._____   Telefax No._____

DATED:_____

_____
Signature of party signing certificate and pleading

Printed name_____

Address_____

_____
City   State   Zip

_____
Telephone (area code and number)

_____
Telefax (area code and number)

IF A NONLAWYER HELPED YOU FILL OUT THIS FORM THEY MUST FILL IN THE BLANKS BELOW: [Fill in **all** blanks]

I, {name of nonlawyer} _____, a nonlawyer, located at {street} _____, {city} _____, {state} _____, {phone} _____, helped {name} _____,who is the [✔ **one** only] _____ petitioner **or**_____ respondent, fill out this form.

Florida Family Law Form 12.922(a), Request to Enter Default

IN THE CIRCUIT COURT OF THE _____ JUDICIAL CIRCUIT, IN AND

FOR _____ COUNTY, FLORIDA

_____,
Petitioner

Case No.: _____

AND

Division: _____

_____,
Respondent.

DEFAULT

A default is entered in this action against the Respondent for failure to serve or file a response or any

paper as is required by law.

DATED: _____

CLERK OF COURT
(SEAL)

By: _____
Deputy Clerk

I CERTIFY THAT THIS DEFAULT WAS:
(✔ check **one** only) _____ mailed, _____telefaxed and mailed, or _____ hand delivered to the person(s) listed
below on *{date}*_____,19_____.

Party or their attorney (if represented)

Name_____

Address_____

_____
City   State   Zip

Telephone No._____

Telefax No._____

Other

Name_____

Address_____

_____
City   State   Zip

Telephone No._____

Telefax No._____

Florida Family Law Form 12.922(b), Default

IN THE CIRCUIT COURT OF THE _____ JUDICIAL CIRCUIT, IN AND

FOR _____ COUNTY, FLORIDA

_____,
Petitioner

Case No.: _____

AND

Division: _____

_____,
Respondent.

MEMORANDUM FOR CERTIFICATE
OF MILITARY SERVICE

TO: U.S. Coast Guard Commander, GPIM-2, Locators, 2100 2nd St.,
S.W., Washington, DC 20593

AFMPC/RMIQL, Attn: Air Force Locator, Randolph
AFB, TX 78150-6001

Department of Navy, Bureau of Navy Personnel, 2 Navy Annex,
Washington, DC 20370-5000

CMC MMSB-10, HQ USMC, Bldg. 2008,
Quantico, VA 22134-5002

Surgeon General, U.S. Public Health Service, Div. of Comm.,
Off. Personnel, 5600 Fishers Lane, Rockville, MD 20857

Army World Wide Locator, U.S. Army Enlisted Records
Center, Fort Benjamin Harrison, IN 46249-5601

Commander, U.S. Army Personnel Center, Officer Locator Branch,
Attn: Locators, 200 Stovall Street, Alexandria, VA 22332

RE: _____   _____
                      [Party]   [Soc. Sec. #]

       This case involves a family matter. It is imperative that a determination be made whether the above named individual, who has an interest in these proceedings, is presently in the military service of the United States, and the date of induction and discharge, if any. This information is necessary to comply with §581 of the Soldier's and Sailor's Civil Relief Act of 1940, as amended. Please supply a certification of verification as soon as possible. My check is enclosed for your search fees. Self-addressed stamped envelopes are enclosed.

Florida Family Law Form 12.912(a), Memorandum for Certificate of Military Service

IN THE CIRCUIT COURT OF THE _____ JUDICIAL CIRCUIT, IN AND

FOR _____ COUNTY, FLORIDA

_____,
Petitioner

Case No.: _____

AND

Division: _____

_____,
Respondent.

NONMILITARY AFFIDAVIT

STATE OF FLORIDA
COUNTY OF _____

_____, being first duly sworn, states
{*Name of person signing below*}

under penalty of perjury:

1. ____ That I know of my own personal knowledge that the respondent is not on active duty in the armed forces of the United States.

2. ____ That I have inquired of the armed forces of the United States and the U.S. Public Health Service to determine whether the respondent is a member of the armed services and am attaching certificates stating that the respondent is not now in the armed forces.

I CERTIFY THAT THE NONMILITARY AFFIDAVIT WAS:
(✔ check **one** only) ____ mailed, ____telefaxed and mailed, or ____ hand delivered to the person(s) listed below on {*date*}_____,19____.

Party or their attorney (if represented)	Other
Name_____	Name_____
Address_____	Address_____
_____	_____
City State Zip	City State Zip
Telephone No._____	Telephone No._____
Telefax No._____	Telefax No._____

Florida Family Law Form 12.912(b), Nonmilitary Affidavit

IN THE CIRCUIT COURT OF THE _____ JUDICIAL CIRCUIT, IN AND

FOR _____ COUNTY, FLORIDA

_____,
Petitioner

AND

Case No.: _____

Division: _____

_____,
Respondent.

CERTIFICATE OF SERVICE

I CERTIFY THAT THE *{name of document(s) served}* _____
_____ WAS: (✔ **one** only) ____ mailed, ____telefaxed and
mailed, or ____ hand delivered to the person(s) listed below on *{date}*_____,19____.

_____
Signature of party

_____
Printed name

_____
Address

_____
City   State   Zip

_____
Telephone (area code and number)

_____
Telefax (area code and number)

<table>
<tr><td><u>Party or their attorney (if represented)</u></td><td><u>Other</u></td></tr>
<tr><td>Name_____</td><td>Name_____</td></tr>
<tr><td>Address_____</td><td>Address_____</td></tr>
<tr><td>_____</td><td>_____</td></tr>
<tr><td>City   State   Zip</td><td>City   State   Zip</td></tr>
<tr><td>Telephone No._____</td><td>Telephone No._____</td></tr>
<tr><td>Telefax No._____</td><td>Telefax No._____</td></tr>
</table>

**IF A NONLAWYER HELPED YOU FILL OUT THIS FORM THEY MUST FILL IN THE
BLANKS BELOW:** [Fill in **all** blanks]

I, *{name of nonlawyer}* _____, a nonlawyer, located at
{street} _____, *{city}* _____, *{state}* _____,
{phone} _____, helped *{name}* _____,who is the
[✔ **one** only] _____ petitioner **or**_____ respondent, fill out this form.

Florida Family Law Form 12.914, Certificate of Service

IN THE CIRCUIT COURT OF THE _____ JUDICIAL CIRCUIT, IN AND

FOR _____ COUNTY, FLORIDA

_____,

Petitioner

AND

Case No.: _____

Division: _____

_____,

Respondent.

AFFIDAVIT FOR SERVICE BY PUBLICATION

_____, states under penalty of perjury that:

1. I have made diligent search and inquiry to discover the name and residence of Respondent: **[Specify details of search] Refer to checklist and list all actions taken (any additional information included such as the date the action was taken and the person with whom you spoke is helpful):**
   _____
   _____
   _____
   _____.

2. The age of Respondent is [✔ **one** only]____over **or** ____under the age of 18 years **or** ____ is unknown.

3. ____ The residence of Respondent is unknown to Affiant.
   ____ The residence of Respondent is in some state or country other than Florida, and Respondent's last known address is: _____
   _____
   [City]   [State]   [Zip]

4. ____ The Respondent, having residence in Florida, has been absent therefrom for more than 60 days prior to the making of this affidavit, or conceals him(her)self so that process cannot be served personally upon him (her), and that Affiant believes that there is no person in the state upon whom service of process would bind said absent or concealed Respondent.

I CERTIFY THAT THE AFFIDAVIT FOR SERVICE BY PUBLICATION WAS:
(✔ check **one** only) ____ mailed, ____telefaxed and mailed, or ____ hand delivered to the person(s) listed below on {date}_____,19_____.

Party or their attorney (if represented)	Other
Name_____	Name_____
Address_____	Address_____
_____	_____
City State Zip	City State Zip
Telephone No._____	Telephone No._____
Telefax No._____	Telefax No._____

Florida Family Law Form 12.913(b), Affidavit for Service by Publication

NOTICE OF ACTION

TO: _____

YOU ARE HEREBY NOTIFIED that an action for modification of the judgment of dissolution of marriage has been filed against you and you are required to serve a copy of your written defenses, if any, to it on *{name of Petitioner}* _____, the Petitioner, whose address is _____

_____

on or before _____, and file the original with the clerk of this court before service on Petitioner or immediately thereafter. If you fail to do so, a default will be entered against you for the relief demanded in the petition.

WARNING: Rule 12.285, Florida Family Law Rules of Procedure, requires certain automatic disclosure of documents and information. Failure to comply can result in sanctions, including dismissal or striking of pleadings.

WITNESS my hand and the seal of this court on _____.

CLERK OF THE COURT

By_____
Deputy Clerk

IN THE CIRCUIT COURT OF THE _____ JUDICIAL CIRCUIT, IN AND

FOR _____ COUNTY, FLORIDA

_____,
Petitioner

Case No.: _____

AND

_____,
Respondent.

Division: _____

NOTICE OF PRODUCTION FROM NON-PARTY

TO: [all parties]

YOU ARE NOTIFIED that after **10 days** from the date of service of this notice the undersigned will

apply to the clerk of this court for issuance of the attached subpoena directed to *{name of person, organization*

or agency} _____,

who is not a party, to produce the items listed at the time and place specified in the subpoena. Objections to

the issuance of this subpoena must be filed with the clerk within **10 days**.

I CERTIFY THAT THIS NOTICE OF PRODUCTION TO NON-PARTY WAS:
(✔ check **one** only) _____ mailed, _____telefaxed and mailed, or _____ hand delivered to the person(s) listed
below on *{date}*_____,19_____.

Party or their attorney (if represented)

Name_____

Address_____

_____
City   State   Zip

Telephone No._____

Telefax No._____

Other

Name_____

Address_____

_____
City   State   Zip

Telephone No._____

Telefax No._____

Florida Family Law Form 12.931(a), Notice of Production from Non-Party

IN THE CIRCUIT COURT OF THE _____ JUDICIAL CIRCUIT, IN AND

FOR _____ COUNTY, FLORIDA

_____,
Petitioner

Case No.: _____

AND

Division: _____

_____,
Respondent.

SUBPOENA FOR PRODUCTION OF DOCUMENTS

THE STATE OF FLORIDA
TO:

YOU MUST go to {place} _____,

on {date}_____, at {time}_____, and bring with you at that time

and place the following:

These items will be inspected and may be copied at that time. You will not have to leave the original items.

You may obey this subpoena by providing readable copies of the items to be produced to the party or their attorney whose name appears on this subpoena on or before the scheduled date of production. You may condition the preparation of the copies upon payment in advance of the reasonable cost of preparation. You may mail or deliver the copies to the attorney whose name appears on this subpoena and thereby eliminate your appearance at the time and place specified above.

If you fail to

(1) appear as specified; or

(2) furnish the records instead of appearing as provided above; or

(3) object to this subpoena,

you may be in contempt of court.

You are subpoenaed by the person whose name appears on this subpoena and, unless excused by that person or the court, you shall respond as directed.

Florida Family Law Form 12.931(b), Subpoena for Production of Documents

You will need to get the information from your local courthouse to fill in this part:

In accordance with the Americans with Disabilities Act of 1990, persons needing a special accommodation to participate in this proceeding should contact _____ for proceedings in court or _____ at _____ for out of court proceedings no later than 7 days before the proceeding. Telephone _____ or _____ for assistance. If hearing impaired, telephone (TDD) _____ for proceedings in court or Florida Relay Service 1-800-955-8771 for out of court proceedings.

Date:_____

                                 Clerk of the Court

                                 By:_____
                                 As Deputy Clerk

Name_____

Address_____

Telephone No._____

     I HEREBY CERTIFY that I gave notice to every other party to this action of the intent to serve a subpoena upon a person who is not a party to this action directing that person to produce documents or things without deposition. I also certify that no objection under Florida Rule of Civil Procedure 1.351 has been received by the undersigned within 10 days of service of this notice, if service was by hand delivery or appropriate facsimile transmission, and within 15 days if service was by mail.

Dated:_____

                                 _____
                                 Signature of party signing certificate and pleading

                                 Printed name_____

                                 Address_____

                                 _____
                                 City   State   Zip

                                 _____
                                 Telephone (area code and number)

                                 _____
                                 Telefax (area code and number)

IF A NONLAWYER HELPED YOU FILL OUT THIS FORM THEY MUST FILL IN THE BLANKS BELOW: [Fill in **all** blanks]

I, {name of nonlawyer} _____, a nonlawyer, located at {street} _____, {city} _____, {state} _____, {phone} _____, helped {name} _____,who is the [✔ one only] _____ petitioner **or**_____ respondent, fill out this form.

Florida Family Law Form 12.931(b), Subpoena for Production of Documents

IN THE CIRCUIT COURT OF THE _____ JUDICIAL CIRCUIT, IN AND

FOR _____ COUNTY, FLORIDA

_____,
Petitioner

Case No.: _____

AND

Division: _____

_____,
Respondent.

SUBPOENA

THE STATE OF FLORIDA

TO:

YOU ARE HEREBY COMMANDED to appear before the Honorable _____

_____, Judge of the Court, at the _____

County Courthouse in _____, Florida, on _____

_____, 19_____, at _____.M., to testify in this action. If you fail to

appear, you may be in contempt of court.

You are subpoenaed to appear by the attorneys or parties designated below, and

unless excused from this subpoena by these attorneys or parties, or the court, you shall

respond to this subpoena as directed.

DATED:_____

(SEAL)

Attorney or Party Requesting Subpoena

CLERK OF THE CIRCUIT COURT

Name:_____
Address:_____

_____
Telephone No:_____

By: _____
Deputy Clerk

IN THE CIRCUIT COURT OF THE _____ JUDICIAL CIRCUIT, IN AND

FOR _____ COUNTY, FLORIDA

_____,
Petitioner

Case No.: _____

AND

Division: _____

_____,
Respondent.

SUBPOENA DUCES TECUM

THE STATE OF FLORIDA

TO:

YOU ARE HEREBY COMMANDED to appear before the Honorable _____

_____, Judge of the Court, at the _____

County Courthouse in _____, Florida, on _____

_____, 19_____, at _____.M., to testify in this action, AND to bring

the following items with you:

If you fail to appear, you may be in contempt of court.

You are subpoenaed to appear by the attorneys or parties designated below, and unless excused from this subpoena by these attorneys or parties, or the court, you shall respond to this subpoena as directed.

DATED:_____

Attorney or Party Requesting Subpoena

(SEAL)
CLERK OF THE CIRCUIT COURT

Name:_____
Address:_____

_____

Telephone No:_____

By:_____
Deputy Clerk

IN THE CIRCUIT COURT OF THE _____ JUDICIAL CIRCUIT, IN AND

FOR _____ COUNTY, FLORIDA

_____,

Petitioner

Case No.: _____

AND

Division: _____

_____,

Respondent.

JOINT PETITION TO MODIFY JUDGMENT DISSOLVING MARRIAGE

The request of the parties shows:

1. We, the parties in this action, were divorced on _____, 19___. A copy of the final judgment dissolving marriage is attached.

2. We have agreed, and hereby stipulate, to a change in the terms of the judgment as indicated below, and request this court to issue an order so modifying our judgment:

❏ Child support shall be ___increased ___decreased to the sum of $_____ per _____, to be paid by way of an income deduction order, until _____, or until further order of this court.

❏ Primary parental responsibility/custody of the minor child(ren) shall be changed to the ___Husband ___Wife, until _____, _____, or until further order of this court.

❏ The non-custodial parent's visitation with the minor child(ren) shall be changed to:

❑ Alimony shall be ___increased ___decreased to the sum of $_____ per _____, to be paid by way of an income deduction order, until _____, or until the death or re-marriage of the recipient of said alimony, or until further order of this court.

❑ Other agreed provisions:

3. We further agree that these modifications are to become effective immediately.

4. The modifications requested are in the best interest of the parties and our minor child(ren).

5. All other provisions of the final judgment not in conflict with the changes indicated above shall remain in full force and effect.

DATED:_____   DATED:_____

_____   _____
Signature   Signature

Name_____   Name_____
Address_____   Address_____

_____   _____
Telephone No._____   Telephone No._____

IF A NONLAWYER HELPED YOU FILL OUT THIS FORM THEY MUST FILL IN THE BLANKS BELOW: [Fill in **all** blanks]

I, {name of nonlawyer} _____, a nonlawyer, located at {street} _____, {city} _____, {state} _____, {phone} _____, helped {name} _____,who is the [✔ one only] _____ petitioner **or**_____ respondent, fill out this form.

IN THE CIRCUIT COURT OF THE _____ JUDICIAL CIRCUIT, IN AND

FOR _____ COUNTY, FLORIDA

_____,
Petitioner

Case No.: _____

AND

Division: _____

_____,
Respondent.

ORDER MODIFYING JUDGMENT DISSOLVING MARRIAGE

THIS CAUSE, having come before the court on the parties' Joint Petition to Modify Judgment Dissolving Marriage,

IT IS HEREBY ORDERED that:

❑ Child support shall be ___increased ___decreased to the sum of $_____ per _____, to be paid by way of an income deduction order, until _____, or until further order of this court.

❑ Primary parental responsibility/custody of the minor child(ren) shall be changed to the ___Husband ___Wife, until _____ _____, _____or until further order of this court.

❑ The non-custodial parent's visitation with the minor child(ren) shall be changed to:

❏ Alimony shall be ___increased ___decreased to the sum of $_____ per _____, to be paid by way of an income deduction order, until

_____

or until the death or remarriage of the recipient of said alimony, or until further order of this court.

❏ Other provisions:

This order is effective immediately, and all other provisions of the final judgment, and any other orders, not in conflict with this order shall remain in full force and effect.

DATED:_____   _____
                                        CIRCUIT JUDGE

Copies furnished to:

Husband or Attorney for Husband   Wife or Attorney for Wife
Name_____   Name_____
Address_____   Address_____

_____   _____
Telephone No._____   Telephone No._____

IF A NONLAWYER HELPED YOU FILL OUT THIS FORM THEY MUST FILL IN THE BLANKS BELOW: [Fill in **all** blanks]

I, *{name of nonlawyer}* _____, a nonlawyer, located at
{street} _____, *{city}* _____, *{state}* _____,
{phone} _____, helped *{name}* _____,who is the
[✔ **one** only] _____ petitioner **or**_____ respondent, fill out this form.

IN THE CIRCUIT COURT OF THE _____ JUDICIAL CIRCUIT, IN AND

FOR _____ COUNTY, FLORIDA

_____,

Petitioner

AND

Case No.: _____

Division: _____

_____,

Respondent.

AFFIDAVIT OF INSOLVENCY

[✔ **all** which apply. Fill in all blanks that apply]

STATE OF FLORIDA

COUNTY OF *{name}*_____

BEFORE ME personally appeared *{name}*_____

who, after being sworn, states:

I am insolvent and unable to pay the charges, costs, or fees otherwise payable by law to any clerk, or sheriff in this civil action because [✔ **one** only]:

_____ a. I am currently receiving public assistance: $_____

per _____ Case No. _____.

_____ b. I am unable to pay those clerk's fees and costs because of indigency, based on the following facts:

INCOME: _____

Employer name and address

Length of employment:_____

Avg. gross pay: $_____   Avg. net pay: $_____

per _____ week _____ month _____ 2 weeks

ASSETS: What I own.   State value of car, home, bank deposits, bonds, stocks, etc.

_____

_____

_____

_____

_____

DEBTS/BILLS: What I owe. List item by item your monthly rent, installment payments, mortgage payments, child support, etc.

Amount of Payment each month   Who I pay it to

_____   _____

_____   _____

_____   _____

_____   _____

_____   _____

_____   _____

Florida Family Law Form 12.901(c), Affidavit of Insolvency

CIVIL COVER SHEET

The civil cover sheet and the information contained herein neither replace nor supplement the filing and service of pleadings or other papers as required by law. This form is required for the use of the Clerk of Court for the purpose of reporting judicial workload data pursuant to Florida Statute 25.075.

NAME OF COURT: FAMILY LAW, CIRCUIT COURT

I. CASE STYLE

_____

PETITIONER,

Case #: _____

vs.

Division: _____

_____

RESPONDENT.

II. TYPE OF CASE

(Place an x in one box only. If the case fits more than one type of case, select the most definite.)

Domestic Relations	Torts	Other Civil
☐ Simplified dissolution	☐ Professional Malpractice	☐ Contracts
☐ Dissolution	☐ Products liability	☐ Condominium
☐ Support - IV-D	☐ Auto negligence	☐ Real property/ Mortgage foreclosure
☐ Support - Non IV-D	☐ Other negligence	
☐ URESA - IV-D		☐ Eminent domain
☐ Domestic violence		☐ Other
☒ Other domestic relations		

III. IS JURY TRIAL DEMANDED IN COMPLAINT?   ☐ Yes   ☒ No

DATE_____

SIGNATURE OF ATTORNEY OR PARTY INITIATING ACTION: _____

ADDRESS_____

_____

PHONE:_____

FINAL DISPOSITION FORM

This form is required for the use of the Clerk of the Court for the purpose of reporting judicial workload data pursuant to Florida Statute 25.075.

NAME OF COURT: FAMILY LAW, CIRCUIT COURT

I. CASE STYLE

_____

PETITIONER,

Case #: _____

vs.

Division: _____

_____

RESPONDENT.

II. MEANS OF FINAL DISPOSITION (Place an "x" in one box only)

❏ Dismissed Before Hearing

❏ Dismissed After Hearing

❏ Disposed by Default

❏ Disposed by Judge

❏ Disposed by Non-Jury Trial

❏ Disposed by Jury Trial

❏ Other

DATE_____

_____
SIGNATURE OF ATTORNEY FOR PREVAILING
PARTY OR PREVAILING PARTY:

ADDRESS:_____

_____

PHONE:_____

ORDER OF REFERRAL TO GENERAL MASTER

THIS CASE IS REFERRED TO THE GENERAL MASTER on the following issues:

1. _____
2. _____
3. _____
4. _____

AND ANY OTHER MATTER RELATED THERETO.

IT IS FURTHER ORDERED that the above motion(s) and responses are referred to General Master *{name}* _____ for further proceedings, pursuant to rule 12.490 of the Florida Family Law Rules of Procedure and current administrative orders of the court. Financial affidavits (Family Law Form 12.901(d) or (e)), shall be filed in accordance with rule 12.285, Florida Family Law Rules of Procedure. The general master is authorized to administer oaths and conduct hearings which may include taking of evidence and shall file a report and recommendations that contain findings of fact, conclusions of law, and the name of the court reporter, if any.

The General Master shall assign a time for the proceedings as soon as reasonably possible after this referral is made and give notice to each of the parties either directly or by directing counsel to file and serve a notice of hearing.

Counties within the State of Florida may have different rules. Please consult the Clerk of the Court or Pro Se Coordinator relating to this procedure.

A REFERRAL TO A GENERAL MASTER REQUIRES THE CONSENT OF ALL PARTIES. YOU ARE ENTITLED TO HAVE THIS MATTER HEARD BY A JUDGE. IF YOU DO NOT WANT TO HAVE THIS MATTER HEARD BY THE GENERAL MASTER, YOU MUST FILE A WRITTEN OBJECTION TO THE REFERRAL WITHIN 10 DAYS OF THE TIME OF SERVICE OF THIS ORDER. IF THE TIME SET FOR THE HEARING IS LESS THAN 10 DAYS AFTER SERVICE OF THIS ORDER, THE OBJECTION MUST BE MADE BEFORE THE HEARING. IF THIS ORDER IS SERVED WITHIN THE FIRST 20 DAYS AFTER SERVICE OF PROCESS, THE TIME TO FILE AN OBJECTION IS EXTENDED TO THE TIME WITHIN WHICH A RESPONSIVE PLEADING IS DUE. FAILURE TO FILE A WRITTEN OBJECTION WITHIN THE APPLICABLE TIME PERIOD IS DEEMED TO BE A CONSENT TO THE REFERRAL.

If either party files a timely objection, this matter shall be returned to the undersigned judge with a notice stating the amount of time needed for hearing.

REVIEW OF THE REPORT AND RECOMMENDATIONS MADE BY THE GENERAL MASTER SHALL BE BY EXCEPTIONS AS PROVIDED IN RULE 12.490(f), FLORIDA FAMILY LAW RULES OF PROCEDURE. A RECORD, WHICH INCLUDES A TRANSCRIPT, MAY BE REQUIRED TO SUPPORT EXCEPTIONS.

YOU ARE ADVISED THAT IN THIS CIRCUIT:
_____ electronic recording is provided by the court. A party may provide a court reporter at that party's expense.
_____ a court reporter is provided by the court.

Florida Family Law For 12.920(a), Order of Referral to General Master

SHOULD YOU WISH TO SEEK REVIEW OF THE REPORT AND RECOMMENDATION MADE BY THE GENERAL MASTER, YOU MUST FILE EXCEPTIONS IN ACCORDANCE WITH RULE 12.490(f), FLORIDA FAMILY LAW RULES OF PROCEDURE. YOU WILL BE REQUIRED TO PROVIDE THE COURT WITH A RECORD SUFFICIENT TO SUPPORT YOUR EXCEPTIONS OR YOUR EXCEPTIONS WILL BE DENIED. A RECORD ORDINARILY INCLUDES A WRITTEN TRANSCRIPT OF ALL RELEVANT PROCEEDINGS. THE PERSON SEEKING REVIEW MUST HAVE THE TRANSCRIPT PREPARED IF NECESSARY FOR THE COURT'S REVIEW.

DONE and ORDERED in {name}_____ County, Florida, on {date}_____, 19____.

_____
CIRCUIT JUDGE

This portion to be filled out by the court:

In accordance with the Americans with Disabilities Act of 1990, persons needing a special accommodation to participate in this proceeding should contact _____ for proceedings in court or _____ at _____ for out of court proceedings no later than 7 days before the proceeding. Telephone_____ or _____ for assistance. If hearing impaired, telephone (TDD) _____ for proceedings in court or Florida Relay Service 1-800-955-8771 for out of court proceedings.

cc:

Petitioner or their attorney (if represented)

Name_____

Address_____

_____

City	State	Zip

Telephone No._____

Telefax No._____

Respondent

Name_____

Address_____

_____

City	State	Zip

Telephone No._____

Telefax No._____

General Master

Name_____

Address_____

_____

City	State	Zip

Telephone No._____

Telefax No._____

IF A NONLAWYER HELPED YOU FILL OUT THIS FORM TO GIVE TO THE JUDGE TO SIGN, THE NONLAWYER WHO HELPED YOU MUST FILL IN THE BLANKS BELOW:

[Fill in **all** blanks]

I, {name of nonlawyer}_____, a nonlawyer, located at {street}_____ {city}_____ {state}_____, {phone}_____, helped {name}_____,who is the [✔ **one** only] _____ petitioner **or** _____ respondent, fill out this form.

Florida Family Law For 12.920(a), Order of Referral to General Master

IN THE CIRCUIT COURT OF THE _____ JUDICIAL CIRCUIT, IN AND

FOR _____ COUNTY, FLORIDA

_____,
Petitioner

Case No.: _____

AND

Division: _____

_____,
Respondent.

NOTICE OF HEARING BEFORE GENERAL MASTER
[Fill in all blanks]

TO: _____

      _____

There will be a hearing before General Master *{name of general master}* _____ _____, on *{date}* _____, 19_____, at *{time}* _____. m., in Room _____ of the_____ Courthouse, on the following matter:_____ _____.

_____ hours/_____ minutes have been reserved for this hearing.

PLEASE GOVERN YOURSELF ACCORDINGLY.

SHOULD YOU WISH TO SEEK REVIEW OF THE REPORT AND RECOMMENDATION MADE BY THE GENERAL MASTER, YOU MUST FILE EXCEPTIONS IN ACCORDANCE WITH RULE 12.490(f), FLORIDA FAMILY LAW RULES OF PROCEDURE. YOU WILL BE REQUIRED TO PROVIDE THE COURT WITH A RECORD SUFFICIENT TO SUPPORT YOUR EXCEPTIONS OR YOUR EXCEPTIONS WILL BE DENIED. A RECORD ORDINARILY INCLUDES A WRITTEN TRANSCRIPT OF ALL RELEVANT PROCEEDINGS. THE PERSON SEEKING REVIEW MUST HAVE THE TRANSCRIPT PREPARED IF NECESSARY FOR THE COURT'S REVIEW.

YOU ARE HEREBY ADVISED THAT IN THIS CIRCUIT:

_____ electronic recording is provided by the court. A party may bring a court reporter at that party's own expense.

_____ a court reporter is provided by the court.

If you are represented by an attorney or plan to retain an attorney for this matter you should notify the attorney of this hearing.

If this matter is resolved, the moving party shall contact the General Master's Office to cancel this hearing.

Florida Family Law Form 12.930(b), Notice of Hearing Before General Master

This part to be filled out by the court:

In accordance with the Americans with Disabilities Act of 1990, persons needing a special accommodation to participate in this proceeding should contact _____ for proceedings in court or _____ at _____ for out of court proceedings no later than 7 days before the proceeding. Telephone _____ or _____ for assistance. If hearing impaired, telephone (TDD) _____ for proceedings in court or Florida Relay Service 1-800-955-8771 for out of court proceedings.

I CERTIFY THAT THE NOTICE OF HEARING BEFORE GENERAL MASTER WAS:
(✔check **one** only) ____ mailed, ____telefaxed and mailed, or ____ hand delivered to the person(s) listed below on {date}_____,19_____.

Party or their attorney (if represented)
Name_____

Address_____

_____
City   State   Zip
Telephone No._____
Telefax No._____

DATED:_____

Other
Name_____

Address_____

_____
City   State   Zip
Telephone No._____
Telefax No._____

_____
Signature of party signing certificate and pleading

Printed name_____
Address_____

_____
City   State   Zip

_____
Telephone (area code and number)

_____
Telefax (area code and number)

IF A NONLAWYER HELPED YOU FILL OUT THIS FORM THEY MUST FILL IN THE BLANKS BELOW: [Fill in **all** blanks]

I, {name of nonlawyer}_____, a nonlawyer, located at {street}_____`{city}_____{state}_____, {phone}_____, helped {name}_____,who is the [✔ **one** only] _____ petitioner **or**_____ respondent, fill out this form.

Florida Family Law Form 12.920(b), Notice of Hearing Before General Master

IN THE CIRCUIT COURT OF THE _____ JUDICIAL CIRCUIT, IN AND

FOR _____ COUNTY, FLORIDA

_____,
Petitioner

Case No.: _____

AND

Division: _____

_____,
Respondent.

FAMILY LAW FINANCIAL AFFIDAVIT (SHORT FORM)

STATE OF FLORIDA
COUNTY OF {name}_____

　　BEFORE ME, this day personally appeared _____,
who being duly sworn, deposes and says that the following information is true and correct according to his/
her best knowledge and belief:

EMPLOYMENT AND INCOME

OCCUPATION: _____
EMPLOYED BY: _____

ADDRESS: _____
　　　　　　　_____

SOC. SEC. # _____
DATE OF BIRTH: _____
PAY PERIOD: _____
RATE OF PAY: _____

If you are employed, but expecting soon to become unemployed or change jobs, describe the change you
expect and why and how it will affect your income. If currently unemployed, describe your efforts to find
employment, how soon you expect to be employed, and the pay you expect to receive.

_____
_____
_____
_____
_____
_____

Florida Family Law Form 12.901(d), Financial Affidavit (Short Form)

EXCEPT IN PROCEEDINGS FOR ADOPTION, <u>SIMPLIFIED</u> DISSOLUTION OF MARRIAGE, ENFORCEMENT, CONTEMPT, AND INJUNCTIONS FOR DOMESTIC OR REPEAT VIOLENCE, ALL OF THE FOLLOWING MUST BE ATTACHED TO THE COPY OF THIS FINANCIAL AFFIDAVIT SERVED ON THE OPPOSING PARTY. THE ATTACHMENTS SHALL NOT BE FILED WITH THE COURT: Your 3 most recent pay stubs, your most recent Federal tax return, and the most recent W-2 forms. If last year's Federal income tax return has not yet been filed, attach W-2s, 1099s, K-1s, and any other document to be attached to your tax return. If the attachments are not made to the copy served on the opposing party, an explanation is required, UNLESS THE PARTIES HAVE AGREED THAT THEY WILL NOT GIVE EACH OTHER THESE DOCUMENTS. See also Florida Family Law Rule of Procedure 12.285.

_____

_____

_____

[✔ one only] _____ YES OR_____ NO: **WE HAVE AGREED TO WAIVE THE REQUIREMENTS OF FLORIDA FAMILY LAW RULE OF PROCEDURE 12.285.**

LAST YEAR'S INCOME	Yours	Other Party's (if known)
1. Gross earned income last calendar year (19___)	$_____	$_____
2. All other income (same year)	$_____	$_____
3. Total income taxes paid on above income (incl. Fed., FICA)	$_____	$_____
4. Net Income	$_____	$_____

AVERAGE GROSS MONTHLY INCOME FROM EMPLOYMENT

Attach more paper, if needed. Items included under "other" should be listed separately with separate dollar amounts.

Present gross income from employment $_____

Bonuses, commissions, allowances, overtime, tips, and similar payment   _____

Business income from sources such as self-employment, partnership, close corporations, and/or independent contracts (gross receipts minus ordinary and necessary expenses required to produce income)   _____

Florida Family Law Form 12.901(d), Financial Affidavit (Short Form)

Disability benefits   _____

Workers' Compensation   _____

Unemployment Compensation   _____

Pension, retirement, or annuity payments   _____

Social Security benefits   _____

Spousal support received from previous marriage   _____

Interest and dividends   _____

Rental income (gross receipts minus ordinary and necessary expenses
    required to produce income)   _____

Income from royalties, trust, or estates   _____

Reimbursed expenses and in kind payments to the extent that they
    reduce personal living expenses   _____

Gains derived from dealing in property (not including nonrecurring gains)   _____

Itemize any other income of a recurring nature   _____

TOTAL MONTHLY INCOME $_____

LESS MONTHLY DEDUCTIONS

See Appendix for how to figure out money amounts for anything that is NOT paid monthly. Attach more paper, if needed. Items included under "other" should be listed separately with separate dollar amounts.

Federal, state, and local income taxes (corrected for filing
    status and actual number of withholding allowances)   _____

FICA or self-employment tax (annualized)   _____

Mandatory union dues   _____

Mandatory retirement   _____

Health insurance payments   _____

Court ordered support payments for the children actually paid   _____

TOTAL DEDUCTIONS $_____

TOTAL NET INCOME $_____

AVERAGE MONTHLY EXPENSES

HOUSEHOLD:		Barber/beauty parlor	_____
		Cosmetics/toiletries	_____
Mtg. or rent payments	$_____	Gifts for special holidays	_____
Property taxes &		Other expenses:	
insurance	_____	_____	_____
Electricity	_____	_____	_____
Water, garbage, & sewer	_____		

Florida Family Law Form 12.901(d), Financial Affidavit (Short Form)

Telephone	_____	INSURANCES:	.
Fuel oil or natural gas	_____		
Repairs and maintenance	_____	Health	_____
Lawn and pool care	_____	Life	_____
Pest control	_____	Other insurance	
Misc. household	_____		
Food and household		_____	_____
items	_____		
Meals outside home	_____		
Other:			

AUTOMOBILE: OTHER EXPENSES NOT LISTED ABOVE:

Gasoline and oil	$_____	Dry cleaning and laundry	_____
Repairs	_____	Affiant's clothing	_____
Auto tags and license	_____	Affiant's medical,	
Insurance	_____	dental, prescriptions	_____
Other:	_____	Affiant's grooming	_____
_____	_____	Affiant's gifts	_____
		Pets:	
		Grooming	_____
		Veterinarian	_____

CHILDREN'S EXPENSES:		Membership dues:	
		Professional dues	_____
Nursery or babysitting	$ _____	Social dues	_____
School tuition	_____	Entertainment	_____
School supplies	_____	Vacations	_____
Lunch money	_____	Publications	_____
Allowance	_____	Religious organizations	_____
Clothing	_____	Charities	_____
Medical, dental,	_____	Bank charges/credit card fees	_____
Prescriptions	_____	Miscellaneous	_____
Vitamins	_____		

OTHER EXPENSES:

_____   _____

_____   _____

_____   _____

TOTAL ABOVE EXPENSES $_____

Florida Family Law Form 12.901(d), Financial Affidavit (Short Form)

PAYMENTS TO CREDITORS:

TO WHOM:	BALANCE DUE	MONTHLY PAYMENTS:
_____	$_____	$_____
_____	_____	_____
_____	_____	_____
_____	_____	_____
_____	_____	_____
_____	_____	_____
_____	_____	_____
_____	_____	_____
_____	_____	_____

TOTAL MONTHLY PAYMENTS TO CREDITORS: $_____

TOTAL MONTHLY EXPENSES: $_____

ASSETS (OWNERSHIP: IF MARITAL, PUT ONE-HALF OF THE TOTAL VALUE UNDER PETI-TIONER AND ONE-HALF UNDER RESPONDENT NO MATTER WHOSE NAME THE ITEM IS IN.

Description	Value	Petitioner	Respondent
Cash on hand	_____	_____	_____
Cash in banks	_____	_____	_____
Stocks/bonds	_____	_____	_____
Notes	_____	_____	_____
Real estate:			
Home:			
_____			
_____	_____	_____	_____
_____	_____	_____	_____
Automobiles:			
_____	_____	_____	_____
_____	_____	_____	_____
_____	_____	_____	_____
Other personal property:			
Contents of home	_____	_____	_____
Jewelry	_____	_____	_____
Life ins./cash surrender value	_____	_____	_____
Other assets:			
_____	_____	_____	_____
_____	_____	_____	_____
_____	_____	_____	_____
TOTAL ASSETS:	$_____	$_____	$_____

Florida Family Law Forms 12.901(d), Financial Affidavit (Short Form)

LIABILITIES

Creditor	Security	Balance	Husband	Wife
_____	_____	_____	_____	_____
_____	_____	_____	_____	_____
_____	_____	_____	_____	_____
_____	_____	_____	_____	_____
_____	_____	_____	_____	_____
_____	_____	_____	_____	_____
TOTAL:	$_____	$_____	$_____	$_____

NET WORTH

Total Assets $_____

Less: Total Liabilities (excluding contingent liabilities)* $_____

New Worth $_____

*If there is a claim for contingent liabilities, it should be set forth in a separate schedule attached.

I AM AWARE THAT ANY MATERIALLY FALSE STATEMENT KNOWINGLY MADE WITH THE INTENT TO DEFRAUD OR MISLEAD SHALL SUBJECT ME TO THE PENALTY FOR PERJURY AND MAY BE CONSIDERED A FRAUD UPON THE COURT.

I CERTIFY THAT THE FAMILY LAW FINANCIAL AFFIDAVIT (SHORT FORM) WAS:
(✔ check **one** only) ____ mailed, ____telefaxed and mailed, or ____ hand delivered to the person(s) listed below on {date}_____,19_____.

Party or their attorney if represented	Other
Name_____	Name_____
Address_____	Address_____
_____	_____
City State Zip	City State Zip
Telephone No._____	Telephone No._____
Telefax No._____	Telefax No._____

Florida Family Law Forms 12.901(d), Financial Affidavit (Short Form)

102

IN THE CIRCUIT COURT OF THE _____ JUDICIAL CIRCUIT, IN AND

FOR _____ COUNTY, FLORIDA

_____,
Petitioner

Case No.: _____

AND

Division: _____

_____,
Respondent.

FAMILY LAW FINANCIAL AFFIDAVIT (LONG FORM)

STATE OF FLORIDA
COUNTY OF {name}_____

BEFORE ME, this date personally appeared {name}_____

_____, who being duly sworn, deposes and says that the following information is true and correct according to his/her best knowledge and belief:

EMPLOYMENT

OCCUPATION: _____
EMPLOYED BY: _____
ADDRESS: _____
_____
DATE OF BIRTH: _____
SOCIAL SECURITY NUMBER: _____
PAY PERIOD: _____
RATE OF PAY: _____

If you are employed, but expecting soon to become unemployed or change jobs, describe the change you expect and why and how it will affect your income. If currently unemployed, describe your efforts to find employment, how soon you expect to be employed, and the pay you expect to receive.

_____
_____
_____
_____
_____
_____

Florida Family Law Form 12.901(e), Financial Affidavit (Long Form)

EXCEPT IN PROCEEDINGS FOR ADOPTION, <u>SIMPLIFIED</u> DISSOLUTION OF MARRIAGE, ENFORCEMENT, CONTEMPT, AND INJUNCTIONS FOR DOMESTIC OR REPEAT VIO-LENCE, ALL OF THE FOLLOWING MUST BE ATTACHED TO THE COPY OF THIS FINANCIAL AFFIDAVIT SERVED ON THE OPPOSING PARTY. THE ATTACHMENTS SHALL NOT BE FILED WITH THE COURT. Your three most recent pay stubs, your most recent Federal tax return, and the most recent W-2 forms. If last year's Federal income tax return has not yet been filed, attach W-2s, 1099s, K-1s, and any other document to be attached to your tax return. If the attachments are not made to the copy of the financial affidavit served on the opposing party, an explanation is required. See also Florida Family Laws Rule Procedure 12.285.

_____
_____
_____
_____

[✔ one only] _____ YES OR_____ NO: **WE HAVE AGREED TO WAIVE THE REQUIREMENTS OF FLORIDA FAMILY LAW RULE OF PROCEDURE 12.285.**

LAST YEAR'S INCOME	Yours	Other Party's (if known)
1. Gross earned income last calendar year (19___)	$_____	$_____
2. All other income (same year)	$_____	$_____
3. Total income taxes paid on above income (incl. Fed., FICA)	$_____	$_____
4. Net Income	$_____	$_____

PRESENT INCOME; AVERAGED ON A MONTHLY BASIS:
Be sure to convert amounts for anything that is NOT paid monthly. Attach more paper, if needed. Items included under "other" should be listed separately with separate dollar amounts.

Florida Family Law Form 12.901(e), Financial Affidavit (Long Form)

Present gross income from employment $_____

Bonuses, commissions, allowances, overtime,
 tips and similar payments   _____

Business income from all other sources such as
 self-employment, partnerships, close
 corporations, and/or independent contracts
 (gross receipts minus ordinary
 and necessary expenses required to
 produce income) (Attach sheet itemizing
 this income and expenses)   _____

Disability benefits/SSI   _____

Workers' Compensation   _____

Unemployment Compensation   _____

Pension, retirement,
 or annuity payments   _____

Social Security benefits   _____

Spousal Support Received from Previous
 Marriage   _____

Interest and dividends   _____

Rental income (gross receipts minus ordinary
 and necessary expenses required to produce income)
 (Attach sheet itemizing the income and expense items)   _____

Income from royalties, trust or estates   _____

Reimbursed expenses and in kind payments to the
 extent that they reduce personal living expenses   _____

Gains derived from dealing in property (not
 including non-recurring gains)   _____

Other: (Itemize any other income on a recurring basis)

_____   _____

_____   _____

TOTAL MONTHLY INCOME: $_____

Florida Family Law Form 12.901(e), Financial Affidavit (Long Form)

LESS DEDUCTIONS ALLOWABLE UNDER SECTION 61.30, FLORIDA STATUTES:

Federal income tax, including
   estimated income tax payments $_____

FICA   _____

Medicare   _____

Mandatory union dues   _____

Mandatory retirement   _____

Health insurance payments, excluding
   portion paid for children
   of the parties   _____

Court ordered child support
   actually paid for children
   from another relationship   _____

Other:

_____   _____

_____   _____

_____   _____

TOTAL DEDUCTIONS: $_____

AVERAGE NET MONTHLY INCOME: $_____

LESS : COURT ORDERED PAYMENTS

      Child support for children
      from another relationship $_____

      Alimony   _____

      Attorneys' fees   _____

      Other: _____

AVERAGE MONTHLY NET INCOME LESS COURT ORDERED PAYMENTS: $_____

AVERAGE MONTHLY EXPENSES:

See instructions for how to figure out money amounts for anything that is NOT paid monthly. Attach more paper, if needed. Items included under "other" should be listed separately with separate dollar amounts.

HOUSEHOLD AND FOOD:

		Meals outside home	_____
		Cable T.V.	
Mortgage or rent payments	$_____	Alarm	_____
Property taxes & insurance	_____	Service contracts on appliances	_____
Condo maintenance fees and		Domestic help	_____
homeowner's association fees	_____	FICA	_____
Electricity	_____	Other:	
Water, garbage & sewer	_____	_____	_____
Telephone	_____	_____	_____
Fuel oil or natural gas	_____	_____	_____
Repairs and maintenance	_____		
Lawn and pool care	_____	Total	$_____
Pest control	_____		
Misc. household	_____		
Food and household items	_____		

Florida Family Law Form 12.901(e), Financial Affidavit (Long Form)

AUTOMOBILE:

Gasoline and oil	$_____
Repairs	
Auto tag and license	_____
Insurance	_____
Payments	_____
Rental/replacements	_____
Alternative transportation (Bus, rail, car pool, etc.)	_____
Tolls and parking	_____
Other:	
_____	_____
_____	_____
TOTAL	$_____

EXPENSES FOR CHILDREN COMMON TO
BOTH PARTIES:

Nursery, babysitting, or day care	$_____
School tuition	_____
School supplies and books, fees	_____
After school activities	_____
Lunch money	_____
Private lessons/tutoring	_____
Allowance	_____
Clothing/uniforms	_____
Entertainment (movies, birthday parties, etc.)	_____
Health insurance	_____
Medical, dental, prescription (unreimbursed only)	_____
Psychiatric/psychological/ counselor	_____
Orthodontic	_____
Vitamins	_____
Barber/beauty parlor	_____
Non-prescription medications	_____
Cosmetics/toiletries and sundries	_____
Gifts from children to others (other children, relatives, teachers, etc.)	_____
Camp or/and other summer activities	_____
Clubs (Boy/Girl Scouts, etc.)	_____
Visitation expense (for nonresidential parent)	_____
Miscellaneous	_____
Other:	
_____	_____
_____	_____
_____	
TOTAL	$_____

INSURANCES:

Health insurance not previously listed	$_____
Life	_____
Other:	
_____	_____
_____	_____
_____	_____
TOTAL	$_____

OTHER EXPENSES FOR AFFIANT
NOT LISTED ABOVE:

Dry cleaning & laundry	$_____
Clothing	_____
Medical, dental & prescription (unreimbursed only)	_____
Psychiatric, psychological, counselor	_____
Non-prescription drugs, cosmetics, toiletries and sundries	_____
Grooming (beauty parlor or barber shop)	_____
Gifts	
_____	
Pets:	
Grooming	_____
Veterinarian	_____
Club dues and membership	
Social clubs	_____
Civic clubs	_____
Professional organizations	_____
Sports and hobbies	_____
Entertainment	_____
Newspapers, magazines, and subscriptions	_____
Vacations	_____
Religious organizations	_____
Bank charges/credit card fees	_____
Education expenses	_____
Postage & stationery	_____
Professional expenses (other than this proceeding)	_____
Other: (include any usual and customary expenses not otherwise mentioned in the above listed items)	
_____	_____
_____	_____
_____	_____
TOTAL	$_____

Florida Family Law Form 12.901(e), Financial Affidavit (Long Form)

PAYMENTS TO CREDITORS:

TO WHOM:	BALANCE DUE	MONTHLY PAYMENTS:
_____	$_____	$_____
_____	_____	_____
_____	_____	_____
_____	_____	_____
_____	_____	_____
_____	_____	_____
_____	_____	_____
_____	_____	_____
_____	_____	_____
_____	_____	_____

TOTAL MONTHLY PAYMENTS TO CREDITORS: $_____

TOTAL MONTHLY EXPENSES: $_____

SUMMARY

Total Monthly Income $_____

Less: Total Monthly Expenses   _____

Surplus (deficit) $_____

Florida Family Law Form 12.901(e), Financial Affidavit (Long Form)

ASSETS (OWNERSHIP: IF MARITAL, PUT ONE-HALF OF THE TOTAL VALUE UNDER PETITIONER AND ONE-HALF UNDER RESPONDENT NO MATTER WHOSE NAME THE ITEM IS IN.

DESCRIPTION	Percentage Of Record Title	Purchase Price & Date of Purchase	Lender & Amount Of Debt (mortgage encumbrances, etc.)	Present Full Fair Market Value	DOLLAR AMOUNTS Petitioner	Respondent	Claim of [✔ check correct column] Marital	Nonmarital
Cash on hand								
Cash in banks								
Stocks/bonds								
Notes								
Money owed to you								
Real estate: Home Other:								
Business Interests (set forth on separate sheet names, share, type of business)								
Automobiles:								

Florida Family Law Form 12.901(e), Financial Affidavit (Long Form)

DESCRIPTION	Percentage Of Record Title	Purchase Price & Date of Purchase	Lender & Amount Of Debt (mortgage encumbrances, etc.)	Present Full Fair Market Value	DOLLAR AMOUNTS Petitioner	DOLLAR AMOUNTS Respondent	Claim of [✔ check correct column] Marital Nonmarital
Boats & other vehicles							
Retirement Plans (Profit Sharing, Pension, IRA, 401Ks, etc.)							
Other Personal Property:							
Furniture & furnishings							
Collectibles							
Jewelry							
Life Ins./cash surrender value							
Other Assets:							
TOTAL ASSETS:		$		$	$	$	

If joint ownership, allocate equally. If not joint, list which party has record title.

Florida Family Law Form 12.901(e), Financial Affidavit (Long Form)

Debts: (OWNERSHIP: IF MARITAL, PUT ONE-HALF OF THE TOTAL DEBT UNDER PETITIONER AND ONE-HALF UNDER RESPONDENT NO MATTER WHOSE NAME THE ITEM IS IN.

Creditor	Security	Balance	Periodic payments Average/per month	Dollar amounts		Marital	Nonmarital
				Petitioner	Respondent	[✔ check correct column]	
Mortgages on real estate:							
Charge/ credit card accounts:		$	$	$	$		
Other debts:							
Contingent debts:							

TOTAL
DEBTS $ _____ $ _____ $ _____ _____

If joint debt, allocate equally. If not joint, list which party owes.

NET WORTH

Total Assets $ _____
Less: Total Debts $ _____
(excluding contingent debts)

Net Worth $ _____

I AM AWARE THAT ANY MATERIALLY FALSE STATEMENT KNOWINGLY MADE WITH THE INTENT TO DEFRAUD OR MISLEAD SHALL SUBJECT ME TO THE PENALTY FOR PERJURY AND MAY BE CONSIDERED A FRAUD UPON THE COURT.

I CERTIFY THAT THE FAMILY LAW FINANCIAL AFFIDAVIT (LONG FORM) WAS: (✔ check **one** only) ____ mailed, ____ telefaxed and mailed, or ____ hand delivered to the person(s) listed below on {date} _____ ,19 ____ .

<u>Party or their attorney (if represented)</u>   <u>Other</u>

Name _____   Name _____

Address _____   Address _____

City _____ State _____ Zip _____   City _____ State _____ Zip _____

Telephone No. _____   Telephone No. _____

Telefax No. _____   Telefax No. _____

IN THE CIRCUIT COURT OF THE _____ JUDICIAL CIRCUIT, IN AND

FOR _____ COUNTY, FLORIDA

_____,

Petitioner

AND

Case No.: _____

Division: _____

_____,

Respondent.

NOTICE OF SERVICE OF STANDARD FAMILY LAW INTERROGATORIES

You are notified that _____ has on

{date} _____, served upon {name of person served} _____

_____ family law standard interrogatories to be answered under oath within 30 days after service of the interrogatories.

I CERTIFY THAT THESE STANDARD FAMILY LAW INTERROGATORIES WERE:
(✔ check **one** only) ____ mailed, ____telefaxed and mailed, or ____ hand delivered to the person(s) listed below on {date}_____,19_____.

Party or their attorney (if represented)

Name_____

Address_____

_____
City   State   Zip

Telephone No._____

Telefax No._____

DATED:_____

Other

Name_____

Address_____

_____
City   State   Zip

Telephone No._____

Telefax No._____

_____
Signature of party signing certificate and pleading

Printed name_____

Address_____

_____
City   State   Zip

_____
Telephone (area code and number)

_____
Telefax (area code and number)

IF A NONLAWYER HELPED YOU FILL OUT THIS FORM THEY MUST FILL IN THE BLANKS BELOW: [Fill in **all** blanks]

I, {name of nonlawyer} _____, a nonlawyer, located at {street} _____, {city} _____, {state} _____, {phone} _____, helped {name} _____,who is the
[✔ **one** only] _____ petitioner **or**_____ respondent, fill out this form.

Florida Family Law Forms 12.930(a), Notice of Service of Standard Family Law Interrogatories

IN THE CIRCUIT COURT OF THE _____ JUDICIAL CIRCUIT, IN AND

FOR _____ COUNTY, FLORIDA

_____,
Petitioner

Case No.: _____

AND

Division: _____

_____,
Respondent.

STANDARD FAMILY LAW INTERROGATORIES

1.   BACKGROUND INFORMATION:

   a.   State your full legal name and any other name by which you have been known.

   b.   State your present residence and employment or business addresses and telephone numbers.

   c.   State your Social Security number.

   d.   State your birthdate.

   e.   List all business, commercial, and professional licenses which you now hold or which you have held in the last 3 years.

   f.   List all of your education after high school, including but not limited to, vocational or specialized training, including the following information:

      (1)   Name and address of each educational institution.

      (2)   Dates of attendance.

      (3)   Degrees or certificates obtained.

2.   EMPLOYMENT:

   a.   For each place of your employment or self-employment during the last 3 years state the following information:

      (1)   Name, address, and telephone number of your employer.

      (2)   Dates of employment.

      (3)   Job title and brief description of job duties.

Florida Family Law Form 12.930(b), Standard Family Law Interrogatories

      (4)   Starting and ending salaries.

      (5)   Name of your direct supervisor.

      (6)   All benefits received, including, for example, health, life, and disability insurance, expense account, use of automobile or automobile expense reimbursement, reimbursement for travel, food, or lodging expenses, payment of dues in any clubs or associations, and pension or profit-sharing plans.

If you have been unemployed at any time during the last 3 years, show the dates of unemployment. If you have not been employed at any time in the last 3 years, give the requested information for your last period of employment.

    b.   If you have been engaged in or associated with any business, commercial, or professional activity within the last 3 years that was not detailed above, state the following information for each such activity:

      (1)   Name, address, and telephone number of each activity.

      (2)   Dates you were connected with such activity.

      (3)   Position title and brief description of activities.

      (4)   Starting and ending salaries.

      (5)   Name of your direct supervisor.

      (6)   All benefits received, including, for example, health, life, and disability insurance, expense account, use of automobile or automobile expense reimbursement, reimbursement for travel, food, or lodging expenses, payment of dues in any clubs or associations, and pension or profit-sharing plans.

If you have not been engaged in any such activities at all in the last 3 years, give the requested information for your last period of such activities.

3.   INCOME:

    a.   For each of the last 3 years, state the following information:

      (1)   Each source of your income.

      (2)   The amount of income you received from each source, including earned, passive, and investment income and capital gains.

    b.   For each of your present employment, self-employment, business, commercial, or professional activities, state the following information:

      (1)   How often and on what days you are paid.

      (2)   An itemization of your gross salary, wages, and income, and all deductions from that gross salary, wages, and income.

Florida Family Law Form 12.930(b), Standard Family Law Interrogatories

(3)   Any additional compensation or expense reimbursement, including, but not limited to, overtime, bonuses, profitsharing, insurance, expense account, automobile or automobile allowance that you have received or anticipate receiving.

(For the purpose of these questions, the definition of income shall be that as contained in section 61.30, Florida Statutes.)

4.   ASSETS:

a.   State the street address and legal description of all real property that you own, use, or hold under a deed, lease, or contract.   For each property, state the following information:

     (1)   The percentage and type interest you hold.

     (2)   The names and addresses of any other persons or entities holding any interest.

     (3)   The date of your acquisition of your interest.

     (4)   The purchase price, the cost of any improvements made since it was purchased, and the amount of any depreciation taken.

     (5)   The present market value.

     (6)   The market value on the date of your separation from your spouse.

     (7)   The market value on the date of the filing of the petition for dissolution of marriage.

b.   List all of the items of tangible personal property, that are owned by you or in which you have had any interest during the last 3 years, including but not limited to, motor vehicles, tools, furniture, boats, jewelry, art objects or other collections, and collectibles. For each item, state the following information:

     (1)   The percentage and type interest you hold.

     (2)   The names and addresses of any other persons or entities holding any interest.

     (3)   The date of your acquisition of your interest.

     (4)   The purchase price.

     (5)   The present market value.

     (6)   The market value on the date of your separation from your spouse.

     (7)   The market value on the date of the filing of the petition for dissolution of marriage.

c.   Other than the financial accounts listed in the answer to interrogatory 5 below, list all of the items of intangible personal property that are owned by you or in which you have had any ownership interest within the last 3 years, including but not limited to, partnership and business interests (including good will), stocks, bonds, receivables, choses in action, and debts owed to you by another entity or person. For each item state the following information:

        (1)   The percentage and type interest you hold.

        (2)   The names and addresses of any other persons or entities holding any interest, and the names and addresses of the persons and entities who are indebted to you or against whom you are claiming a chose in action.

        (3)   The date of your acquisition of your interest.

        (4)   The purchase price.

        (5)   The present market value or the amounts you claim are owed as receivables, choses in action, or debts.

        (6)   The market value or the amounts you claim are owed as receivables, choses in action, or debts, on the date of your separation from your spouse.

        (7)   The market value, or the amounts you claim are owed as receivables, choses in action, or debts, on the date of the filing of the petition for dissolution of marriage.

d.   List all policies of insurance that you hold, own, or in which you have any interest. If the owner of any policy is anyone other than yourself, state the name and address of such person or entity. For each policy, state the following information:

        (1)   The name of the insurance carrier and the name, address, and telephone number of the agent.

        (2)   The policy number.

        (3)   The type of insurance.

        (4)   The face value of any life insurance or annuity policy.

        (5)   The date the policy was acquired.

        (6)   The beneficiary.

        (7)   The cash surrender value.

        (8)   The loan value.

        (9)   The amount and nature of any loans outstanding against the policy.

e.   If you are the beneficiary of any estate, trust, insurance policy, or annuity state the following information for each one:

   (1)   Identification of the estate, trust, insurance policy, or annuity.

   (2)   The nature and amount of the benefit.

   (3)   The value of the benefit.

   (4)   Whether the benefit is vested or contingent.

f.   If you have established any trusts, state the following information:

   (1)   The date the trust was established.

   (2)   The names and addresses of the trustees.

   (3)   The names and addresses of the beneficiaries.

   (4)   The names and addresses of the persons or entities who possess the trust documents.

   (5)   Each asset that is held in each trust, with its present fair market value.

g.   Other than the financial accounts listed in your answer to interrogatory 5 below, list all other assets that you own, in which you have any interest, or of which you have the use and benefit that has not already been listed. For each asset, state the following:

   (1)   The name of the asset.

   (2)   The date you acquired the asset or the date you first obtained the use or benefit of it.

   (3)   The name and address of the person or entity from whom the asset was acquired or who allows you the use and benefit of it.

   (4)   The fair market value on the date you acquired the asset or the use or benefit of it.

   (5)   The fair market value on the date of your separation from your spouse.

   (6)   The fair market value on the date of the filing of the petition for dissolution of marriage.

   (7)   The present fair market value.

5.   FINANCIAL ACCOUNTS:

a.   Are you an owner, participant, or alternate payee in any pension, profit sharing, deferred compensation, or retirement plan? If so, please state the following:

   (1)   The precise legal name of the plan, and the name and address of the plan administrator or trustee.

Florida Family Law Form 12.930(b), Standard Family Law Interrogatories

118

(2)   A description of the type of plan, whether profit sharing, defined benefit, defined contribution, IRA, Keogh, or other.

(3)   The account balance of any money held for your benefit or to which you are entitled, and your accrued monthly benefit.

(4)   The location and last valuation date of said asset, the amount currently vested, and the schedule of vesting.

(5)   An itemization of any loans that you have made against the plan during the last 5 years, the outstanding balance of the loans, and the amounts of the loans.

b.   List all accounts, including checking, money market, brokerage, or any other investments that you have had any legal or equitable interest in, regardless of whether the interest is or was held in your own name individually, in your name with another person, or in any other name, within the last 3 years. Give the name and address of each institution, the name in which each account is or was maintained, the account numbers, and the names of each person authorized to make withdrawals from the accounts. State the present balance in each account, giving the largest balance during the last 12 months.

c.   State whether, during the past 3 years, you have prepared any financial statements, loan applications, or lists of your assets and liabilities. If so, for each document state: the date of preparation; the purpose for which the document was prepared; the name and address of the person or firm who prepared the document; and the names and addresses of any persons or financial institutions to whom the statements, applications, or lists were presented.

d.   State the names, addresses, and telephone numbers of your accountant and any other persons who possess your financial records, and as to each state which records they possess.

e.   State the location of all safes, vaults, or other similar depositories in which you maintained property at any time during the period commencing 1 year before the initiation of the action pending before this court until the date of furnishing answers to this interrogatory. State the names and addresses of all banks or other depositories where you had a safe deposit box; where you were a signatory or co-signatory on a safe deposit box; where you have access to a safe deposit box; or where you maintained property in a safe deposit box at any time during the period commencing 1 year before the initiation of the action before this court until the date of your answering this interrogatory. Provide the name and address of each other person who has had access to any such depository during the same time period. List any items removed from any depository by you or your agent during that time, together with the present location and fair market value of each item.

6.   LIABILITIES:

a.   List all of your liabilities, debts, and other obligations, indicating for each: the name and address of the creditor; the nature of the security, if any; the payment schedule; the current status of your payments; and the total amount of arrearage, if any.

b.   List all charge accounts and credit cards upon which you are a signatory, which you use, or which are issued to you. For each account listed give the account number, the current status of your payments, the balance presently owed, and the minimum monthly payments.

7.   LIVING EXPENSES:

    a.   Complete Florida Family Law Form 12.901(d) or 12.901(e) and, if applicable, Florida Family Law Form 12.901(g), child support worksheet. Both of these forms are attached. You do not need to do this if a financial affidavit complying with Family Law Form 12.901(d) or 12.901(e) and/or Florida Family Law Form 12.901(g) has been filed with the court and served on the parties.

8.   MISCELLANEOUS:

    a.   List all other assets that you own, have an interest in, or have the use or benefit of, setting forth for each your interest in the asset and its value. For each, set forth the date of your acquisition, receipt, or inheritance, or the date of your first being given use or benefit; the party from whom it was received; the value on the date of your acquisition or use; the value on the date of marriage; the value on the date of the filing of the petition for dissolution of marriage; and the present value.

    b.   If you are claiming a special equity in any assets, list the asset, the amount claimed as special equity, and all facts upon which you rely in your claim.

    c.   If the mental or physical condition of a spouse or child is an issue, identify the person and state the name and address of all health care providers involved in the treatment of that person.

I AM AWARE THAT ANY MATERIALLY FALSE STATEMENT KNOWINGLY MADE WITH THE INTENT TO DEFRAUD OR MISLEAD SHALL SUBJECT ME TO THE PENALTY FOR PERJURY AND MAY BE CONSIDERED A FRAUD UPON THE COURT.

DATED:_____

I CERTIFY THAT THE ANSWERS TO THESE STANDARD FAMILY LAW INTERROGATORIES WERE:
(✔ check **one** only) ____ mailed, ____telefaxed and mailed, or ____ hand delivered to the person(s) listed below on {date}_____,19_____.

Party or their attorney if represented   Other

Name_____   Name_____

Address_____   Address_____

_____   _____
City   State   Zip   City   State   Zip

Telephone No._____   Telephone No._____

Telefax No._____   Telefax No._____

Florida Family Law Form 12.930(b), Standard Family Law Interrogatories

IN THE CIRCUIT COURT OF THE _____ JUDICIAL CIRCUIT, IN AND

FOR _____ COUNTY, FLORIDA

_____,
Petitioner

AND

Case No.: _____

Division: _____

_____,
Respondent.

CERTIFICATE OF COMPLIANCE WITH FAMILY LAW RULE 12.285

I CERTIFY that the following documents were delivered, on the date(s) indicated below, to the ❑ Petitioner ❑ Respondent, as required by Rule 12.285 of the Florida Family Law Rules of Procedure: (✔ check **all that apply and fill in all appropriate blanks**)

❑ Family Law Financial Affidavit   Date served:_____

❑ Delivery of all other documents referred to in Family Law Rule 12.285 has been waived.

❑ Answers to the Standard Family Law Interrogatories   Date served:_____

❑ _____   Date served:_____

❑ _____   Date served:_____

❑ _____   Date served:_____

❑ _____   Date served:_____

❑ _____   Date served:_____

❑ _____   Date served:_____

❑ _____   Date served:_____

❑ _____   Date served:_____

❑ _____   Date served:_____

❑ See attached list of additional documents.

Dated:_____

_____
Signature of party

_____
Printed name

_____
Address

_____
City   State   Zip

_____
Telephone (area code and number)

_____
Telefax (area code and number)

Party or their attorney (if represented)

Name_____

Address_____

_____
City   State   Zip

Telephone No._____

Telefax No._____

Other

Name_____

Address_____

_____
City   State   Zip

Telephone No._____

Telefax No._____

WAIVER OF RECEIPT OF DOCUMENTS

I HEREBY WAIVE my right to receive copies of documents pursuant to Rule 12.285 of the Florida Family Law Rules of Procedure. This waiver includes, but is not limited to, a waiver of my right to receive answers to the Standard Family Law Interrogatories.

Dated:_____

_____
Signature of party signing waiver

_____
Printed name

_____
Address

_____
City   State   Zip

_____
Telephone (area code and number)

_____
Telefax (area code and number)

IF A NONLAWYER HELPED YOU FILL OUT THIS FORM THEY MUST FILL IN THE BLANKS BELOW: [Fill in **all** blanks]

I, {name of nonlawyer} _____, a nonlawyer, located at {street} _____, {city} _____, {state} _____, {phone} _____, helped {name} _____,who is the [✔ **one** only] _____ petitioner **or**_____ respondent, fill out this form.

DATED:_____

_____
Signature of party signing certificate

Printed name_____

Address_____

_____
City   State   Zip

_____
Telephone (area code and number)

_____
Telefax   (area code and number)

IF A NONLAWYER HELPED YOU FILL OUT THIS FORM THEY MUST FILL IN THE BLANKS BELOW: [Fill in **all** blanks]

I, {name} _____, a nonlawyer, located at {street} _____, {city} _____, {state} _____, {phone} _____, helped {name} _____,who is the [✔ **one** only] _____ petitioner **or**_____ respondent, fill out this form.

DATED:_____

_____
Signature of party signing certificate and pleading/affidavit

Printed name_____

Address_____

_____
City   State   Zip

_____
Telephone (area code and number)

_____
Telefax (area code and number)

STATE OF FLORIDA
COUNTY OF {name}_____

     Sworn to (or affirmed) and subscribed before me on {date}_____, 19____,
by {name}_____.

_____
NOTARY PUBLIC—STATE OF FLORIDA

_____
[Print, type, or stamp commissioned name of notary]

[✔ one only]
____ Personally known
____ Produced identification   Type of identification produced_____

**IF A NONLAWYER HELPED YOU FILL OUT THIS FORM THEY MUST FILL IN THE BLANKS
BELOW:** [Fill in **all** blanks]

I, {name of nonlawyer}_____, a nonlawyer, located at
{street}_____{city}_____{state}_____,
{phone}_____, helped {name}_____,who
is the [✔ one only] _____ petitioner **or**_____ respondent, fill out this form.

WITNESS TESTIMONY WORKSHEET

PURPOSE OF WITNESS:

PART I
Please state your name and address.
Do you know the parties in this case?
How do you know them?

PART II
What is your occupation?
How long have you been in your current occupation?
Where are you employed?
How long have you been employed there?
Please describe your educational background, and employment history.

PART III

IN THE CIRCUIT COURT OF THE _____ JUDICIAL CIRCUIT, IN AND

FOR _____ COUNTY, FLORIDA

_____,

Petitioner

AND

Case No.: _____

Division: _____

_____,

Respondent.

PETITION TO MODIFY ALIMONY

The ___Husband ___Wife requests that the judgment entered on _____, 19___,

under which the ___Husband ___Wife is ordered to pay the sum of $_____ per _____ alimony,

be modified to provide for:

❏ A(n) ___increase ___decrease to the sum of $_____ per _____.

❏ The termination of alimony effective _____.

❏ The award of rehabilitative alimony to be changed to permanent alimony in the amount of $_____ per _____, continuing until the death or remarriage of the ___Husband ___Wife, or until further order of the court.

❏ The award of permanent alimony to be changed to rehabilitative alimony in the amount of $_____ per _____, continuing until _____, or until further order of the court.

❏ Other (specify):

This petition is based upon a change in the circumstances of the parties, as indicated by the attached

Affidavit Regarding Alimony and the parties' financial affidavits to be filed in connection with this petition.

DATED:_____

_____

Signature

Petitioner

Name_____

Address_____

_____

Telephone No._____

IF A NONLAWYER HELPED YOU FILL OUT THIS FORM THEY MUST FILL IN THE BLANKS BELOW: [Fill in **all** blanks]

I, {name of nonlawyer} _____, a nonlawyer, located at {street} _____, {city} _____, {state} _____, {phone} _____, helped {name} _____,who is the [✔ **one** only] _____ petitioner **or**_____ respondent, fill out this form.

IN THE CIRCUIT COURT OF THE _____ JUDICIAL CIRCUIT, IN AND

FOR _____ COUNTY, FLORIDA

_____,
Petitioner

AND

Case No.. _____

Division: _____

_____,
Respondent.

AFFIDAVIT REGARDING ALIMONY

STATE OF FLORIDA)
COUNTY OF)

    BEFORE ME this day personally appeared _____,
who, being first duly sworn on oath, deposes and says:
1. The affiant is the petitioner in this action.
2. The affiant is in need of, and is entitled to, a modification of alimony, as requested in the Petition, based upon the following circumstances:

_____
AFFIANT

Acknowledged before me on _____, by _____,
                      [date]   [name]
who ___ is personally known to me/ _____ produced _____
                                                             [document]
as identification, and who did take an oath.

_____
NOTARY PUBLIC—STATE OF FLORIDA

Name:_____
Commission No.:_____
My Commission Expires:_____

IF A NONLAWYER HELPED YOU FILL OUT THIS FORM THEY MUST FILL IN THE BLANKS BELOW: [Fill in **all** blanks]

I, {name of nonlawyer} _____, a nonlawyer, located at
{street} _____, {city} _____, {state} _____,
{phone} _____, helped {name} _____,who is the
[✔ one only] _____ petitioner **or**_____ respondent, fill out this form.

IN THE CIRCUIT COURT OF THE _____ JUDICIAL CIRCUIT, IN AND

FOR _____ COUNTY, FLORIDA

_____,
Petitioner

Case No.: _____

AND

Division: _____

_____,
Respondent.

ORDER MODIFYING ALIMONY

THIS CAUSE, having come on for hearing on _____, 19____, and the court having considered all of the evidence presented and being fully advised in the premises,

IT IS HEREBY ORDERED that the judgment dissolving marriage in the above matter be modified as follows:

☐ The amount of alimony shall be ___increased ___decreased to the sum of $_____ per _____ .

☐ Alimony shall be terminated_____.

☐ The award of rehabilitative alimony shall be modified to provide for permanent alimony in the amount of $_____ per _____, which shall continue until the death or remarriage of the ___Husband ___Wife, or until further order of this court.

☐ The award of permanent alimony shall be modified to provide for rehabilitative alimony in the amount of $_____ per _____, which shall continue until_____.

or until further order of this court.

☐ Other:

All other provisions of the judgment, and any other orders not in conflict with this order, shall remain in full force and effect.

Any income deductions orders shall be modified to conform to this order, and shall otherwise remain in effect. In the event there is no existing income deduction order, an income deduction order shall be issued.

This order shall be effective retroactive to the date of filing of the Petition to Modify Alimony, unless an alternative date has been specified above.

ORDERED in _____, Florida, this _____ day of _____, 19_____.

_____
Circuit Judge

cc:

IF A NONLAWYER HELPED YOU FILL OUT THIS FORM THEY MUST FILL IN THE BLANKS BELOW: [Fill in **all** blanks]

I, {name of nonlawyer} _____, a nonlawyer, located at {street} _____, {city} _____, {state} _____, {phone} _____, helped {name} _____,who is the [✔ one only] _____ petitioner **or**_____ respondent, fill out this form.

129

IN THE CIRCUIT COURT OF THE _____ JUDICIAL CIRCUIT, IN AND

FOR _____ COUNTY, FLORIDA

_____,
Petitioner

AND

Case No.: _____

Division: _____

_____,
Respondent.

**PETITION/REQUEST FOR MODIFICATION/CHANGE OF
CHILD SUPPORT AND OTHER RELIEF**

[✔ check all which apply. Fill in all blanks that apply]

The _____Petitioner/____ Respondent, files this Petition for Modification and claims:

1. This is an action for modification of the last order/judgment addressing child support previously entered by this court on the *{date}*_____. A copy of that order is attached.

2. That order/judgment, required the **obligor** to pay child support in the amount of $_____ each pay period:
    _____weekly____biweekly____twice a month____monthly

3. That since the entry of the last child support determination there has been a substantial and permanent change of circumstances as follows:

a. **Obligor's** income has ____increased or ____decreased. Please explain: _____
_____

b. **Payee's** income has ___increased or ___decreased. Please explain: _____
_____

c. The child's/children's needs have ____increased or ____decreased. Please explain:
_____

d. List any other changes that have taken place since the last child support determination that you feel are reasons why the child support in effect at this time should be changed.
_____

e. The child support calculations under the Child Support Guidelines support a change. A guideline worksheet (Family Law Form 12.901(g) is attached). Please explain:
_____

f. Other:_____
_____

Florida Family Law Form 12.904(b), Petition for Modification of Child Support

WHEREFORE, the [✔ one only]_____ Petitioner **or**_____ Respondent respectfully demands that the child support be modified and such other relief be granted as the court deems appropriate.

I CERTIFY THAT THE PETITION/REQUEST FOR MODIFICATION/CHANGE OF CHILD SUP-PORT AND OTHER RELIEF WAS: (✔ one only) _____ mailed, _____telefaxed and mailed, or _____ hand delivered to the person(s) listed below on *{date}*_____,19_____.

Party or their attorney (if represented)
Name_____
Address_____
_____
City   State   Zip
Telephone No._____
Telefax No._____

Other
Name_____
Address_____
_____
City   State   Zip
Telephone No._____
Telefax No._____

DATED:_____

_____
Signature of party signing certificate and pleading

Printed name_____
Address_____
_____
City   State   Zip

_____
Telephone (area code and number)

_____
Telefax (area code and number)

STATE OF FLORIDA
COUNTY OF *{name}*_____

        Sworn to (or affirmed) and subscribed before me on *{date}*_____, 19____
by *{name}*_____.

_____
NOTARY PUBLIC—STATE OF FLORIDA

_____
[Print, type, or stamp commissioned name of notary]
[✔ one only]
_____ Personally known
_____ Produced identification   Type of identification produced_____

IF A NONLAWYER HELPED YOU FILL OUT THIS FORM THEY MUST FILL IN THE BLANKS BELOW: [Fill in **all** blanks]

I, *{name}* _____, a nonlawyer, located at
{street} _____*{city}* _____*{state}* _____,
{phone} _____, helped *{name}* _____,who is the
[✔ one only] _____ petitioner **or**_____ respondent, fill out this form.

IN THE CIRCUIT COURT OF THE _____ JUDICIAL CIRCUIT, IN AND

FOR _____ COUNTY, FLORIDA

_____,
                    Petitioner

                                                    Case No.: _____

AND

                                                    Division: _____

_____,
                    Respondent.

CHILD SUPPORT GUIDELINES WORKSHEET

CHILD SUPPORT SUMMARY

Number of Children (Section I):   _____

	FATHER	MOTHER
Total actual income (Section III)	$_____	$_____
Imputed income	_____	_____
Less total deductions (Section IV)	_____	_____
Total Net Monthly Income	$ _____	$ _____

COMBINED NET MONTHLY INCOME ....$_____

	FATHER	MOTHER
Basic obligation (from chart)	$_____	$_____
Pro rate financial responsibility	____%	____%
Pro rate share of basic obligation	$_____	$ _____
Additions to basic obligation (Section II) Pro rate share of 75% of child care costs equaling $_____	$ _____	$ _____
Health insurance premiums of $_____	.$_____	$_____
Statutory child support obligation	$_____	$_____
Statutory adjustments (Section V)	$_____	$_____
Adjustment for secondary residential parent paying child care expenses	$_____	$_____

Florida Family Law Form 12.901(g), Child Support Guidelines Worksheet

Adjustment for secondary residential
  parent paying child(ren)'s health
  insurance premiums $_____ $_____

Total child support responsibility of
  primary residential parent ....$_____

Total child support responsibility of
  secondary residential parent ....$_____

SECTION I — CHILDREN

NAME	DATE OF BIRTH	AGE
_____	_____	_____
_____	_____	_____
_____	_____	_____
_____	_____	_____

SECTION II — ADDITIONS TO BASIC OBLIGATION

Child(ren)'s health insurance costs $_____
75% of allowable child care costs due
  to job search or education to enhance income
  or current employment
  Allowable amount: $_____

TOTAL ADDITIONS TO BASIC OBLIGATION $_____

SECTION III — INCOME

	FATHER	MOTHER
AVERAGE GROSS INCOME FROM EMPLOYMENT	$_____	$_____
Bonuses, commissions, allowances, overtime, tips, and similar payments	$_____	$_____
Business income from sources such as self-employment, partnerships, close corporations, or independent contracts (gross receipts minus ordinary and necessary expenses required to produce income) (Attach sheet itemizing this income)	$_____	$_____
Disability benefits/SSI	$_____	$_____
Workers' compensation	$_____	$_____
Unemployment compensation	$_____	$_____
Pension, retirement, or annuity payments	$_____	$_____
Social Security benefits	$_____	$_____
Spousal support received from previous marriage(s)	$_____	$_____

Florida Family Law Form 12.901(g), Child Support Guidelines Worksheet

Interest and dividends	$_____	$_____
Rental income (gross receipts minus ordinary and necessary expenses required to produce income) (Attach sheet itemizing the income and expense items)	$_____	$_____
Income from royalties, trusts, or estates	$_____	$_____
Reimbursed expenses or in-kind payments to the extent that they reduce personal living expenses	$_____	$_____
Gains derived from dealing in real property (not including nonrecurring gains)	$_____	$_____
TOTAL GROSS MONTHLY INCOME	$_____	$_____

SECTION IV — DEDUCTIONS

Federal income tax, including estimated income tax payments	$_____	$_____
FICA or self-employment taxes	$_____	$_____
Medicare tax	$_____	$_____
Mandatory union dues	$_____	$_____
Mandatory retirement	$_____	$_____
Health insurance and dental payments excluding portion paid for child(ren) of the parties	$_____	$_____
Ordered support actually paid for child(ren) not of this relationship	$_____	$_____
TOTAL DEDUCTIONS	$_____	$_____

SECTION V — ADJUSTMENTS

Extraordinary medical, psychological, educational, or dental expenses	$_____	$_____
Independent income of child(ren)	$_____	$_____
Payment of both child support and spousal support for a parent that regularly has been paid and for which there is a demonstrated need	$_____	$_____
Seasonal variations in a parent's income	$_____	$_____
Age of the child, taking into consideration the greater needs of older children	$_____	$_____
Special needs that have been met traditionally within the family budget even though the fulfilling of those needs will cause support to exceed the guidelines	$_____	$_____
The child(ren) spend(s) a substantial amount of time with the nonresidential parent, thereby reducing expenses of the residential parent	$_____	$_____
Refusal of the nonresidential parent to become involved in the activities of the child(ren)	$_____	$_____
Due consideration given to the residential parent's homemaking services	$_____	$_____
Visitation with nonresidential parent for more than 28 consecutive days	$_____	$_____
Total available assets of obligee, obligor, and Child(ren)	$_____	$_____
Impact of IRS dependency exemption and waiver of that exemption	$_____	$_____

Florida Family Law Form 12.901(g), Child Support Guidelines Worksheet

Application of the child support guidelines requires the obligor to pay more than 55% of gross income for single support order $_____ $_____

Any other adjustment that is needed to achieve an equitable result which may include reasonable and necessary expenses jointly incurred during the marriage $_____ $_____

Residency of subsequently born or adopted children with the obligor, including consideration of the subsequent spouse's income, only in the case of upward modification proceeding $_____ $_____

TOTAL ADJUSTMENTS $_____ $_____

SECTION VI — APPLICABLE SECTION OF CHART
[Insert applicable section of child support guidelines table]

OR

Combined income in this case exceeds $10,000 per month. Calculations in this Worksheet are based on the basic obligation of $_____. This is the minimum amount of support provided by the guidelines, plus

_____% multiplied by the amount of income over $10,000 per month (section 61.30(6), Florida Statutes).

cc:

Petitioner or their attorney (if represented)
Name_____

Address_____

_____
City   State   Zip

Telephone No._____

Telefax No._____

Other
Name_____

Address_____

_____
City   State   Zip

Telephone No._____

Telefax No._____

Respondent
Name_____

Address_____

_____
City   State   Zip

Telephone No._____

Telefax No._____

IF A NONLAWYER HELPED YOU FILL OUT THIS FORM THEY MUST FILL IN THE BLANKS BELOW: [Fill in **all** blanks]

I, {name of nonlawyer} _____, a nonlawyer, located at {street} _____, {city} _____, {state} _____, {phone} _____, helped {name} _____, who is the [✔ **one** only] _____ petitioner **or**_____ respondent, fill out this form.

Florida Family Law Form 12.901(g), Child Support Guidelines Worksheet

IN THE CIRCUIT COURT OF THE _____ JUDICIAL CIRCUIT, IN AND

FOR _____ COUNTY, FLORIDA

_____,
Petitioner

Case No.: _____

AND

Division: _____

_____,
Respondent.

FINAL JUDGMENT MODIFYING CHILD SUPPORT

[✔ **all** which apply. Fill in **all** blanks that apply]

THIS CAUSE was heard on _____ upon the _____ Petitioner's _____ Respondent's Petition for Modification of Child Support. Having heard the testimony of the parties, having reviewed the court file in this action and financial affidavits of the parties and being otherwise fully advised, it is:

1.   The Court has jurisdiction of the parties and the subject matter of this proceeding.

2.   Florida is the home state of the minor child(ren) or there is significant connection with this State and accordingly it has jurisdiction to determine child custody, visitation, and support under the Uniform Child Custody Jurisdiction Act.

3.   [✔ **one** only] ___Petitioner **or** ___Respondent [✔ **one** only] _____ was **or** _____ was not duly served by process of law and a default, ❑ Family Law Form 12.922(b), _____ was or _____ was not properly entered.

4.   The last order governing child support was entered on *{date}*_____. A copy of that order is attached.

5.   There [✔ **one** only] _____ has **or** _____ has not been a substantial change in the circumstances of the parties since the entry of the last order governing child support, specifically, _____

_____

_____

_____

_____.

6.   It [✔ **one** only] _____ is **or** _____ is not in the best interest of the minor child(ren) that the current child support order be changed because:_____

_____

_____

_____.

Florida Family Law Form 12.994(b), Final Judgment Modifying Child Support

7. Child Support
   [Fill in **all** blanks that apply]
   a. Petitioner's net income is: _____. **OR**
      Petitioner's imputed net income is: _____, based upon the following:
      _____
      _____.

   b. Respondent's net income is: _____. **OR**
      Respondent's imputed net income is: _____, based upon the following:
      _____
      _____.

[✔ all that apply]

_____ c. Child support should be set by Florida's child support guidelines (see section 61.30 Florida Statutes).

_____ d. The calculations and conclusion included in the child support guidelines worksheet ❑ Family Law Form 12.901(g)) filed in this case by [✔ **one** only] _____ petitioner **or** _____ respondent are adopted by this court and incorporated in this order.

THE COURT **MUST** MAKE SPECIFIC, WRITTEN FINDINGS WHY AWARDING THE AMOUNT OF CHILD SUPPORT REQUIRED BY SECTION 61.30, FLORIDA STATUTES, WOULD BE UNJUST OR INAPPROPRIATE IF THE AMOUNT AWARDED IS DIFFERENT FROM THE GUIDELINES AMOUNT BY PLUS OR MINUS FIVE PERCENT (5%).

_____ e. Child support should **not** be set by Florida's child support guidelines (see section 61.30 Florida Statutes). The basis for ordering [✔ **one** only] _____ more **or** _____ less than the guidelines amount of child support pursuant to section 61.30, Florida Statutes is:

_____
_____
_____
_____
_____
_____
_____
_____.

   f. Past Due Child Support/ Arrearages. The [✔ **one** only] _____ petitioner **or** _____ respondent has a total child support arrearage of $_____, this is based upon payments missed on the following dates in the following amounts _____
_____
_____.

   g. _____ Medical insurance [✔ **one** only] ___is **or** ____is not reasonably available to the
      [✔ **one** only] _____ petitioner **or** _____ respondent for the child(ren) and
      [✔ **one** only] _____ petitioner **or** _____ respondent should be required to provide it.

   h. _____ Dental insurance [✔ **one** only] ___is **or** ____is not reasonably available to the
      [✔ **one** only] _____ petitioner **or** _____ respondent for the child(ren) and
      [✔ **one** only] _____ petitioner **or** _____ respondent should be required to provide it.

Florida Family Law Form 12.994(b), Final Judgment Modifying Child Support

8. THE COURT **MUST** MAKE SPECIFIC, WRITTEN FINDINGS OF FACT EXPLAINING WHY ATTORNEYS' FEES ARE BEING GRANTED AND EXPLAINING THE BASIS OF THE AMOUNT AWARDED.

1. The [✔ **one** only] _____ husband's **or** _____ wife's request for fees and costs is DENIED.

2. The [✔ **one** only] _____husband's **or** _____wife's request for fees and costs is GRANTED.

[✔ **all** that apply]
_____ Attorneys' fees, _____ suit money, and/or _____ costs be awarded to:
[✔ **one** only] _____ petitioner **or** _____ respondent.

The basis for granting this award and for the determination of the amount is:

_____ _____
_____
_____

Therefore, upon consideration of the above findings, it is hereby ORDERED AND ADJUDGED that:

A. The Petition/Request to Modify Child Support is [✔ **one** only] _____ GRANTED **or** _____ DENIED.

B. CHILD SUPPORT
1. _____ Child support of $_____ to be paid by the
   [✔ **one** only] _____ petitioner **or** _____ respondent
   [✔ **one** only] _____weekly_____biweekly_____twice a month_____monthly.

This support shall continue until the first of the parties' minor children reaches the age of 18, or if the child(ren) are between the ages of 18 and 19 and are still in high school performing in good faith with a reasonable expectation of graduation, until the child(ren) reaches the age of 19. At that time the child support will be recomputed under the then-current Child Support Guidelines.

2. _____ The [✔ **one** only] _____ petitioner **or** _____ respondent shall pay the sum of $_____ per _____ for _____ children, for past due child support. This payment for past due child support shall last for _____ months/years, until all past due support and interest are paid. Interest on past due child support shall be added to obligor's debt at the rate of _____% per annum until paid.

3. _____ Unusual or uninsured medical/dental expenses for the children be provided by:
[✔ **one** only] _____ petitioner **or** _____ respondent **or** _____ petitioner and respondent each pay one-half

4. _____ Medical insurance to be provided by
[✔ **one** only] _____ petitioner **or** _____ respondent for the child(ren).

5. _____ Dental insurance to be provided by
[✔ **one** only] _____ petitioner **or** _____ respondent for the child(ren).

6. _____ Life insurance shall be maintained for the benefit of the minor child(ren) as beneficiaries **or** as stated in the *{name trust}* _____ for the benefit of the minor children created *{date}* _____ with the [✔ **one** only] _____ petitioner **or** _____ respondent or other *{specify}* _____as owner as follows: [✔ **one** only] _____ none ordered **or** _____ by petitioner with a benefit amount of $ _____ **or** _____ by respondent with a benefit amount of $ _____.

Florida Family Law Form 12.994(b), Final Judgment Modifying Child Support

138

7. All payments of child support and alimony shall be as follows:
   [✔ all which apply]
   _____ Directly to the person the court has ordered will be paid the support.
   _____ Payment will be through the Central Depository by the attached order ❑ Family Law Form 12.991(a).
   _____ Payment will be by income deduction order, ❑ Family Law Form 12.991(b), which is attached.

C. _____ Attorneys' fees, suit money, and costs be awarded to:
   [✔ one only] _____ petitioner or _____ respondent in the amount of $ _____(fees),
$_____ (costs), $_____ suit money. The basis for granting or denying this award and for the amount of any fees and costs awarded is given in the findings of fact in this judgment.

D. This court awards the petitioner the following further relief in this cause:
_____
_____

F. The court reserves jurisdiction to enforce the terms of this order and all documents incorporated into it (e.g., parties' stipulation/agreement, child support guidelines worksheet, etc.).

DONE and ORDERED in {name} _____ County, Florida, on {date} _____, 19_____.

_____
CIRCUIT JUDGE

cc:

Petitioner or their attorney (if represented)
Name_____
Address_____

_____
City   State   Zip
Telephone No._____
Telefax No._____

Other
Name_____
Address_____

_____
City   State   Zip
Telephone No._____
Telefax No._____

Respondent or their attorney (if represented)
Name_____
Address_____

_____
City   State   Zip
Telephone No._____
Telefax No._____

IF A NONLAWYER HELPED YOU FILL OUT THIS FORM TO GIVE TO THE JUDGE TO SIGN, THE NONLAWYER WHO HELPED YOU MUST FILL IN THE BLANKS BELOW:
[Fill in all blanks]

I, {name of nonlawyer}_____, a nonlawyer, located at {street}_____{city}_____{state}_____, {phone}_____, helped {name}_____,who is the [✔ one only] _____ petitioner or _____ respondent, fill out this form.

Florida Family Law Form 12.994(b), Final Judgment Modifying Child Support

IN THE CIRCUIT COURT OF THE _____ JUDICIAL CIRCUIT, IN AND

FOR _____ COUNTY, FLORIDA

_____,
Petitioner

Case No.: _____

AND

Division: _____

_____,
Respondent.

ORDER REQUIRING PAYMENT THROUGH CENTRAL DEPOSITORY
[✔ check all which apply. Fill in all blanks that apply]

IT IS ORDERED AND ADJUDGED that all payments of child support shall be as follows:

_____ **Obligor** will make the payments ordered - Fill out A & B below, NOT C.

_____ Payment will be by income deduction order and **payor** is **not** the **obligor** - Fill out A, B, & C.

A.   PAYOR INFORMATION

1.   Name:_____   DOB:_____

Social Security No:_____   Phone:_____

Street:_____

City:_____   State:_____   Zip:_____

2.   Employer:_____Phone:_____

Street:_____

City:_____   State:_____   Zip:_____

Other sources of income:_____

_____

_____

_____

Florida Family Law Form 12.991(a), Order Requiring Payment Through Central Depository

B.   PAYEE INFORMATION

1.   Name:_____   DOB:_____

      Social Security No:_____   Phone:_____

      Street:_____

      City:_____   State:_____   Zip:_____

2.   Children for whom support is to be paid:

Name	Date of Birth	Age	Sex	Social Security No.
_____	_____	_____	_____	_____
_____	_____	_____	_____	_____
_____	_____	_____	_____	_____
_____	_____	_____	_____	_____
_____	_____	_____	_____	_____

C. PAYOR INFORMATION (fill out only if **payor** is NOT **obligor**)

2.   Name (**obligor's** employer):_____

      Named agent for service:_____

      Street:_____

      City:_____   State:_____   Zip:_____

      Telephone:_____   Telefax:_____

D.   MANNER AND METHOD OF PAYMENT
      [✔ check all which apply, fill in amount, pay period and number of children]

1.   Regular Child Support
      [✔ **one** only]

      _____   The **payor** shall pay the sum of $_____ per _____ for _____ children, plus the clerk's processing fee as set forth in paragraph 8 below.

      _____   The **payor** shall pay the sum of $_____ per _____ for _____ children, from which the clerk shall deduct its processing fee.

Florida Family Law Form 12.991(a), Order Requiring Payment Through Central Depository

2.   Past Due Child Support/ Arrearages.
      _____   The **payor** shall pay the sum of $_____ per _____ for _____ children, and the clerk's processing fee, for past due child support. This payment for past due child support shall last for _____ months/years, until all past due support, fees to the central depository and interest are paid. Interest on past due child support shall be added to obligor's debt at the rate of _____% per annum until paid.

3.   Alimony
      [✔ **one** only]
      _____   The **payor** shall pay the sum of $_____ per _____ for alimony, plus the clerk's processing fee as set forth in paragraph 8 below.

      _____   The **payor** shall pay the sum of $_____ per _____ for alimony, from which the clerk shall deduct the processing fee.

4.   Past Due Alimony/ Arrearages.
      _____   The **payor** shall pay the sum of $_____ per _____, plus the clerk's processing fee, for past due alimony. This payment for past due alimony shall last for _____ months/years, until all past due alimony is paid.

5.   Payments shall begin on the date of entry of this order and payments shall continue to be made the way this order says they will be paid and in the amount this order says will be paid unless and until this court orders something else.

6.   Payments shall be sent to:

CLERK OF COURT, CENTRAL DEPOSITORY

Street:_____

City:_____   State:_____   Zip:_____

Telephone:_____   Telefax:_____

7.   Payment shall be made by cash, check, or money order. For identification and accounting purposes, you must write the court case number on each payment made by check or money order and be attached on a separate sheet of paper with any cash payment. If payment is made by check, the clerk may require the payor to fill out a form.

8.   Any depository processing fees as allowed in section 61.181, Florida Statutes, shall be paid with each payment. The amount of the service fee is 4% of the total payment, but not less than $1.25 nor more than $5.25.

9.   The parties affected by this order must tell the central depository right away if there is any change of name, address, employer, place of employment, or source of income.

Florida Family Law Form 12.991(a), Order Requiring Payment Through Central Depository

DONE and ORDERED in _____ County, Florida, on this _____ day

of _____, 19_____.

_____

CIRCUIT JUDGE

cc:

Petitioner or their attorney (if represented)

Name_____

Address_____

_____
City   State   Zip

Telephone No._____

Telefax No._____

Other

Name_____

Address_____

_____
City   State   Zip

Telephone No._____

Telefax No._____

Respondent or their attorney (if represented)

Name_____

Address_____

_____
City   State   Zip

Telephone No._____

Telefax No._____

IF A NONLAWYER HELPED YOU FILL OUT THIS FORM TO GIVE TO THE JUDGE TO SIGN, THE NONLAWYER WHO HELPED YOU MUST FILL IN THE BLANKS BELOW:
[Fill in **all** blanks]

I, {name of nonlawyer} _____, a nonlawyer, located at {street} _____, {city} _____, {state} _____, {phone} _____, helped {name} _____, who is the [✔ one only] _____ petitioner **or** _____ respondent, fill out this form.

Florida Family Law Form 12.991(a), Order Requiring Payment Through Central Depository

IN THE CIRCUIT COURT OF THE _____ JUDICIAL CIRCUIT, IN AND

FOR _____ COUNTY, FLORIDA

_____,
Petitioner

Case No.: _____

AND

Division: _____

_____,
Respondent.

CHILD SUPPORT INCOME DEDUCTION ORDER
[✔ check all which apply, Fill in all blanks that apply]

      THIS COURT entered an order on _____ establishing support obligations owed by the **obligor**, *{name}* _____, whose social security number is _____. In compliance with section 61.1301, Florida Statutes,

      IT IS ADJUDGED:

INCOME DEDUCTION: From all income due and payable to **obligor**_____, the following amounts shall be deducted:

A. ONGOING SUPPORT:
    1. _____ Child support of $_____ [✔ **one** only]
        each pay period: ____weekly____biweekly____twice a month____monthly

    2. _____ Spousal support of $_____ [✔ **one** only]
        each pay period: ____weekly____biweekly____twice a month____monthly

B. PAST DUE SUPPORT/ARREARAGE: Payments of previously ordered support not paid.
    1. _____ Child support of $_____ [✔ **one** only]
        each pay period: ____weekly____biweekly____twice a month____monthly
    2. _____ Spousal support of $_____ [✔ **one** only]
        each pay period: ____weekly____biweekly____twice a month____monthly
    3. TOTAL: $_____ is past due.
    4. INTEREST: of _____% through_____,19__.
        Interest continues to accrue at the rate of 12% annually on the unpaid principal, or $_____ per day.

    5. PAYMENT OF PAST DUE CHILD/SPOUSAL SUPPORT:
        An additional $_____ shall be withheld each pay period: [✔ **one** only]
        ____weekly____biweekly____twice a month____monthly until full payment is made of this arrearage with interest.

Florida Family Law Form 12.991(b), Child Support Income Deduction Order

C. RETROACTIVE SUPPORT: The court has ordered that the new support amount began on the date the petition asking for it was filed. Retroactive support is the difference between how much support was paid from the date the petition was filed to the date the order was entered and how much support would have been paid if the new amount had begun when the petition was filed.

1. _____ Child support of $_____ [✔ **one** only]
each pay period: _____weekly____biweekly____twice a month____monthly

2. _____ Spousal support of $_____ [✔ **one** only]
each pay period: _____weekly____biweekly____twice a month____monthly

3. TOTAL: $_____ is past due.

4. PAYMENT OF PAST DUE CHILD/SPOUSAL SUPPORT:
An additional $_____ shall be withheld each pay period: [✔ **one** only]
_____weekly____biweekly____twice a month____monthly until full payment is made of this retroactive support.

D. PAST PUBLIC ASSISTANCE:

3. TOTAL: $_____ past public assistance was awarded in this matter and is due and owing.

4. PAYMENT OF PAST DUE CHILD/SPOUSAL SUPPORT:
An additional $_____ shall be withheld each pay period: [✔ **one** only]
_____weekly____biweekly____twice a month____monthly until full payment is made of this past public assistance.

E. ATTORNEYS' FEES AND COSTS: **obligor** has been ordered to pay to the **payee**
____ attorneys' fees in the amount of $_____ and
____ costs in the amount of $_____, totalling $_____.
Immediately after support arrearages in subsection (1)(b) are paid in full, an additional $_____ shall be withheld each pay period: [✔ **one** only]
_____weekly____biweekly____twice a month____monthly until full payment is made. If there is no support arrearage, this amount shall be withheld immediately.

F. SERVICE FEE: Any depository service fees as provided in section 61.181, Florida Statutes shall be paid with each payment. The amount of the service fee is 4% of the total payment, but not less than $1.25 nor more than $5.25.

G. AMOUNT OF DEDUCTION: The total amount to be withheld [add (a)-(f) above] each pay period is $_____, or _____55%____65% of the disposable income of the obligor, whichever is lower.

H. PLACE OF PAYMENT: The **payor (obligor's** employer) shall make the total amount in (g) above payable to and send it directly to:

CLERK OF COURT, CENTRAL DEPOSITORY

Street:_____
City:_____ State:_____ Zip: _____
Telephone: _____ Telefax::_____

I. CONSUMER CREDIT PROTECTION ACT: The maximum amount to be deducted shall not exceed amounts allowed under section 303(b) of the Consumer Credit Protection Act, 15 U.S.C. section 1673(b), as amended. The maximum amount to be deducted shall not exceed 50% of the disposable income where there is a second family, 60% where there is not second family, and an additional 5% of either limit if the arrearage equals or exceeds 12 weeks of support payments. A copy of the Consumer Credit Protection Act is attached to and made a part of this order.

Florida Family Law Form 12.991(b), Child Support Income Deduction Order

J. EFFECTIVE DATE: This income deduction order
_____shall become effective immediately **OR** _____shall be effective upon a delinquency in an amount equal to one month's support $_____. A Notice to **Payor** and a Statement of Rights, Remedies, and Duties of the **Obligor** are attached to and made a part of this order.

K. DURATION: This income deduction order supersedes any income deduction order that may have been entered earlier in this case. This order shall stay in effect unless and until it is changed by this court or until the support duty ends by operation of law.

L. ATTORNEYS' FEES: This court reserves jurisdiction for an award of attorneys' fees, costs, and suit money incurred by the **payee** regarding the entry of this order.

CONSUMER CREDIT PROTECTION ACT
GARNISHMENT RESTRICTIONS

(a) Except as provided in subsection (b) of this section, the total disposable earnings of a person for any workweek which can be garnished (kept from the **obligor** and sent directly to the **payee**) **cannot be more than**:

(1) 25% of **obligor's** disposable earnings for that week, or

(2) the amount by which **obligor's** disposable earnings for that week exceed 30 times the Federal minimum hourly wage prescribed by section 206(a) of Title 29 in effect at the time the earnings are payable, whichever is less. In the case of earnings for any pay period other than a week, the Secretary of Labor shall by regulation prescribe a multiple of the federal minimum hourly wage equivalent in effect to that set forth in paragraph (2).

EXCEPTIONS

(b)(1) The restrictions of subsection (a) of this section do not apply in the case of:

(A) any order for the support of any person issued by a court of competent jurisdiction or in accordance with an administrative procedure, which is established by state law, affords substantial due process, and is subject to judicial review.

(B) any order of any court of the United States having jurisdiction over cases under Chapter 13 of Title 12.

(C) any debt due for a state or federal tax.

(2) The total disposable earnings of a person for any workweek which can be garnished (kept from the **obligor** and sent directly to the **payee**) **cannot be more than**:
(A) when such individual is supporting a spouse or dependent child (other than a spouse or child with respect to whose support such order is used), 50% of such individual's disposable earnings for that week; and
(B) when such individual is not supporting such a spouse or dependent child described in clause (A), 60% of such individual's disposable earnings for that week;

except that, with respect to the disposable earnings of any individual for any workweek, the 50% specified in clause (A) shall be deemed to be 55% and the 60% specified in clause (B) shall be deemed to be 65%, if and to the extent that such earnings are subject to garnishment to enforce a support order with respect to a period which is prior to the twelve-week period which ends with the beginning of such workweek.

Florida Family Law Form 12.991(b), Child Support Income Deduction Order

(c) Execution or enforcement of garnishment order or process is prohibited.

No court of the United States or any state, and no state (or officer or agency thereof), may make, execute, or enforce any order of process in violation of this section.

15 U.S.C. section 1673.

NOTICE TO PAYOR

[✔ check all which apply, Fill in all blanks that apply]

RE: **Obligor's** name: _____

SSN:_____

YOU ARE HEREBY NOTIFIED:

1. Deduction from **Obligor's** Income. You are required to begin an income deduction in compliance with the income deduction order entered by the court and pay that amount to the **payee** or the depository, whichever the court order setting support says to make payment to. A copy of that order and any notice of delinquency is enclosed for your payroll records. The amount actually deducted, plus all administrative charges, shall not be in excess of the amount allowed under section 303(b) of the Consumer Credit Protection Act, 15 U.S.C. section 1673(b). If payment is ordered through the court depository, payments shall be made payable to and send it directly to:

CLERK OF COURT, CENTRAL DEPOSITORY

Address_____

_____

City	State	Zip

Telephone No. _____

Telefax No._____

Each payment must have the **obligor's** name and case number clearly written on it.

2. Effective Date. You must begin the income deduction no later than the first payment date which occurs more than 14 days after the date you get this notice.

3. Forward Payments. You must send to the **payee** or the court depository (whichever the court order says to send payments to), within 2 days after each payment date, the amount to be kept from the **obligor's** wages/income and a statement saying if the money sent pays all or part of the payment due as set out in the income deduction order or notice of delinquency, and giving the exact date the money was taken from the **obligor's** wages/income and sent to the **payee** directly or through the central depository.

4. Your Liability. If you do not take out the right amount of money from the **obligor's** wages/income, you are liable for the money you should have kept out, and costs, interest, and reasonable attorneys' fees.

5. Your Costs. You may take out and keep from the **obligor's** wages\income an additional $5.00 for the first deduction and $2.00 for each deduction after that to cover your administrative costs.

6. Duration. The income deduction order and this [✔ **one** only]
____notice to **payor OR**
____notice of delinquency
are binding upon you until released in writing by the **payee**, by court order, or until you stop giving wages/income to the **obligor**.

Florida Family Law Form 12.991(b), Child Support Income Deduction Order

7. Duty to Report. Penalty if You Do Not. You must tell the

_____ **payee**

_____ depository

when you are no longer giving wages/income to the **obligor**. You must also give the **obligor's** last-known address, and the name and address of the **obligor's**

_____ new payor

_____ new employer, if known. You face a civil penalty not to exceed $250.00 for the first violation and $500.00 for any violation after that if you do not give tell the payee/depository obligor's new payor/ employer if you know it. Penalties shall be paid to the **payee**.

8. Duty to Cooperate. Penalty if You Do Not. You may not discharge/fire, refuse to employ, or take disciplinary action against an **obligor** because of an income deduction order. You face a civil penalty not to exceed $200.00 for the first violation or $500.00 for any violation after that. Penalties shall be paid to the **payee** if any support is owing. If no support is owing, the penalty shall be paid to the **obligor**.

9. **Obligor's** Rights. The obligor may bring a civil action against you if you refuse to employ the **obligor**, discharge the **obligor**, or otherwise discipline the **obligor** because of an income deduction order. The **obligor** is entitled to reinstatement and all wages and benefits lost, plus reasonable attorneys' fees and costs.

10. Priority Under Law. The income deduction order has priority over all other legal processes under state law pertaining to the same income. Payment in compliance with the income deduction order is a complete defense by you against any claims of the **obligor** or **obligor's** creditors as to the sums paid.

11. Your Convenience. When you get income deduction orders requiring that the income of 2 or more **obligors** be deducted and sent to the same depository, you may combine the amounts that are to be paid to the depository in a single payment as long as you clearly identify the portion of the payment that is for to each **obligor**.

12. Conflict. If you receive more than one income deduction order against the same **obligor**, contact the court for further instructions.

STATEMENT OF RIGHTS, REMEDIES, AND DUTIES IN REGARD TO INCOME DEDUCTION ORDER
[✔ check all which apply, Fill in all blanks that apply]

A. Fees of $_____ shall be imposed. Interest of $_____ shall be imposed.

B. UNTIL the total arrearage, retroactive support, interest, costs and fees are paid in full
$_____ shall be deducted from each pay period: [✔ **one** only]
_____weekly____biweekly____twice a month____monthly.

AFTER all of those amounts are paid in full
$_____ shall be deducted from each pay period: [✔ **one** only]
_____weekly____biweekly____twice a month____monthly.

The amounts deducted may not be in excess of that allowed under section 303(b) of the Consumer Credit Protection Act, 15 U.S.C. section 1673(b), as amended.

C. The income deduction order applies to current and subsequent **payors** and periods of employment.

D. A copy of the income deduction order will be served on the **obligor's payor** or **payors**.

E. Enforcement of the income deduction order may be contested only on the ground of mistake of fact regarding the amount of support owed pursuant to a support order, the arrearage, or the identity of the obligor.

F. The **obligor** is required to notify the **payee** within 7 days of changes in the **obligor's** address and **payors** and the addresses of his **payors**.

DONE and ORDERED in {name}_____ County, Florida, on {date} _____.

_____
CIRCUIT JUDGE

cc:

Petitioner or their attorney (if represented)	Respondent or their attorney (if represented)
Name_____	Name_____
Address_____	Address_____
_____	_____
City State Zip	City State Zi p
Telephone No._____	Telephone No._____
Telefax No._____	Telefax No._____
Clerk of the Central Depository	**Payor or their attorney (if represented)**
Name_____	Name_____
Address_____	Address_____
_____	_____
City State Zip	City State Zip
Telephone No._____	Telephone No._____
Telefax No._____	Telefax No._____

IF A NONLAWYER HELPED YOU FILL OUT THIS FORM TO GIVE TO THE JUDGE TO SIGN, THE NONLAWYER WHO HELPED YOU MUST FILL IN THE BLANKS BELOW:
[Fill in **all** blanks]
I, {name of nonlawyer} _____, a nonlawyer, located at {street} _____, {city} _____, {state}_____, {phone} _____, helped {name} _____,who is the
[✔ **one** only] _____ petitioner **or** _____ respondent, fill out this form.

Florida Family Law Form 12.991(b), Child Support Income Deduction Order

IN THE CIRCUIT COURT OF THE _____ JUDICIAL CIRCUIT, IN AND

FOR _____ COUNTY, FLORIDA

_____,

                     Petitioner

AND

                              Case No.: _____

                              Division: _____

_____,

                    Respondent.

MOTION FOR HEALTH INSURANCE COVERAGE

1. On *{date}*_____, this court ordered the child(ren)'s [✔ one only]
_____ father or _____ mother to provide health insurance coverage for the following child(ren):

Name	Date Of Birth	Age	Soc. Sec. No.
_____	_____	_____	_____
_____	_____	_____	_____
_____	_____	_____	_____
_____	_____	_____	_____
_____	_____	_____	_____

2. Notice to [✔ **one** only] _____ Petitioner **or** _____ Respondent:
[✔ **one** only]
_____ a. On _____, which is at least 15 days before filing this application,
I gave written notice of my intent to seek this order to _____
_____ by [✔ **one** only]____certified mail ____personal service.
_____ b. The requirement of written notice has been waived by the other party.

3. I ask the court to order the employer, or other person providing health insurance coverage to enroll or maintain the child(ren) on any health insurance coverage available to father/mother.

I CERTIFY THAT THE MOTION FOR HEALTH INSURANCE COVERAGE WAS:
[✔ check **one** only] _____ mailed, ____telefaxed and mailed, or _____ hand delivered to the person(s)
listed below on *{date}*_____,19_____.

Party or their attorney (if represented)   Other
Name_____   Name_____
Address_____   Address_____
_____   _____
City   State   Zip   City   State   Zip
Telephone No._____   Telephone No._____
Telefax No._____   Telefax No._____

Florida Family Law Form 12.940(a), Motion for Health Insurance Coverage

IN THE CIRCUIT COURT OF THE _____ JUDICIAL CIRCUIT, IN AND

FOR _____ COUNTY, FLORIDA

_____,
Petitioner

Case No.: _____

AND

Division: _____

_____,
Respondent.

ORDER FOR HEALTH INSURANCE COVERAGE

TO: ALL EMPLOYERS (OR FUTURE EMPLOYERS), or any other person providing health insurance coverage for OBLIGOR *{name of person who was ordered to provide health insurance}* _____:

YOU ARE HEREBY ORDERED TO:

1. Begin or maintain health insurance coverage on the child(ren). You may deduct any premium or costs from the wages or earnings of the OBLIGOR *{name of person who was ordered to provide health insurance}* _____.

2. If the OBLIGOR works for you, or if you have health insurance coverage available to OBLIGOR, you must give him or her a copy of this order within 10 days after you receive it.

3. If no health insurance coverage is available to the OBLIGOR, complete and sign the DECLA-RATION OF NO HEALTH INSURANCE COVERAGE form and mail the declaration within 20 days to the attorney or person requesting the insurance coverage.

DONE and ORDERED in *{name}* _____ County, Florida, on *{date}*_____, 19_____.

_____
CIRCUIT JUDGE

Florida Family Law Form 12.940(b), Order for Health Insurance Coverage

cc:
Petitioner or their attorney (if represented)   Respondent or their attorney (if represented)
Name_____   Name_____
Address_____   Address_____

_____   _____
City   State   Zip   City   State   Zip
Telephone No._____   Telephone No._____
Telefax No._____   Telefax No._____

Obligor's employer
Name_____
Address_____

_____
City   State   Zip
Telephone No._____
Telefax No._____

IF A NONLAWYER HELPED YOU FILL OUT THIS FORM TO GIVE TO THE JUDGE TO SIGN, THE NONLAWYER WHO HELPED YOU MUST FILL IN THE BLANKS BELOW: [Fill in **all** blanks]

I, {name of nonlawyer}_____, a nonlawyer, located at {street}_____{city}_____{state}_____, {phone}_____, helped {name}_____,who is the [✔ **one** only] _____ petitioner **or** _____ respondent, fill out this form.

Florida Family Law Form 12.940(b), Order for Health Insurance Coverage

IN THE CIRCUIT COURT OF THE _____ JUDICIAL CIRCUIT, IN AND

FOR _____ COUNTY, FLORIDA

_____,
Petitioner

Case No.: _____

AND

Division: _____

_____,
Respondent.

INSTRUCTIONS TO EMPLOYER OR OTHER
PERSON PROVIDING HEALTH INSURANCE

1. If the obligor works for you or health insurance is available through your company, you must give obligor a copy of this order within 10 days after you receive it.
2. Unless you receive a motion to quash the assignment of insurance benefits, you must take steps to begin or maintain health insurance coverage for the specified child(ren) within the shortest possible time consistent with group plan enrollment rules.
3. The obligor's existing health coverage shall be replaced only if the child(ren) are not provided benefits under the existing coverage where they reside.
4. If the obligor is not enrolled in a plan and there is a choice of several plans, you may enroll the child(ren) in any plan that will reasonably provide benefits of coverage where they live, unless the court has ordered coverage by a specific plan.
5. If no coverage is available, complete the declaration of no health insurance coverage on this page, and mail the declaration by first class mail to the attorney or applicant seeking the coverage within 30 days of your receipt of this order. Keep a copy of the form for your records.
6. If coverage is provided, you must supply evidence of coverage to both parents and any person having custody of the child(ren).
7. Upon request of the parents or person having custody of the child(ren), you must provide all forms, identification cards, and other documentation necessary for submitting claims to the insurance carrier to the extent you provide them to other covered individuals.
8. You must notify the applicant of the effective date of the coverage of the child(ren).
9. You will be liable for any amounts incurred for health care services which would have otherwise been covered under the insurance policy, if you willfully fail to comply with the terms of the order attached. You can also be held in contempt of court. Florida law forbids your firing or taking any disciplinary action against any employee because of the health insurance coverage order.

EMPLOYEE INFORMATION

The attached order tells your employer or other person providing health insurance coverage for you to enroll or maintain the named child(ren) in a health insurance plan available to you and to deduct the appropriate premium amount or costs, if any, from your wages or other compensation.

Florida Family Law Form 12.940(c), Instructions to Employer or Other Person Providing Health Insurance

EMPLOYER'S DECLARATION OF NO HEALTH INSURANCE COVERAGE

I, (name)_____ as (position)_____
for (company)_____ located at _____
_____, whose telephone is_____, HEREBY
DECLARE THAT NO HEALTH INSURANCE COVERAGE IS AVAILABLE TO OBLIGOR:
_____ because (state reasons):

DATED:_____

_____
Signature of party signing certificate
Position_____
Printed name_____
Address_____
_____
City   State   Zip
_____
Telephone (area code and number)
_____
Telefax   (area code and number)

STATE OF FLORIDA
COUNTY OF _____

        Sworn to (or affirmed) and subscribed before me on *{date}*_____, 19____
by *{name}*_____.

_____
NOTARY PUBLIC—STATE OF FLORIDA

_____
[Print, type, or stamp commissioned name of notary]

____   Personally known
____   Produced identification   Type of identification produced _____

Florida Family Law Form 12.940(c), Instructions to Employer or Other Person Providing Health Insurance

154

IN THE CIRCUIT COURT OF THE _____ JUDICIAL CIRCUIT, IN AND

FOR _____ COUNTY, FLORIDA

_____,
Petitioner

Case No.: _____

AND

Division: _____

_____,
Respondent.

**PETITION/REQUEST TO MODIFY/CHANGE PRIMARY
RESIDENCY/CUSTODY OF CHILDREN**

This petition of [✔ **one** only] _____ Petitioner **or** _____ Respondent shows:

1. [✔ **one** only] _____ Petitioner **or** _____ Respondent has primary parental responsibility, including primary residential responsibility (custody). The last order granting primary parental responsibility in this case was entered (dated) by the court on *{date}*_____, 19_____. A copy of the order is attached.

2. My completed Uniform Child Custody Jurisdiction Act Affidavit (Family Law Form 12.901(f)) is also attached.

3. Since the last order granting primary parental responsibility was entered, there has been a substantial change in circumstances as follows (briefly list below the changes that have taken place since the last order granting primary parental responsibility and the reasons why you feel the primary parental responsibility in effect at this time should be changed - if necessary, you may add additional sheets of paper):

_____
_____
_____
_____
_____
_____
_____

4. A change in primary parental responsibility, including primary residential responsibility (custody), is in the best interest of my child(ren) for the following reason(s): _____
_____
_____
_____
_____
_____
_____
_____

Florida Family Law Form 12.903(b), Petition to Modify Custody

5. If I am granted primary parental responsibility, I will need, and
[✔ one only] _____ Petitioner **or** _____ Respondent (the other person in the case) has the ability to pay reasonable child support.

WHEREFORE, I am asking that the court enter an order:

1. CUSTODY
Granting [✔ one only] _____ Petitioner **or** _____ Respondent primary parental responsibility, including primary residential responsibility (custody).

2. CHILD SUPPORT
Awarding child support to [✔ one only] _____ Petitioner **or** _____ Respondent

(a) Amount [✔ one only]
_____ Child support should be set by Florida's child support guidelines (see section 61.30, Florida Statutes).

_____ Child support should NOT be set by Florida's child support guidelines (see section 61.30, Florida Statutes).
The court should do this because: _____
_____
_____
_____
_____
_____

(b) Method of Payment: [✔ check all which apply]
_____ Directly to the person the court has ordered will be paid the support.
_____ Payment will be through the central depository by the attached order (Family Law Form 12.991(a).
_____ Payment will be by income deduction order (Family Law Form 12.991(b)) which is attached.

(c) _____ Unusual or uninsured medical/dental expenses for the children be paid by: [✔ one only]
_____ Petitioner **or** _____ Respondent **or** _____ Petitioner and Respondent each pay one-half.

(d) _____ Medical insurance[✔ one only] ___is **or** _____is not reasonably available to the
[✔ one only] _____petitioner **or** _____respondent for the child(ren) and
[✔ one only] _____ petitioner **or** _____respondent should be required to provide it.

(e) _____ Dental insurance[✔ one only] ___is **or** _____is not reasonably available to the
[✔ one only] _____petitioner **or** _____respondent for the child(ren) and
[✔ one only] _____ petitioner **or** _____respondent should be required to provide it.

(f) _____ Life insurance for the benefit of the children be provided by:
[✔ one only] _____ Petitioner _____ Respondent

Florida Family Law Form 12.903(b), Petition to Modify Custody

156

I CERTIFY THAT THE PETITION/REQUEST TO MODIFY/CHANGE PRIMARY RESPONSIBILITY/ CUSTODY OF CHILDREN WAS: [✔ check one only] _____ mailed, _____telefaxed and mailed, or _____ hand delivered to the person(s) listed below on *{date}*_____,19_____.

Party or their attorney (if represented)

Name_____

Address_____

_____
City   State   Zip

Telephone No._____

Telefax No._____

DATED:_____

Other

Name_____

Address_____

_____
City   State   Zip

Telephone No._____

Telefax No._____

_____
Signature of party signing certificate and pleading

Printed name _____

Address _____

_____
City   State   Zip

_____
Telephone (area code and number)

_____
Telefax (area code and number)

STATE OF FLORIDA
COUNTY OF *{name}*_____

     Sworn to (or affirmed) and subscribed before me on *{date}*_____, 19____ by *{name}*_____.

_____
NOTARY PUBLIC—STATE OF FLORIDA

_____
[Print, type, or stamp commissioned name of notary]
[✔ **one** only]
_____ Personally known
_____ Produced identification   Type of identification produced_____

IF A NONLAWYER HELPED YOU FILL OUT THIS FORM THEY MUST FILL IN THE BLANKS BELOW: [Fill in **all** blanks]

I, *{name}* _____, a nonlawyer, located at *{street}* _____*{city}* _____*{state}* _____, *{phone}* _____, helped *{name}* _____,who is the [✔ **one** only] _____ petitioner **or**_____ respondent, fill out this form.

Florida Family Law Form 12.903(b), Petition to Modify Custody

Form 44

IN THE CIRCUIT COURT OF THE _____ JUDICIAL CIRCUIT, IN AND

FOR _____ COUNTY, FLORIDA

_____,
Petitioner

Case No.: _____

AND

Division: _____

_____,
Respondent.

UNIFORM CHILD CUSTODY JURISDICTION ACT (UCCJA) AFFIDAVIT

1.   The name and present address of each child (under 18) in this case is:

2.   The places where the child(ren) has/have lived within the last 5 years are:

3.   The name(s) and present address(es) of persons with whom the child(ren) has/have lived within the last 5 years are:

4.   I do not know of, and have not participated (as a party, witness, or in any other capacity) in, any other court decision, order, or proceeding (including divorce, separate maintenance, child neglect, dependency, or guardianship) concerning the custody or visitation of the child(ren) in this state or any other state, except: [specify case name and number and court's name and address].

Florida Family Law Form 12.901(f), Uniform Child Custody Jurisdiction Act (UCCJA) Affidavit

158

5.   I do not have information of any pending proceeding (including divorce, separate maintenance, child neglect, dependency, or guardianship) concerning the custody or visitation of the child(ren), in this state or any other state except: [specify case name and number and court's name and address].

Check: That proceeding ____is continuing ____has been stayed by the court.

____Temporary action by this court is necessary to protect the child(ren) because the child(ren) has/have been subjected to or threatened with mistreatment or abuse or is/are otherwise neglected or dependent. Attach explanation.

6.   I do not know of any person who is not already a party to this proceeding who has physical custody of, or who claims to have custody or visitation rights with, the child(ren), except: [state name(s) and address(es)].

I acknowledge a continuing duty to advise this court of any custody or visitation proceeding (including dissolution of marriage, separate maintenance, child neglect, or dependency) concerning the child(ren) in this state or any other state about which information is obtained during this proceeding.

I CERTIFY THAT THIS UNIFORM CHILD CUSTODY JURISDICTION ACT (UCCJA) AFFIDAVIT WAS:
(✔ check **one** only) ____ mailed, ____telefaxed and mailed, or ____ hand delivered to the person(s) listed below on {date}_____,19____.

Party or their attorney (if represented)	Other
Name_____	Name_____
Address_____	Address_____
_____	_____
City State Zip	City State Zip
Telephone No._____	Telephone No._____
Telefax No._____	Telefax No._____

Florida Family Law Form 12.901(f), Uniform Child Custody Jurisdiction Act (UCCJA) Affidavit

Form 45

IN THE CIRCUIT COURT OF THE _____ JUDICIAL CIRCUIT, IN AND

FOR _____ COUNTY, FLORIDA

_____,
Petitioner

Case No.: _____

AND

Division: _____

_____,
Respondent.

MOTION FOR APPOINTMENT OF GUARDIAN AD LITEM

The [✔ **one** only] ____ Petitioner **or** ____ Respondent asks this court to appoint a guardian ad litem and states:

1. Matters before court: ____primary residential parent ____parental responsibility ____visitation

2. Child(ren) Name(s)   Date Of Birth   Age   Sex   Presently residing with

_____   _____ ____ ____ _____
_____   _____ ____ ____ _____
_____   _____ ____ ____ _____
_____   _____ ____ ____ _____
_____   _____ ____ ____ _____

3. A guardian ad litem is necessary to protect the best interests of the child(ren).

4. There [✔ **one** only] ____ is **or** ____ is not a history of domestic violence between the parties.

5. Other court-ordered social investigations are:
   ____Custody investigation unit home study
   ____Other {specify} _____

I CERTIFY THAT THE MOTION FOR APPOINTMENT OF GUARDIAN AD LITEM WAS:
[✔ **one** only] ____ mailed, ____telefaxed and mailed, or ____ hand delivered to the person(s) listed below on {date}_____,19____.

Party or their attorney (if represented)   Other
Name _____   Name _____
Address _____   Address _____
_____   _____
City   State   Zip   City   State   Zip
Telephone No. _____   Telephone No. _____
Telefax No. _____   Telefax No. _____

Florida Family Law Form 12.942(a), Motion for Appointment of Guardian Ad Litem

160

IN THE CIRCUIT COURT OF THE _____ JUDICIAL CIRCUIT, IN AND

FOR _____ COUNTY, FLORIDA

_____,
                    Petitioner

AND   Case No.: _____

_____,   Division: _____
                    Respondent.

ORDER APPOINTING GUARDIAN AD LITEM

The court hereby appoints the State of Florida Guardian ad Litem Program for the _____ Judicial Circuit to assign a certified Guardian ad Litem in this cause on behalf of the minor child(ren). It is further **ORDERED** as follows:

1. Powers of Guardian. The guardian ad litem, as party to this cause and a representative of the child(ren) shall have the powers, privileges and responsibilities to the extent necessary to advance the best interest of the child(ren); including, but not limited to, the following:

a. Notice Required Prior to Certain Interviews. The guardian ad litem may investigate the allegations of the pleadings affecting the child and, **after proper notice to interested parties to the litigation**, may interview witnesses, or any other person having information concerning the welfare of the child; **provided, however, that no such notice shall be required prior to any interview with the child or the parties** as this order shall serve as notice of the guardian ad litem's intent to interview the child and the parties. Receipt of notice does not give the parties or the parties' attorneys any rights to attend or participate in such interviews of non-parties. However, except for scheduling matters, the guardian ad litem shall not have any communication with any of the parties represented by an attorney unless all attorneys participate or consent to non-participation.

b. Court Order Required to Inspect Records Other Than Court File and School Records. The guardian ad litem, **through counsel**, may petition the court for an order directed to a specified person, agency, or organization, including, but not limited to, hospitals, medical doctors, dentists, psychologists and psychiatrists, which order directs that the guardian ad litem be allowed to inspect and copy any records and documents which relate to the minor child or to the child's parents or other custodial persons or household members with whom the child resides. **Such order shall be obtained only after notice to all parties and hearing thereon; provided, however, that upon presentation of this order to the appropriate person or office, the guardian ad litem is authorized, pursuant to section 61.403(2), Florida Statutes, to inspect and copy any school and/or daycare records or medical records relating to the child(ren) without a hearing or consent of the parent(s).**

Florida Family Law Form 12.942(b), Order Appointing Guardian Ad Litem

c. <u>Court Order Required for Expert Examinations</u>. The guardian ad litem, **through counsel**, may request the court to order expert examinations of the child, the child's parents, or other interested parties in the action, by medical doctors, dentists, and other providers of health care including psychiatrists, psychologists, or other mental health professions.

d. <u>Guardian's Right To Discovery and Other Relief</u>. A guardian ad litem, **acting through counsel**, may file such pleadings, motions, or petitions for relief as the guardian ad litem deems appropriate or necessary and may request and provide discovery.

e. <u>Presence of Guardian At Depositions and Hearings</u>. The guardian ad litem, **through counsel**, may compel the attendance of witnesses; **provided, however, that a guardian ad litem may be present and appear without counsel at such proceedings but may not participate unless permitted by the court.**

f. <u>Party to Agreement</u>. The guardian ad litem appointed to this cause is a party and must be advised of any agreement or plan entered into in this cause. The guardian ad litem shall submit his/her recommendations to the Court regarding any stipulation or agreement, whether incidental, temporary, or permanent, which affect the interest or welfare of the child(ren), within ten (10) days after the date such stipulation or agreement is served upon the guardian ad litem.

2. <u>Parties to Provide Notice to Guardian ad Litem</u>. The guardian ad litem shall be given reasonable written notice by any party who shall schedule judicial hearings, depositions or judicial conferences, and shall have the right to be present. Written notice to the guardian ad litem shall be mailed or delivered to the Guardian ad Litem Program, Circuit Court of the _____ Judicial Circuit, {city} _____, Florida.

3. All parties are ordered to make themselves and their child(ren) available for interview by the guardian ad litem.

4. <u>Reports and Recommendations</u>. The guardian ad litem shall file a written report which may include recommendations and a statement of the wishes of the child. The report must be filed and served on all parties at least 20 days prior to the hearing at which it will be presented unless the court waives such time period. The guardian ad litem shall file and serve such other reports as directed by the Court.

5. <u>Confidentiality</u>. The parties and their counsel shall maintain as confidential the report of the guardian ad litem, and all supporting documents, exhibits, reports and other information. No party or counsel may disclose any information or document, or any part of the guardian's report except with the approval of the Court.

DONE and ORDERED in {name} _____ County, Florida, on {date} _____, 19_____.

_____
CIRCUIT JUDGE

Florida Family Law Form 12.942(b), Order Appointing Guardian Ad Litem cc:

Petitioner or their attorney (if represented)	Respondent or their attorney (if represented)
Name_____	Name_____
Address_____	Address_____
_____	_____
City State Zip	City State Zip
Telephone No._____	Phone No._____
Telefax No._____	Fax No._____

Guardian ad Litem Office

Name_____

Address_____

_____

City   State   Zip

Telephone No._____

Telefax No._____

IF A NONLAWYER HELPED YOU FILL OUT THIS FORM TO GIVE TO THE JUDGE TO SIGN, THE NONLAWYER WHO HELPED YOU MUST FILL IN THE BLANKS BELOW: [Fill in **all** blanks]

I, {name of nonlawyer} _____, a nonlawyer, located at {street} _____{city}_____{state}_____, {phone} _____, helped {name} _____,who is the [✔ **one** only] _____ petitioner **or**_____ respondent, fill out this form.

Florida Family Law Form 12.942(b), Order Appointing Guardian Ad Litem

163

IN THE CIRCUIT COURT OF THE _____ JUDICIAL CIRCUIT, IN AND

FOR _____ COUNTY, FLORIDA

_____,
Petitioner

AND

Case No.: _____

Division: _____

_____,
Respondent.

**FINAL JUDGMENT OF MODIFICATION OF PARENTAL
RESPONSIBILITY AND VISITATION**

THIS CAUSE, was heard on *{date}* _____ upon the Petition for Modification of Parental Responsibility and/or Visitation. The court, having heard the testimony of the parties and appropriate witnesses, having reviewed the pleadings contained in the court file, and being more fully advised and informed, hereby makes the following findings of fact and conclusions of law:
[✔ **all** that apply]

1. The Court has jurisdiction of the parties and the subject matter of this proceeding.

2. Florida is the home state of the minor child(ren) or there is significant connection with this State and accordingly it has jurisdiction to determine child custody, visitation, and support under the Uniform Child Custody Jurisdiction Act.

3. Respondent [✔ **one** only] _____ was **or** _____ was not duly served by process of law and a default,
    ❏ Family Law Form 12.922(b), _____ was **or** _____ was not properly entered.

4. The last order governing primary parental responsibility or visitation was entered on *{date}* _____. A copy of that order is attached.

5. There [✔ **one** only] _____ has **or** _____ has not been a substantial change in the circumstances of the parties since the entry of the last order governing primary parental responsibility or visitation, specifically,

_____
_____
_____
_____
_____.

6. It [✔ **one** only] _____ is **or** _____ is not in the best interest of the minor child(ren) that the current parenting arrangement be changed because: _____

_____
_____
_____.

Florida Family Law Form 12.993, Final Judgment of Modification of Parental Responsibility

7. Child Support
[Fill in **all** blanks that apply]
a. Petitioner's net income is: _____. OR
   Petitioner's imputed net income is: _____, based upon the following:
   _____
   _____.

b. Respondent's net income is: _____. OR
   Respondent's imputed net income is: _____, based upon the following
   _____
   _____.

[✔ **all** that apply]

_____ c. Child support should be set by Florida's child support guidelines (see section 61.30 Florida
         Statutes).

_____ d. The calculations and conclusion included in the child support guidelines worksheet ❑ Family
         Law Form 12.901(g) filed in this case by [✔ **one** only] _____ petitioner **or** _____ respondent are
         adopted by this court and incorporated in this order.

THE COURT MUST MAKE SPECIFIC, WRITTEN FINDINGS WHY AWARDING THE AMOUNT OF
CHILD SUPPORT REQUIRED BY SECTION 61.30, FLORIDA STATUTES, WOULD BE UNJUST OR
INAPPROPRIATE IF THE AMOUNT AWARDED IS DIFFERENT FROM THE GUIDELINES AMOUNT
BY PLUS OR MINUS FIVE PERCENT (5%).

_____ e. Child support should not be set by Florida's child support guidelines (see section 61.30 Florida
         Statutes). The basis for ordering [✔ **one** only] _____ more **or** _____ less than the guidelines
         amount of child support pursuant to section 61.30, Florida Statutes is:
         _____
         _____
         _____
         _____
         _____
         _____
         _____
         _____
         _____
         _____
         _____.

f. _____ Medical insurance [✔ **one** only] ___is **or** ____is not reasonably available to the
         [✔ **one** only] _____ petitioner **or** _____ respondent for the child(ren) and
         [✔ **one** only] _____ petitioner **or** _____ respondent should be required to provide it.

g. _____ Dental insurance [✔ **one** only] ___is **or** ____is not reasonably available to the
         [✔ **one** only] _____ petitioner **or** _____ respondent for the child(ren) and
         [✔ **one** only] _____ petitioner **or** _____ respondent should be required to provide it.

Florida Family Law Form 12.993, Final Judgment of Modification of Parental Responsibility

8. THE COURT MUST MAKE SPECIFIC, WRITTEN FINDINGS OF FACT EXPLAINING WHY ATTORNEYS' FEES ARE BEING GRANTED AND EXPLAINING THE BASIS OF THE AMOUNT AWARDED.

    [✔ **all** that apply]

    _____ Attorneys' fees, _____ suit money, and/or _____ costs be awarded to:
[✔ **one** only] _____ petitioner **or** _____ respondent.

The basis for granting this award and for the determination of the amount is:

_____
_____
_____
_____
_____
_____
_____
_____
_____.

    Therefore, upon consideration of the above findings, it is hereby ORDERED AND ADJUDGED that:

A. The Petition/Request to Modify/Change Primary Residency/Custody of Child(ren) is
    [✔ **one** only]
    _____ GRANTED **or** _____ DENIED based on the findings of fact regarding changed circumstances and best interests of the child set out previously in this order.

B. PRIMARY RESIDENCY/VISITATION [Fill in **all** blanks that apply]
    [✔ **one** only]
    1. Parental responsibility over the minor child(ren) shall be changed as follows:
        _____ a. Primary Residency to _{specify}_ _____.
        _____ b. Sole to _{specify}_ _____.
        _____ c. Other (e.g., certain decisions with one parent such as education, medical, religious training etc.): _____
        _____.

    2. Parental decision making responsibility over the minor child(ren) shall be as follows:
    [✔ **one** only]
        _____ Shared to: [✔ **one** only] _____father **or** _____ mother **or**
        _____Other _{Specify other person(s) and issue(s)}_:_____
        _____
        _____.

        _____ Sole to: [✔ **one** only] _____father **or** _____ mother **or**
        _____Other _{Specify other person(s) and issue(s)}_:_____
        _____
        _____.

Florida Family Law Form 12.993, Final Judgment of Modification of Parental Responsibility

3. Child visitation rights by the noncustodial parent shall be :

[✔ **one** only]

_____ There shall be no visitation by the noncustodial parent pending further orders from the court.

_____ Liberal

_____ Reasonable

_____ Scheduled (schedule attached)

_____ Supervised as scheduled (schedule attached)

_____ As follows:

_____ a. Alternating weekends from _____ p.m. on Fridays until _____ p.m. on Sundays.

[✔ **all** that apply]

(1) ___ if there is a school holiday on Friday, visitation will begin at _____ p.m. on Thursday.

(2) ___ if there is a school holiday on Monday visitation will continue until _____ p.m. on Monday.

(3) ___ weekend visitation shall not change regardless of Friday or Monday school holidays.

(4) ___ if there is a school holiday on Monday or Friday the entire weekend shall be treated as a holiday an alternated in odd and even years under the holiday part of this order.

_____ b. One day of contact/visitation during the week in which there is no weekend visitation, for a period of _____ hours on the day of the week of _____.

_____ c. Alternating legal holiday periods as follows which are also school holiday periods:

_____ Spring Break [✔ **one** only] _____ odd years **or** _____ even years

_____ Thanksgiving Holiday [✔ **one** only] _____ odd years **or** _____ even years

_____ Winter Holiday period [✔ **one** only] _____ odd years **or** _____ even years (odd or even is established by the first day of the holiday)

_____ Alternating other legal school holidays or religious holidays: *{specify}*

_____

_____

_____

_____

_____.

_____ d. A continuous period during the summer for _____ weeks.
Contact with the other parent during this summer period will be as follows:

_____

_____.

_____ e. Alternating the child(ren)'s respective birthdays.

_____ f. Spending each parent's respective birthdays with that parent.

_____ g. Mother's Day and Father's Day with the appropriate parent.

_____ h. Unlimited phone communications at reasonable hours.

_____ i. Unlimited written communications.

C. CHILD SUPPORT

1. _____ Child support of $_____ to be paid by the
[✔ **one** only] _____ petitioner **or** _____ respondent
[✔ **one** only] _____weekly_____biweekly_____twice a month_____monthly.

This support shall continue until the first of the parties' minor children reaches the age of 18, or if the child(ren) are between the ages of 18 and 19 and are still in high school performing in good faith with a reasonable expectation of graduation, until the child(ren) reaches the age of 19. At that time the child support will be recomputed under the then-current Child Support Guidelines.

2. _____ Unusual or uninsured medical/dental expenses for the children be provided by:
[✔ **one** only] _____ petitioner **or** _____ respondent **or** _____ petitioner and respondent each pay one-half

3. _____ Medical insurance to be provided by
[✔ **one** only] _____ petitioner **or** _____ respondent for the child(ren).

4. _____ Dental insurance to be provided by
[✔ **one** only] _____ petitioner **or** _____ respondent for the child(ren).

5. _____ Life insurance shall be maintained for the benefit of the minor child(ren) as beneficiaries or as stated in the *{name of trust}* _____ for the benefit of the minor children created *{date}* _____ with the [✔ one only] _____petitioner **or** _____respondent or other {specify} _____ _____as owner as follows
[✔ **one** only] _____ none ordered **or** _____ by petitioner with a benefit amount of $_____ **or** _____ by respondent with a benefit amount of $_____.

6. All payments of child support shall be as follows:
[✔ check **all** which apply]
_____ Directly to the person the court has ordered will be paid the support.
_____ Payment will be through the Central Depository by the attached order ❑ Family Law Form 12.991(a).
_____ Payment will be by income deduction order, ❑ Family Law Form 12.991(b), which is attached.

D. _____ Attorneys' fees, suit money, and costs be awarded to:
[✔ **one** only] _____ petitioner **or** _____ respondent in the amount of $_____(fees), $_____ (costs), $_____ suit money. The basis for granting or denying this award and for the amount of any fees and costs awarded is given in the findings of fact in this judgment.

Florida Family Law Form 12.993, Final Judgment of Modification of Parental Responsibility

E. This court awards the petitioner the following further relief in this cause:

_____

_____.

F. The court reserves jurisdiction to enforce the terms of this order and all documents incorporated into it (e.g., parties' stipulation/agreement, child support guidelines worksheet, etc.).

DONE and ORDERED in {name} _____ County, Florida, on {date} _____, 19_____.

_____
CIRCUIT JUDGE

cc:

Petitioner or their attorney (if represented)	Respondent or their attorney (if represented)
Name_____	Name_____
Address_____	Address_____
_____	_____
City State Zip	City State Zip
Telephone No._____	Telephone No._____
Telefax No._____	Telefax No._____

Other
Name_____
Address_____
_____
City   State   Zip
Telephone No._____
Telefax No._____

IF A NONLAWYER HELPED YOU FILL OUT THIS FORM TO GIVE TO THE JUDGE TO SIGN, THE NONLAWYER WHO HELPED YOU MUST FILL IN THE BLANKS BELOW:
[Fill in **all** blanks]
I, {name of nonlawyer} _____, a nonlawyer, located at {street} _____{city}_____{state}_____, {phone} _____, helped {name} _____,who is the [✔ one only] _____ petitioner **or** _____ respondent, fill out this form.

Florida Family Law Form 12.993, Final Judgment of Modification of Parental Responsibility

IN THE CIRCUIT COURT OF THE _____ JUDICIAL CIRCUIT, IN AND

FOR _____ COUNTY, FLORIDA

_____,

Petitioner

AND

Case No.: _____

Division: _____

_____,

Respondent.

SUPPLEMENTAL PETITION/REQUEST TO MODIFY/CHANGE VISITATION

The petition of [✔ one only] ____ Petitioner or ____ Respondent shows:

1. The last order on visitation in this case was entered (dated) by the court on {date} _____, 19____. A copy of the order is attached.

2. Paragraph(s) _____ of the attached order describe(s) the present visitation.

3. Since the last order on visitation, there has been a substantial change in circumstances as follows: Briefly list below the changes that have taken place since the last order on visitation and the reasons why you feel the visitation in effect at this time should be changed. (if necessary, you may add additional sheets of paper):_____

_____

_____

_____.

4. This is in the child(ren)'s best interest because: _____

_____

_____.

WHEREFORE, I ask that the court to change the visitation as follows (list the changes you want in the visitation):_____

_____

_____.

I CERTIFY THAT THE SUPPLEMENTAL PETITION/REQUEST TO MODIFY/CHANGE VISITA-
TION WAS: [✔ check one only] ____ mailed, ____telefaxed and mailed, or ____ hand delivered to the
person(s) listed below on {date} _____,19____.

Party or their attorney (if represented)

Name_____

Address_____

_____

City   State   Zip

Telephone No._____

Telefax No._____

Other

Name_____

Address_____

_____

City   State   Zip

Telephone No._____

Telefax No._____

Florida Family Law Form 12.903(a), Supplemental Petition to Modify Visitation

Index

Affidavit for Service by Publication, 17, 79
Affidavit of Insolvency, 25, 90
Affidavit Regarding Alimony, 34, 127
Alimony, 10, 31-38, 57
Attorneys (See "Lawyers")

Bar association, 5, 30

Case number, 14
Case style, 13
Central Depository, 38, 45
Certificate of Compliance With Family
    Law Rule 12.285, 35, 121
Certificate of Service, 15, 20, 36, 78
Certified mail, 15
Clerk, 14
Child abuse, 48
Child care costs, 41, 58
Child custody (see "Custody")
Child support, 10, 39-46, 58, 63
Child support enforcement, 16
Child Support Guidelines Worksheet, 40, 42, 43, 131
Child Support Income Deduction Order, 38, 45, 53, 144
Child visitation (see "Visitation")
Civil Cover Sheet, 14, 36, 43, 51, 56, 91
Combined income (and child support), 39, 41
Court clerk (See "Clerk")
Court costs, 15
Court reporters, 52
Courtroom manners, 24
Custody, 10, 47-53, 57

Deductions from income, 40, 58
Default, 18, 19, 36, 75
Department of Health and Rehabilitative Services
    (see "HRS")
Divorce judgments, 13, 31
Documents (as evidence), 24, 53

Employers (getting information from),
Evidence, rules of, 7, 23
Expert witnesses, 52

Family Law Financial Affidavit, 12, 20, 21, 34, 42, 50,
    56, 60, 97, 103
Filing, 14, 36, 43, 51
Filing fee, 15
Final Disposition Form, 25, 37, 38, 92
Florida Digest, 8
Florida Jurisprudence, 8
Florida Rules of Court, 8, 59-62
Florida Statutes, 8, 57-59, 63
Forms, 8, 13

Forms (instructions),
    Form - 1, 15
    Form - 2, 15
    Form - 3, 20
    Form - 4, 20
    Form - 5, 20
    Form - 6, 19
    Form - 7, 19
    Form - 8, 18
    Form - 9, 18
    Form - 10, 15
    Form - 11, 17
    Form - 12, 17
    Form - 13, 21
    Form - 14, 22
    Form - 15, 22
    Form - 16, 23
    Form - 17, 11
    Form - 18, 12
    Form - 19, 25
    Form - 20, 14
    Form - 21, 25
    Form - 22, 21
    Form - 23, 21
    Form - 24, 34, 42, 50
    Form - 25, 34, 42, 50
    Form - 26, 36
    Form - 27, 35
    Form - 28, 35
    Form - 29, 18
    Form - 30, 13, 17
    Form - 31, 33, 52
    Form - 32, 33
    Form - 33, 34
    Form - 34, 37
    Form - 35, 42
    Form - 36, 42
    Form - 37, 44
    Form - 38, 38, 45
    Form - 39, 38, 45
    Form - 40, 45
    Form - 41, 46
    Form - 42, 46
    Form - 43, 49
    Form - 44, 50
    Form - 45, 50
    Form - 46, 50
    Form - 47, 53, 56
    Form - 48, 55

General Master, 19
Gross income (and child support), 39, 40, 58
Guardian ad litem, 50

Hearings, 9, 24, 37
Hearing notices, 9, 19, 69, 95
Hearing preparation, 24, 36, 43, 51, 56
Hearsay, 23
HRS, 49

Imputed income, 40, 58
Income, (See "Gross" and "Net" income)
Income deduction, 38
Insolvency, 25
Instructions to Employer or Other Person
    Providing Health Insurance, 41, 46, 58, 153
Interrogatories, 35, 42

Joint custody, 47
Joint petition, 11, 86
Judgment (See "Orders")

Law library, 8
Lawyers, 27
Legal forms (See "Forms")
Legal research, 8
Lump sum alimony, 31

Mail, service by, 15
Manners (in court), 24
Mediation, 26
Memorandum for Certificate of Military Service, 18, 76
Motions:
    for Appointment of Guardian ad litem, 51, 160
    for Health Insurance Coverage, 45, 150
    to Set Final Hearing/Trial, 19, 20, 71

Names, 14
Neglect (See "Abuse")
Negotiating, 11
Net income (and child support), 39, 40
Newspapers, 17
Nonmilitary Affidavit, 18, 77
Notice of Action, 17, 80
Notice of Hearing, 19, 20, 69
Notice of Hearing Before General Master, 20, 21, 95
Notice of Production From Non-Party, 21, 81
Notice of Service of Standard Family
    Law Interrogatories, 36, 113
Notifying your ex-spouse, 15
Notifying witnesses, 52

Opening statement, 37, 43, 56
Orders (court):
    Alimony, 37
    Appointing Guardian ad Litem, 51, 161
    Child support, 44, 136
    Custody, 53
    for Health Insurance Coverage, 46, 151
    in general, 25
    Income deduction, 38

Modify Judgment Dissolving Marriage, 12, 88
of Referral to General Master, 20, 21, 93
Requiring Payment Through Central Depository,
    38, 45, 53, 140
Setting Matter for Final Hearing or Status
    Conference, 19, 20, 72
Visitation, 56, 164

Parental responsibility, 47
Permanent alimony, 31
Personal service, 15
Petition to modify:
    Alimony, 33, 126
    Child support, 42, 130
    Custody, 49, 155
    Divorce judgment (joint), 11
    Visitation, 55, 170
Presenting your case, 25, 36, 43, 51, 56
Process Service Memorandum, 15, 22, 23, 68
Primary residence (of children), 47
Private investigators, 52
Publication, 16

Questioning witnesses, 51
Quitting a job, 33, 40

Rehabilitative alimony, 31
Relevancy, 23
Remarriage (and alimony), 33
Request to Enter Default, 18, 19, 74
Research, legal, 8
Retirement (and alimony), 33
Rules of evidence, 7, 23

Service, 15
Service by mail, 15
Service by publication, 16
Sheriff, 15, 52
Southern Reporter, 8
Special needs, 49, 59
Standard Family Law Interrogatories, 35, 114
Statutes (see "*Florida Statutes*")
Subpoena, 21, 22, 52, 84
Subpoena Duces Tecum, 23, 52, 85
Subpoena for Production of Documents, 22, 23, 82
Summons, 15, 66

Taxes, 26
Typing forms, 14

Uniform Child Custody Jurisdiction Act
    Affidavit, 50, 56, 158

Visitation, 10, 55

Witness Testimony Worksheet, 24, 51, 125
Witnesses, 23, 51-53

Florida Legal Guides

•With Florida Supreme Court-approved forms, where available•

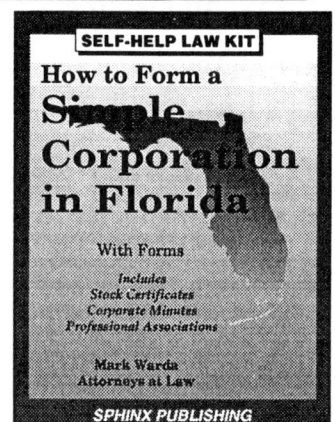

SELF-HELP LAW KIT
How to File for **Divorce** in **Florida**

With Forms

Includes
Child Support
Child Custody &
Visitation
Property Division

Edward A. Haman
Attorneys at Law

SPHINX PUBLISHING

SELF-HELP LAW KIT
Landlords' Rights & Duties in Florida

With Forms
and Caselaw

Includes
Security Deposit Rules
Eviction Procedures
Residential and Commercial

Mark Warda
Attorneys at Law

SPHINX PUBLISHING

SELF-HELP LAW KIT
How to Win in **Small Claims Court** in **Florida**

With Forms

Explain
Rules of Evidence
Court Procedures
Collecting Your Judgment

Mark Warda
Attorneys at Law

SPHINX PUBLISHING

SELF-HELP LAW KIT
How to Form a **Simple Corporation** in **Florida**

With Forms

Includes
Stock Certificates
Corporate Minutes
Professional Associations

Mark Warda
Attorneys at Law

SPHINX PUBLISHING

Florida Power of Attorney Handbook .... $ 9.95

How to Change Your Name in Florida, 3rd Ed. $14.95

How to File a Florida Contruction Lien (and Collect!), 2nd Ed. $19.95

How to File a Guardianship in Florida $19.95

How to File an Adoption in Florida $19.95

How to File for Divorce in Florida, 4th Ed. $21.95

How to Form a Nonprofit Corporation in Florida, 3rd Ed. $19.95

How to Form a Simple Corporation in Florida, 3rd Ed. $19.95

How to Form Your Own Partnership Agreement (Southeastern Edition) $19.95

How to Make a Florida Will, 4th Ed. .... $ 9.95

How to Modify Your Florida Divorce Judgment, 3rd Ed. $21.95

How to Probate an Estate in Florida, 2nd Ed. $24.95

How to Register Your Own Trademark (Southeastern Edition) $21.95

How to Start a Business in Florida, 4th Ed. $16.95

How to Win in Small Claims Court in Florida, 5th Ed. $14.95

Land Trusts in Florida, 4th Ed. $24.95

Landlords' Rights and Duties in Florida, 6th Ed. $19.95

Winning in Florida Traffic Court $14.95

Women's Legal Rights in Florida $19.95

Also available: Self-help law books for Alabama, Georgia, Illinois, Massachusetts, Minnesota, Michigan, North Carolina, South Carolina, and Texas

Books from other publishers

Represent Yourself in Court A step-by-step guide to preparing and trying a civil lawsuit. — $29.95

Patent It Yourself, 5th Ed. Explains every step of the patent process; a complete legal guide for inventors. — $44.95

The Inventor's Notebook, 2nd Ed. How to develop, document, protect, finance, and market your invention. — $19.95

Copyright Your Software — $39.95

How to Win Your Personal Injury Claim How to settle an injury claim on your own. — $24.95

Beat the Nursing Home Trap: A Consumer's Guide to Choosing and Financing Long-Term Care — $18.95

Who Will Handle Your Finances If You Can't? — $19.95

The Living Together Kit, 8th Ed. Includes estate planning, living together agreements, buying real estate, etc. — $24.95

Simple Contracts for Personal Use, 2nd Ed. Clearly written legal form contracts for all ocassions. — $16.95

Stand Up to the IRS Know your rights when dealing with IRS: deductions, penalties, liens, and much more. — $21.95

The Independent Paralegal's Handbook, 4th Ed. — $29.95

How to Write a Business Plan, 4th Ed. Finance your business and make it work. — $21.95

A Legal Guide for Lesbian and Gay Couples, 8th Ed. — $24.95

Your Rights in the Workplace: A Complete Guide for Employees, 3rd Ed. — $18.95

Sexual Harassment on the Job, 2nd Ed. Explains the rights of employees who are sexually harassed. — $18.95

Dog Law A legal guide for dog owners and their neighbors. — $12.95

Guerrilla Real Estate Investing — $29.95

Order Form

To order these publications, please fill in the information requested and send check or money order to Sphinx Publishing, PO Box 25, Clearwater, FL 34617.

☐ Check Enclosed   ☐ Money Order Enclosed

We accept Visa, MasterCard, American Express and Discover cards.

Card number:

☐☐☐☐ ☐☐☐☐ ☐☐☐☐ ☐☐☐☐

Expiration date:

☐☐☐   ☐ American Express   ☐ Visa
        ☐ MasterCard   ☐ Discover

Ship to:

Name_____

Address _____

City_____State_____

Zip_____ Phone_____

For **Credit Card Orders** call:
1-800-226-5291
or fax this form to 1-800-408-3291

DISCOVER   VISA   MasterCard   American Express

Quantity	Title	Price	Total Price

*Shipping: **In Florida:** UPS: (1-3 books) $3.25, each add'l .50¢
Priority Mail: (1-2 books) $3.00, each add'l. $1.00
4th class mail: (1 book) $1.50 , each add'l. 50¢
Other States: UPS: (1-3 books) $3.75, each add'l .50¢
Priority Mail: (1-2 books) $3.00, each add'l. $1.00
[NOTE: Books from other publishers are only sent UPS]

Subtotal: $_____
Sales Tax (FL residents) $_____
*Shipping: $_____
Total: $_____

Prices subject to change

Signature

Sphinx Publishing Presents
Self-Help Law Books
Laymen's Guides to the Law

Victims' Rights

The Complete Guide to Crime Victim Compensation

- Who qualifies
- How to qualify
- How to apply
- How much is available
- Rights of relatives
- Who to contact

William L Ginsburg
Attorney at Law

SELF-HELP LAW KIT

How to File Your Own Bankruptcy (or How to Avoid It)

With Forms

Includes
Chapter 7 (Discharge of Debts)
Chapter 13 (Payment Plan)

Edward A. Haman
Attorney at Law

SPHINX PUBLISHING

SELF-HELP LAW KIT

Living Trusts and Simple Ways to Avoid Probate

With Forms

Karen Ann Rolcik
Attorney at Law

SPHINX PUBLISHING

SELF-HELP LAW KIT

How to Register Your Own Trademark

With Forms

Includes
Choosing Your Mark
Searching Your Mark
State & Federal Registration
Protecting Your Mark

Mark Warda
Attorney at Law

SPHINX PUBLISHING

Every state has funds available to compensate victims of violent crime, but few are aware of this fact. Find out all about who qualifies, how much can be paid, and where and how to apply. Summary of laws for all states. 161 pages; $12.95.

Everything needed to file for bankruptcy in any state without a lawyer. Includes all of the forms and instructions for either Chapter 7 or Chapter 13 personal bankruptcies; with state-by-state exemptions. 143 pages; $19.95.

This book cuts through the legal jargon and explains in simple language what everyone needs to know about the probate process, and how to avoid it through living trusts and other devices. Includes forms & instructions. 144 pages; $19.95.

This complete guide to protecting a trademark explains state and federal registration, and protection available without registration. Includes all forms for filing your own federal registration. 159 pages; $19.95

What our customers say about our books:

"It couldn't be more clear for the lay person."   -R.D.

"I want you to know I really appreciate your book. It has saved me a lot of time and money." -L.T.

"Your real estate contracts book has saved me nearly $12,000.00 in closing costs over the past year." -A.B.

"...many of the legal questions that I have had over the years were answered clearly and concisely through your plain English interpretation of the law." -C.E.H.

"If there weren't people out there like you I'd be lost. You have the best books of this type out there." -S.B.

"...your forms and directions are easy to follow..." -C.V.M.

Sphinx Law Books
• Written by lawyers •
• Simple English explanation of the law •
• Forms and instructions included •

Sphinx books are available directly from the publisher, or from your local bookstores.

For credit card orders call 1-800-226-5291, or write P.O. Box 25, Clearwater, FL 34617

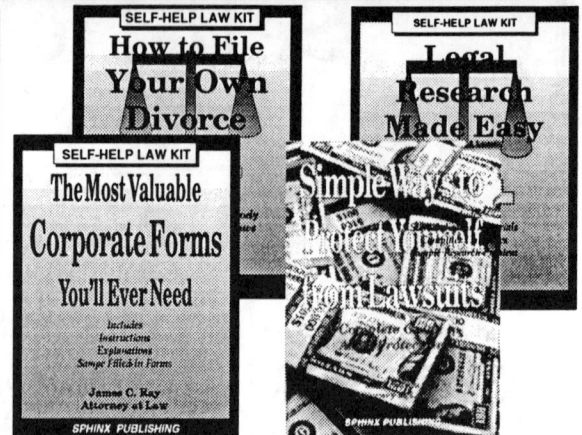

Our National Titles Are Valid In All 50 States

Grandparents' Rights,
by Attorney Traci Truly

"Highly recommended. . ."
—*Library Journal*

". . . forthrightly explains maneuvering through court proceedings without getting lost in the fray. . .covers all relevant laws."
—*Booklist*

SELF-HELP LAW KIT
How to File Your Own Divorce

SELF-HELP LAW KIT
The Most Valuable Corporate Forms You'll Ever Need
Includes
Instructions
Explanations
Sample Filled-in Forms
James C. Ray
Attorney at Law
SPHINX PUBLISHING

SELF-HELP LAW KIT
Legal Research Made Easy
Simple Ways to Protect Yourself From Lawsuits
SPHINX PUBLISHING

"This movement toward self-help demands attention...Sphinx [books] are staples of legal how-to collections."   —*Library Journal*

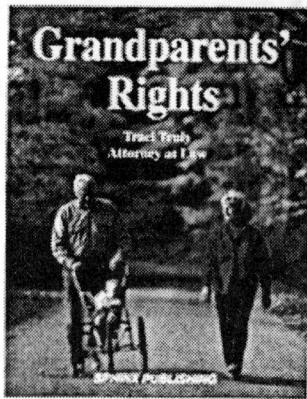

National Title	ISBN Number	Price
Crime Victims' Guide to Justice	1-57248-048-3	19.95
Debtors' Rights, A Legal Self-Help Guide, 2nd ed.	1-57248-023-8	12.95
Defend Yourself Against Criminal Charges	1-57248-059-9	19.95
Divorces From Hell	1-57248-017-3	10.95
Grandparents' Rights	1-57248-001-7	19.95
Guia de Inmigración a Estados Unidos (Spanish ed. Immigration Guide)	0-913825-99-9	19.95
Help Your Lawyer Win Your Case	1-57248-021-1	12.95
How to Buy a Condominium or Townhome	1-57248-061-0	16.95
How to File Your Own Bankruptcy, 3rd Ed.	0-913825-98-0	19.95
How to File Your Own Divorce, 2nd Ed.	1-57248-045-9	19.95
How to Form Your Own Corporation	0-913825-61-1	19.95
How to Negotiate Real Estate Contracts, 2nd Ed.	1-57248-035-1	16.95
How to Negotiate Real Estate Leases, 2nd Ed.	1-57248-036-X	16.95
How to Register Your Own Copyright	1-57248-002-5	19.95
How to Register Your Own Trademark	0-913825-88-3	19.95
How to Write Your Own Living Will	1-57248-060-2	9.95
How to Write Your Own Premarital Agreement	0-913825-69-7	19.95
Jurors' Rights	1-57248-031-9	9.95
Lawsuits of the Rich & Famous	0-913825-95-6	10.95
Legal Malpractice and Other Claims Against Your Lawyer	1-57248-032-7	18.95
Legal Research Made Easy	1-57248-008-4	14.95
Living Trusts & Simple Ways to Avoid Probate	1-57248-019X	19.95
The Most Valuable Business Forms You'll Ever Need	1-57248-022-X	19.95
The Most Valuable Corporate Forms You'll Ever Need	1-57248-007-6	24.95
Neighbor vs. Neighbor: Legal Rights of Neighbors in Dispute	0-913825-41-7	12.95
The Power of Attorney Handbook, 2nd Ed.	1-57248-044-0	19.95
Simple Ways to Protect Yourself From Lawsuits	1-57248-020-3	24.95
Social Security Benefits Handbook	1-57248-033-5	14.95
Software Law: A User Friendly Legal Guide for Software Developer's	1-57248-049-1	24.95
Successful Real Estate Brokerage Management	0-913825-86-7	19.95
U.S.A. Immigration Guide, 2nd Ed.	1-57248-000-9	19.95
Victims' Rights: The Complete Guide to Crime Victim Compensation	0-913825-82-4	12.95
Winning Your Personal Injury Claim	1-57248-052-1	19.95